Catherine de' Medici

HUGH ROSS WILLIAMSON

Catherine de' Medici

A Studio Book

The Viking Press · New York

This book was devised and produced by
Park and Roche Establishment, Schaan

Published in 1973 by The Viking Press, Inc.
625 Madison Avenue, New York, N.Y.10022

Designed by Crispin Fisher
Picture research: Nicole Bourgeois

SBN 670–20696–2
Library of Congress catalog card number: 73–6072

Printed in Italy by Amilcare Pizzi S.A., Milano

End-paper illustration: *The League, sixteenth-century engraving.*

Half-title illustration: *Medal depicting Catherine de' Medici.*

Title-page illustration: see page 82.

Contents

List of colour plates

To
Neville Hill Archer

The Little Duchess

She was born in the Medici Palace at Florence on 13 April 1519 and three days later, the eve of Palm Sunday, she was christened Caterina Maria Romola. From the walls of the tiny chapel on the first floor her forbears, as represented in the celebrated fresco of *The Journey of the Magi* which Fra Angelico's pupil, Benozzo Gozzoli, had painted half a century earlier, impassively witnessed the baptism of the last of their line.

Her great-grandfather, Lorenzo the Magnificent, depicted as the youngest of the Three Kings, was astride the great white horse he had ridden in a memorable tournament. At the head of the crowded retinue following the Kings were Lorenzo's father, Piero the Gouty, and Piero's father, Cosmo *Pater Patriae*, the founder of the greatness of the Medici.

In another part of the palace the child's parents lay dying; her father, Lorenzo de' Medici, Duke of Urbino, from raging consumption induced by his dissolute life, her mother, Madeleine de la Tour d'Auvergne, a Bourbon, of puerpal fever. Within a fortnight Madelaine was dead, to be followed six days later by her husband who, in his twenty-seven years, had brought nothing but discredit on the family name. At less than a month old, 'the little Duchess', as she was called, was an orphan, left alone in the vast treasure-house of a palace in charge of servants. The poet Ariosto, musing on the cradle between the coffin, wrote as if speaking for Florence:

> *Verdeggio un ramo sol con poca foglia*
> *E fra tema e speranza sto sospesa*
> *Se lo me lasci il verno, o lo mi taglia*

Only a branch shows a little green in its leaves and I am divided between fear and hope whether the winter will leave it to me or kill it.

Opposite: *Catherine's father, Lorenzo de' Medici, Duke of Urbino, painted at the time of his marriage by Raphael; he died three weeks after her birth.*

11

Within a week, however, her relative, Cardinal Giulo de' Medici, arrived in great haste from Rome to undertake the guardianship of the so-precious baby girl. He had been sent by the Pope, Leo X, who was also a Medici. As Sovereign Pontiff Leo—Giovanni de' Medici—naturally issued the order; but the relationship between the two men was such that the real decision was Giulio's.

The Pope and the Cardinal were cousins, the former, Giovanni, the second son of Lorenzo the Magnificent, the latter, Giulio, the bastard of Lorenzo's brother. There were only two years between them—Giovanni at the time of their great-niece, Catherine's birth, was 43, Giulio 41—and as Giulio had been entirely brought up in 'il Magnifico's' household and treated like a son, they regarded themselves as brothers rather than cousins.

Giulio was the genius of the family, absorbed in dreams of the restoration of its greatness—dreams given an edge of desperation during the eighteen years of exile which followed the expulsion of the Medici from Florence in 1494 when Giovanni and Giulio were in their teens. Their return in 1512 coincided with the election of Giovanni as Pope (although he had not yet been ordained priest) and the first part of Giulio's plan was fulfilled.

The new Pope reciprocated by creating his foster-brother a Cardinal in defiance of the Church's law prohibiting such an honour in the case of illegitimacy.

If Cardinal Giulio was his house's genius, he was also its evil genius. In him the qualities of generosity and magnanimity, of unselfish service to the state and clemency to opponents, which had been so long inherent in the men and women of the Medici that they were assumed as a matter of course, were completely lacking. His handsome exterior and his graceful manner concealed a cold-hearted disposition and a character burdened by no scruples whatever. His final aim was so to aggrandize his family that even the form of republican government in Florence should be destroyed and in its place a despotic monarchy of Tuscany set up and a crown placed on a Medici head—preferably his own.

The carrying-out of the plan involved, among other things, an alliance with France and, in pursuit of it, he had arranged the marriage of Catherine's parents, which had taken place at Amboise in the presence of the King, Francis I, and had been graced with festivities on a more splendid scale than had ever before been seen in Europe. And now that, in less than a year, both bride and bridegroom were dead, Cardinal Giulio sped with an almost unseemly haste to Florence to instal himself in the Medici Palace and to take charge of the orphaned offspring of the marriage who could perhaps be used, when the time came, in the furtherance of the dynastic schemes which had met with so dramatically sudden a check.

For five months he administered the government of Florence, in so far as such a thing was possible, to the general satisfaction of the citizens.

It was no mean feat. The Florentines' addiction to democracy bordered on the eccentric. The government was vested in the Signoria, which consisted of the elected representatives of the guilds *(priori delle arti)* who held office for two months only, during which they all lived together in the great Palazzo della Signoria. At their head was the *gonfaloniere*, who was also elected for two months. The judicial power was exercised by three non-Florentines, who were invited for a year and who at the end of that period

Catherine's great-uncles; in Raphael's portrait, Giovanni (right) is shown as Pope Leo X, and his cousin Giulio as the Cardinal de' Medici.

were required to render a minute account of their administration to a syndicate of native Florentines appointed to examine it. When, at any point, the gonfalonier raised the gonfalon, the standard of the state, all citizens were required to rise and assist in the enforcement of law, just as when he rang the great bell, the *vacca,* in the tower of the Signorial Palace, the entire male population had to assemble in the square below so that a decision might be taken 'by popular acclamation'. These rules, with various other checks and counter-checks, ensured that, in theory at least, Florence was 'the most republican republic the world has ever seen.'

The Medici, middle-class traders with a money-lending interest, fitted perfectly into this background. They were definitely—even defiantly—'of the people', consistently hostile to the aristocracy, good democrats all. They behaved always as the equals of artisans and small shopkeepers, at ease with people of all classes, courteous, benevolent, undistinguished in appearance, modest and generous. In the offices to which they were from time to time elected, they served Florence conscientiously and well. For the rest they got on quietly with their own business.

They got on with it, in fact, so well that by the time Cosmo became head of the house and brought it from semi-obscurity into the full glare of history —the mid-1400s—the Medici owned banks in sixteen of the capital cities of Europe, including Paris, London, Bruges and Rome; (the golden 'florin' had become eponymously the general European standard of value), and they were, as far as could be ascertained, the wealthiest family of the West.

As wealth is the only effective power in a democracy, the Medici, once they had limitless money to manipulate a constitution which might have been designed as a test of proficiency in the art of bribery, were able to become, whatever they were called, the real rulers of Florence. Their unassuming demeanour deflected envy. At a time when Lorenzo the Magnificent was in practice the arbiter of the politics of all Italy and was so recognised by the sovereigns of France and England, he was careful to speak to any citizen as to an equal. The accommodating affability of generations of tradesmen intent on pleasing their customers had hardened into a habit, so that 'absence of arrogance' so dear to the Florentines eventually became a Medici instinct.

For another trait of the *nouveau riche*—the desire to surround themselves with the latest fashionable art—the world remains grateful, since that art at the time included the work of, among others, Fra Angelico, Lippi, Ghirlandaio, Botticelli, Masaccio, Leonardo da Vinci, Michelangelo, Raphael, Donatello, Verrocchio, Brunelleschi and Bramante.

Opposite: *Santi di Tito's painting of Machiavelli, whose treatise* Il Principe, *written for Catherine's father, became known as her 'bible'.*

If their absence of arrogance and their sensitivity to art could be seen as the public enlargement of private characteristics, the magnificent spectacles the Medici provided had a more calculated motive. 'One who wishes to obtain the reputation of liberality among men must not omit every kind of sumptuous display' was one of the maxims contained in the book, *Il Principe,* which the shrewd political observer, Niccolò Machiavelli, for many years secretary to the Signoria, dedicated to Catherine's father, five years before she was born.

Machiavelli, then in retirement, had spent his life in Florence during the greatest days of the Medici—he was born the year that Lorenzo the Magnificent became head of the house—and his portrait of the prince who should redeem Italy from chaos owned much to his observation of them. They are eminently recognisable, for instance, in one of the most famous passages: 'It is necessary to be a great dissembler and men are so simple and ready to obey present necessities that one who deceives will always find those who allow themselves to be deceived. It is well to seem pious, faithful, humane, religious, sincere, and also to be so; but you must have a mind so watchful that when it is needful to be otherwise you may be able to change to the opposite qualities. It must be understood that a prince cannot observe all those things that are good in men, being often obliged, in order to maintain the State, to act against faith, against charity, against humanity and against religion. And, therefore, he must have a mind disposed to adapt itself according to the wind not to deviate from the good if possible but able to do evil if necessitated.'

When, fifty years later, *The Prince* was the rage (in both senses) of Europe and the name of Machiavelli had given a new adjective to languages, it was said that the book was Catherine de' Medici's bible, with the implication that, as Queen-Mother of France she had accidentally discovered an Italian author. What people overlooked—and still tend to overlook—is that it was specifically written for her.

When the Cardinal Giulio returned to Rome he took the five-months old Catherine with him. The Pope took her in his arms, noticed that she was 'well and lively', shed an expected tear, made an appropriate classical quotation: '*Secum fert aerumnas Danaum*'—She brings with her the calamities of the Greeks—and entrusted her to the care of her aunt, Clarice Strozzi. In doing so, he made the wisest of decisions. Clarice was Lorenzo's sister and the Pope had always contended that it would have been well for the family had Clarice been the man and Lorenzo the woman. Now, in giving the last of the Medici to Clarice to train, he did what he could to correct Nature's unfortunate mistake. Not the least of Clarice's admirable qualities was her detestation of Cardinal Giulio.

Catherine had been in Rome less than two years when Pope Leo died and Cardinal Giulio made the conventional preparations to succeed him. But on this occasion neither his diplomacy nor his bribery was unaccountably able to secure the necessary amount of votes in the Conclave, and to the astonishment of Europe an earnestly pious Fleming who had been tutor to the Emperor Charles V was elected and mounted the Papal throne as Adrian VI. Cardinal Giulio, in unconcealed chagrin, left Rome and devoted himself to family affairs in Florence. However, in a mere twenty months Adrian VI died, almost certainly poisoned, and this time, after a stormy seven weeks' session, Giulio was successful and on 19 November 1523 became Pope Clement VII.

Almost immediately he concluded a secret treaty with Francis I, but

Pope Clement VII and the Emperor Charles V meet to discuss Italian affairs in general and the siege of Florence in particular; painting by Vasari.

Contemporary engraving of Martin Luther, founder of Protestantism.

early in 1525 when the French suffered a crushing defeat at Pavia and the King himself was taken prisoner he made haste to desert him and ally himself instead with the victor, the young Emperor Charles V.

As a result of the chaos which prevailed in Italy after Pavia, with the victorious Imperial army, an unpaid rabble of 25,000 mercenaries in search of plunder, marching on Rome, it was felt that the Eternal City was no longer a safe refuge. Catherine and her aunt returned, in consequence, to Florence. Clarice naturally took up residence in the newly-built Strozzi Palace, while Catherine went back to the Medici Palace, a quarter of a mile away, where the new Pope had installed, as his representative in the government of Florence, his accommodating creature, Silvio Passerini, Cardinal of Cortona. In Passerini's charge were already two other young Medicis, Ippolito and Alessandro.

Ippolito, as the son of one of her father's brothers, was Catherine's first cousin. He was 16, two years older than Alessandro who—if Pope Clement was to be believed—was Catherine's half-brother, her father's bastard by a negress. Most people, however, did not believe it. The inordinate affection that Giulio, both as Cardinal and Pope, showed to this stupid and repulsive youth (who was described by a contemporary as 'a creature who would have disgraced even the worst epochs of the decadence of ancient Rome') roused the suspicion that he was Giulio's own bastard, while the Pope's final action in forcing 'the Moor'—as Alessandro was called on account of his swarthy complexion, his black curly hair and his thick negroid lips—on Florence as its ruler, instead of the admirable Ippolito, confirmed the suspicion. The truth, however, was naturally kept from Catherine, whom her new guardian, Cardinal Passerini, taught to regard him as her half-brother.

That inconceivable yet expected event, the siege and sack of Rome, took place in the May of 1527. Tales of destruction and atrocity far exceeding the pillage and cruelty of the Huns, the Vandals and the Goths of earlier centuries soon reached Florence to terrify the eight-year-old girl on whom one aspect of the sack made an indelible impression which was to influence her fundamental policy when she was Queen-Mother of France.

The invading troops were mainly Spanish and German (as Charles V was King of Spain as well as Emperor) and the largest section consisted of 13,000 German *reiters* who had volunteered to serve without pay provided that no limit was set to their pillaging. Their commander was von Frundsberg, notorious for his brutality, who always wore round his neck a heavy gold chain with which, so he said, he intended to strangle the Pope. He and his men were Lutherans, followers of the new creed which came into being the year after Catherine's birth when the Pope excommunicated its founder, Martin Luther, a renegade Augustinian monk.

The religious fanaticism of the Germans added a doctrinal edge to the sack. One of their captains, dressed in papal vestments, ordered his companions, arrayed as Cardinals, to kiss his feet and accompany him to the Vatican where, to the sound of trumpets and fifes, Luther was proclaimed Pope. An ass caparisoned in a cope was led into St. Peter's where a priest was ordered to cense it and offer it a consecrated Host. On his refusal he was hacked to pieces.

In later years Catherine had to face eight rebellions of French Protestants in which the threat to call in German *reiters* and let them loose on France was a constant factor in policy. On the first occasion, Gaspard de Coligny, Admiral of France, the Protestant leader, actually offered them the sack of Paris as a bribe. To ward off such a calamity, Catherine would stretch her statecraft to the limit. As Queen-Mother of France she never outgrew the impressions she gained as the 'Duchessina' of Florence.

In the days that followed the sack of Rome, her experiences deepened her apprehensions. When news came to Florence that the Pope was virtually a prisoner in the Castel St. Angelo, there was an immediate uprising of the people to throw off the Medici rule as represented by the hated Cardinal Passerini and his charges. On 19 May 1527 the Florentine populace rose and at the Palazzo della Signoria the decision was taken that the republican form of government should be in every respect restored but that Ippolito, Alessandro and Catherine should be permitted to reside in the city as private citizens and be exempted from all taxes for the next five years.

In the Medici Palace, Passerini and the two young men debated whether the offer should be accepted or whether, since there were signs of the mob preparing to plunder the palace, they would be wiser to leave Florence while they could. Catherine sat and listened. Suddenly her aunt Clarice burst into the room and, in a voice so loud that it could be heard in the Via Larga outside she bitterly taunted the trembling Cardinal on having brought the affairs of the Medici to such a pass, contrasting it with the way things were managed 'by my ancestors, who were *true* Medici and who with benevolence and gentleness gained the loyalty of the Florentines and so found them constant in adversity. But *you*'—she turned to Alessandro—'who by your conduct have betrayed the secret of your birth and convinced the world that you are not a true Medici; and not you only but Clement also, wrongfully Pope and now rightfully prisoner in St. Angelo, why are you surprised that all are this day against you? Now, therefore, depart from a house to which you have no claim and a city which has no affection for you. For in this evil hour the family honour depends on *me*.'

Passerini and the two boys took her advice and made a hurried departure by the door at the back of the palace while the mob began to pour in from the

Via Larga and start plundering the great house. The representatives of the people refused to allow Catherine and her aunt to leave the city. The little Duchess was to be kept as a hostage in the case of any future difficulties with Pope Clement.

To gain what safety she could for her charge, Clarice Strozzi, while herself refusing to leave the Medici Palace, arranged for Catherine to live in the convent of Santa Lucia, where, for the next six months, the child was looked after by the nuns.

In a very short time, however, the plague visited Florence and so increased in virulence that by the end of November there had been 14,000 deaths. It had even invaded the convent of Santa Lucia and for her safety Catherine was moved to the great convent of the Murate, on the other side of the city, which was free of it. On the night of December 7, she walked through the deserted streets, accompanied by two attendants and on her arrival, as one of the Murate sisters recorded, the nuns 'caressed her with every possible show of affection, principally because she was only a little creature, only eight years and eight months, of most engaging manners and eminently capable of securing the affection of everyone for her own sake, but also because of the convent's grateful memory of the benefits received from Lorenzo the Magnificent, her great-grandfather and from Leo the Tenth and from Clement the Seventh.'

Two days later, in Rome, Clement VII managed to escape from the Castel St. Angelo. Disguised as one of his servants, he walked unchallenged through the gates, wearing a long false beard and a large tattered hat, a basket on his arm and an empty bag over his shoulder. With a single peasant for his companion, he procured a cart and through the night drove to his summer residence at Orvieto. On his regaining his liberty, one emotion overtopped all others—the desire for revenge.

That Florence should revolt again and once more send his family into exile was more intolerable to him even than the sack of Rome and his other misfortunes. It so obsessed him that he made another secret arrangement with the Emperor, undertaking to crown him with the crown of Charlemagne, to marry Alessandro to the Emperor's illegitimate daughter and to make them Duke and Duchess of Florence when the city should be recaptured and its republican constitution finally destroyed. To this end he hired for 30,000 florins and the promise of the plunder of Florence the same ruffians who had sacked Rome. They marched to besiege it, with 'By the glorious sack of Florence' as their favourite oath. As the historian of the Popes has it: 'With astonishment did men behold Clement so completely change his policy that the very army by which the horrors of the sack of Rome had been perpetrated before his eyes and himself held so long a

Catherine's native city as it was in her day.

captive, he now launched upon his native city.'

During the terrible eleven months' siege, Catherine was being educated intensively by the aristocratic nuns of the Murate. In the months before the actual arrival of the Imperial and Papal forces before the walls of the city, she found there such peace and affection and security as made them indelible in memory. Over fifty years later, she made the Murate a valuable grant of some of her property in Tuscany, writing to the Abbess: 'The notable and unceasing zeal for God's service, as well as the uprightness and purity of life which in my childhood I observed to reign in your convent (where possibly some may still be alive who knew me as a young girl) have induced me to show my gratitude to your convent for the continual and devout prayers you have offered up for the soul of the King my husband and for me.'

And in another letter she recalled in verse the garden by the river and the view she saw daily:

Detail from the 'Carta della Catena', Florence in 1490.

Monti superbi, la cui fronte Alpina
 Fa di se contro i venti argine e sponda!
 Valle beate, per cui d'onda in onda
L'Arno con passo signoril cammina!

Glorious mountains, whose Alp-like summits
Make against the winds a barrier and a defence!
Happy valleys, through which in wave on wave
The Arno with lordly step takes his way!

But once the besieging army encamped outside Florence the atmosphere changed dramatically. She became the object of suspicion and hatred. One member of the Signoria proposed that she should be suspended from the walls in a basket as a target for the enemy fire; another that she should be put in a brothel.

Even the Murate nuns, because they were mainly members of the Florentine aristocracy and presumed to favour the Medici, fell under the suspicion
of the Government, who spread the rumour that the little baskets of pastry
which the Sisters were accustomed to send to their relatives in the city
contained six round buns which were to be construed as the six *palle*, the
red balls which were the armorial bearings of the Medici. At a time when the
shout of the crowds was *Abbasso le Palle!* this was treason. The Signoria
decided that Catherine must be removed from the Murate.

Consequently in the middle of the night of 19 July 1530, the nuns were
aroused by a prolonged knocking at the door by a party of Senators who
presented an official order for the delivery to them of 'the girl Catherine
de' Medici'. The Duchissina, fearing death in the dark, managed to persuade
the Mother Superior to postpone the handing over till the morning. She then
went to her own room, cut off all her hair and put on a nun's habit. 'Will
they dare now to remove me?' she said. 'When they come back in the morning, it will appear to everyone that they are guilty of carrying off a nun from
her convent.'

The entire sisterhood spent the remaining hours of the night in prayer in
the chapel and in the morning when the Senators returned, this time with a
horse for Catherine, they unavailingly tried to persuade her to change into
lay clothes. 'She refused with wonderful firmness and resolution' recorded
one of the nuns, 'declaring that at least all the world should see that she was a
nun taken forcibly from her convent.' The battle of wills continued for over
an hour. At last she consented to mount the horse and, escorted by a considerable number of gentlemen marching on either side to keep the crowds
away, she was taken away from the Murate. Whatever destination the
Senators had intended, they had now no option but to take her to another
convent and she found herself back at the Santa Lucia nunnery, whose
puritan and plebeian sisters could at least be trusted to follow the republican
line in political matters.

A month later Florence surrendered and Catherine as soon as she regained
her freedom returned joyfully to the Murate where she remained until the
spring when the Pope, having arranged for Alessandro to take up residence
as Duke of Florence, recalled her to Rome.

Opposite: *Detail from Gozzoli's fresco in the Medici Palace, showing
Catherine's great-grandfather, Lorenzo the Magnificent, on horseback.*

Overleaf: *Vasari's painting on the siege of Florence in 1530, during which
Catherine was virtually a prisoner.*

The Bride

Catherine arrived in Rome on 12 October 1530 and remained there for eighteen months in a household presided over by her great-aunt, Leo X's sister, which included Ippolito. He, to his great annoyance, had been made a Cardinal by the Pope in order to facilitate Alessandro's appointment as Duke of Florence. One of the very few accounts of Catherine in Rome is given by the Venetian Ambassador.

'The Duchessina is of a rather vivacious nature but shows an amiable disposition. She was educated by the nuns of the Convent of the Murate in Florence and she has very good manners. She is small and thin, her face is not refined and she has the big eyes characteristic of the Medici. The Most Reverend Cardinal de' Medici (Ippolito) is very envious of the Duke Alessandro because it seems to him that the Pope did him a great injustice in putting the Duke instead of him at the head of the government of Florence. I have also heard it whispered by some that the Cardinal de' Medici wants to put off his ecclesiastical robes and to take as his wife the little Duchess, his third cousin, with whom he lives on the best possible terms and is also very much loved by her. Indeed there is no other in whom she confides so much or whose counsel she is apt to seek.'

The Milanese Ambassador also gave a picture of the young Catherine: 'I have seen her twice on horseback, but not sufficiently well to give a complete picture of her. She seems to me rather large for her age, fairly good-looking without the help of any cosmetic, a blonde with a rather stout face. But she appears very young and I do not believe she can be called or considered a woman for a year and a half longer. It is said that she has good feelings and a very acute and adroit mind for her age.'

Nubile or not, Catherine had been in Rome less than six weeks when her

Opposite: *Titian's portrait of Cardinal Ippolito, who was Catherine's cousin, confidant and friend, and who might well have married her.*

29

uncle the Duke of Albany—her mother's elder brother—arrived in Rome as the representative of the King of France to negotiate her marriage with Francis I's second son, Henry Duke of Orléans. By this alliance, Pope Clement hoped to counterbalance the influence of the Emperor and in the secret terms of the marriage-treaty he made several concessions incompatible with his promises to Charles V. This however was of comparatively little importance since he had no intention of keeping any of them.

The actual sum of 130,000 écus for Catherine's dowry was, in the circumstances, modest enough and far less than Francis originally demanded, but it was more than compensated for by Clement's promise to give, in addition to Parma, 'the cities of Pisa, Livorno, Reggio and Modena to his said niece and consequently to her future husband'. Though the contract was signed in 1531, the date of the wedding was postponed for at least eighteen months, and at the end of April 1532, Catherine returned to Florence to make the necessary preparations.

Clarice Strozzi was dead, Alessandro was occupying the Medici Palace and Catherine's aunt, Maria—the daughter of the Lucrezia Salviati who had been in charge of her in Rome—was living in widowed retirement in her villa twenty miles from Florence, devoting her life to the bringing up of her only son. Catherine, therefore, returned to the Murate, though Maria Salviati often visited her in the capacity of general guardian and was, moreover, prepared to accompany her, as her nearest living female relative, to her wedding at Marseilles.

Alessandro, much as he disliked his supposed half-sister, felt that he must make some contribution to her marriage. He imposed a forced loan on the citizens of Florence of 35,000 scudi which according to the historian was entirely spent on 'the equipage of the Duchessina, in embroidery and jewels and clothes and velvet and gold bed-curtains and housings for horses,' instead of on the fortifications of Florence for which it was officially raised.

On 1 September 1533 Catherine, accompanied by her aunt Maria Salviati and her cousin Catherine Cibò (whose grandfathers were Lorenzo the Magnificent and Pope Innocent VIII) and a considerable retinue left Florence for Spezia where her uncle Albany was awaiting her with a fleet of twenty-seven ships to take her to France. The royal galley had been specially constructed with a state-room which ran from mainmast to rudder, covered with crimson damask strewn with golden lilies. The awnings were purple, the rooms were hung with cloth of gold, the rowing-benches, occupied by three hundred rowers dressed in damascened satin of red and gold, were chained to the sides with silver chains.

Catherine landed at Nice and remained there while Albany returned with some of the galleys to Leghorn to fetch the Pope, who had refused to travel overland because it would have necessitated a visit to Florence. After Clement with his retinue (which included Ippolito who had been recalled from Turkey for the occasion), had joined Catherine, they proceeded in different vessels, as etiquette prescribed, to Marseilles where they arrived on October 11th.

For two months the city had been making preparations for the event, supervised by Anne de Montmorency, Grand Master and Marshal of France, the trusted friend of the King, Francis I.

By the end of September the Chancellor, the Cardinals, the great nobles and the principal ladies of the court of France had arrived at Marseilles. On October 8th, the King, the Queen and the Dauphin had taken up their temporary residence at Aubagne, a village one post from Marseilles on the road to Aix. With them were the two younger princes, Henry of Orléans and Charles of Angoulême.

Henry, the bridegroom-elect, was fourteen and a half, a mere thirteen days older than Catherine. He was a dull, taciturn youth and, though physically robust, with a temperament scarred by his imprisonment in Madrid where, after the French defeat at Pavia, he and his elder brother, the Dauphin, had been held as hostages for their father. It was said that when the captivity ended and the Constable of Castile asked the princes to forgive any ill-treatment they might have received, Henry answered by breaking wind. He returned to France with a violent and undying hatred of the Emperor and a permanent grudge against his father. Francis, on his part, who adored the Dauphin, disliked Henry and the tension between them was further increased by the boy's feeling of inadequacy beside his splendid father whose almost legendary personality is best summed up in an ambassadorial report: 'The King has such a royal presence that anyone seeing him without knowing who he was would say at once: "That is the King".' Francis had about him an aura of light and laughter; Henry, with his listless, bruised eyes and slow mind, was never known to laugh.

With grave courtesy the boy received the Pope when on Sunday 12 October Clement's galley crossed the harbour so that he could make a processional entry into the city. The Holy Father's right hand held that of Henry, his left his younger brother Charles's. Together they genuflected to the Blessed Sacrament. Then the Pope placed the Host in a tabernacle and, according to the custom observed in all long Papal journeys, put it on a white horse, led by two footmen holding white silk reins and preceded by a third ringing a golden bell to warn the crowds to prostrate themselves in adoration to the Blessed Sacrament.

On the Monday the King and the Dauphin made their state entry with a splendour that eclipsed the Pope's and on the Tuesday the Queen and the princesses with their ladies in six 'triumphal cars' attended by thirty damsels

Pope Clement VII (Giulio de'
Medici); painting by Bronzino.

Catherine at the time of her
marriage; from a Book of Hours.

on magnificently caparisoned horses entered, giving the citizens of Marseilles
a penultimate pageant.

Catherine entered last of all—on horseback. Her twelve ladies were also
mounted, but to demonstrate that she, no less than the French ladies, possessed a carriage and was riding from choice, her 'carriage of black velvet'
with two pages on the horses followed her in the procession.

On 28 October, the marriage ceremony was performed by the Pope in
the Cathedral. At its conclusion the bride was taken to the royal residence
by Francis himself 'who led her by the arm, she being covered with brocade,
with a corsage of ermine filled with pearls and diamonds.' Catherine's
jewels were the talk of the occasion. As part of her dowry, the Pope had given
her twenty-seven thousand gold *scudi's* worth—a belt of gold with eight
great balas rubies and a diamond in the middle, a pendant set with a great
diamond, ruby and emerald, a string of eighty pearls, a rose of twenty
diamonds, many rings and, above all, a set of seven especially magnificent
pearls, 'the largest and finest that ever were seen', which she subsequently
gave to her daughter-in-law, Mary Queen of Scots, and which are now

Rock crystal cabinet by Vincentino made as a gift from Clement VII to King Francis I on the occasion of Catherine's wedding.

among the English crown jewels. To these the bridegroom and his father had added a sapphire tablet and a diamond cut *en dos d'âne*.

Clement, on his part, had presented King Francis with a casket made by Valerio Vincentino, the greatest cutter of precious stones of the day, which the Pope had paid the artist the unprecedented sum of 2000 golden crowns to make. It was carved from transparent rock crystal and lined with silver so as to give the appearance of relief to the twenty-four engravings of scenes from the life of Christ. It contained a pyx of fine enamel set with rubies for the reservation of the Host. Vincentino's casket was generally considered the most valuable of all the wedding gifts.

At the marriage supper Catherine sat between her husband and the Dauphin at the head of a long table lined by Cardinals, while the King and the Pope presided over another, and a third was occupied by a galaxy of

Overleaf: Vasari's painting of Pope Clement VII marrying his niece Catherine to Henry Duke of Orleans, second son of King Francis I of France, in Marseilles on 28 October 1533.

ladies chaperoned by the Grande Sénéchale de Normandie, Diane de Poitiers.

'Marseilles on that occasion', wrote a chronicler, 'was honoured by the most celebrated assembly that perhaps had ever met in Europe, comprising the entire court of Rome and the entire court of France of both sexes.' In consequence, Catherine, surrounded by her past, met immediately her future. Among the plethora of cardinals was not only Ippolito but the young Cardinal de Guise and the even younger Cardinal de Coligny, Odet, who was given the honour on that particular occasion.

The new Duchesse d'Orléans had an opportunity to study the women whose influences made the court a battleground where she would henceforth have to fight for survival. The Queen was a nonentity—the Emperor's sister whom Francis had been forced to take as his second wife as part of the bargain for his release after Pavia—but the King's sister and his mistress, Margaret of Navarre and the Duchesse d'Etampes, were forceful enough. Margaret, indeed, as a patroness of the arts and as an 'advanced' thinker was known in Italy, but it was only proximity which revealed her essential nature and the mainspring of her actions. This was a passionate and unwavering love for her brother Francis, who was two years her junior and who, with the long nose and sideways glance from heavy-lidded eyes, so resembled her facially. 'I was yours before you were born; you are more to me than father, mother and husband. Compared with you, husband and children count as nothing' she had written to him and the avowal was a key to court politics. Whoever was loved by the one was approved by the other and, from the moment of Catherine's arrival, Margaret held out her arms in friendship.

The golden-haired Madame d'Etampes, 'la plus belle des savants et la plus savante des belles', the King's mistress and governess to the young Princesses, had been chosen for Francis by his mother and his sister and exercised no individual authority. What Francis and Margaret approved, she approved; and, as Margaret had already signified her approval of Catherine, there was no difficulty to be expected by the bride in that quarter.

La Grande Sénéchale, Diane de Poitiers, was a different matter. She was thirty-one, the widow of Louis de Brézé, le Grand Sénéchal. She had lived, impeccable in widowhood, preserving what little beauty she had by the application of much cold water but no cosmetics to her skin. When the two young princes, the Dauphin and Henry, had arrived back from their captivity in Madrid, their father had been so shocked by the change in them that he ordered their tutors to cross them in nothing 'in order to remove the fear of

Opposite: *Painting by Jean Clouet of Francis I, Catherine's father-in-law, who all his life gave her his friendship.*

subjection they felt in Spain.' The result was that Henry at the age of eleven could be justly described as 'M. d'Orléans who does nothing but give blows and whom no man can master,' and Francis thought it time to try to civilize him. For this process he entrusted him to Diane who, seventeen years his senior, supplied something of the maternal solicitude which his step-mother the Queen notably withheld.

The years were to change the formal relationship between the Sénéchale and her charge into a devoted love which, despite the disparity of their ages, lasted for twenty-two years and ensured that when Henry became king it was not Catherine de' Medici but Diane de Poitiers, the uncrowned queen, who dictated France's policy. Of that future misery, the bride had no hint at the marriage-feast, nor would anyone there—except, perhaps Diane with her cold, sphinx-like smile—have entertained it as the remotest of possibilities.

Supper over, the bride and groom were seen officially to bed in the manner prescribed by protocol. The Pope had insisted on immediate consummation and he remained in Marseilles for thirty-four days hoping for evidence of conception. He was disappointed and returned to Rome after giving Catherine his blessing and the advice '*A figlia d'inganno non manca mai la figliuolanza*' —a clever woman can always have children.

But Catherine had none for ten years.

Queen Claude, consort of Francis I, mother of Catherine's husband.

Duchess of Orléans

'M. d'Orléans is married to Madame Catherine de' Medici,' the Venetian Ambassador reported, 'which dissatisfies the entire nation. It is thought that Pope Clement deceived the King in this alliance.'

He had indeed done so. Not only did he make no effort, once he had returned to Rome, to implement his promise to cede Parma, Pisa, Livorno, Reggio and Modena to France, but it was discovered that the greater part of the jewels he had given Catherine were not his to give, since they were the property of the Holy See and not of whatever individual happened temporarily to occupy the Papal Throne.

On Clement's death, eleven months after the wedding, French opinion was confirmed by Italian behaviour. There were nightly attacks on his tomb and had it not been for respect for Ippolito, Cardinal de' Medici, the body would have been dragged through the city by a hook. A guard had to be set over it after the inscription: 'To Clement the Seventh, Pontifex Maximus, whose invincible valour was only exceeded by his clemency' had been changed to: 'To Inclement, Pontifex Minimus whose conquered valour was only exceeded by his avarice.'

Clement had left Philip Strozzi, Clarice's widower, as his ambassador in France, chiefly because his enormous wealth and ability might have obstructed Alessandro in Florence. In the circumstances, however, Strozzi's financial expertise in appearing to extricate the Vatican from Clement's commitments and in bringing procrastination to a fine art justified the new appointment from the Papal point-of-view, even if it provoked Francis to remark: '*J'ai reçu la fille toute nue.*'

The King, however, did not withdraw his affection from his daughter-in-law. Catherine, despised by the nobility and disliked by the populace who saw it as a slur on the national honour that an Italian bourgeoise should intrude into the royal family of France, could rely on the friendship of Francis who, from the day he received her at Marseilles, realised that she

39

Catherine's Italian advisers:

Left: *Philippe Strozzi, painted by the school of Clouet. Strozzi's wife Clarice was Catherine's aunt and mentor; and Strozzi himself was Rome's first ambassador to Paris after Catherine's marriage.*

Centre: *René de Biragues, sculpted in bronze by Germain Pilon. The banker Birago was entitled René de Biragues and became Chancellor of France.*

Right: *Albert de Gondi, son of the banker Antonio Gondi, painted by the school of Clouet. Albert was entitled Comte de Retz, and became Marshal of France.*

had a livelier wit and a better education than the court ladies who vied with each other in insulting her. He made her a member of his famous *Petite Bande,* the exclusive bevy of young women who attended him from palace to palace—he seldom stayed in one place for more than a fortnight—who hunted with him and dined with him and jested with him and composed *risqué* riddles for him and kept him young.

Despite the King's favour and the friendship of his mistress, Madame d'Etampes, Catherine felt inevitably isolated, the more so as her continuing childlessness emphasised the failure of the marriage on every level. The recall of Strozzi to Rome deprived her of his avuncular care and was not altogether compensated for by the subsequent arrival of his eldest son, Piero, at the head of a band of harquebusiers, magnificently mounted and equipped, offering himself for service to King Francis. He was followed by his brothers, Leone and Lorenzo—Clarice had had ten children, seven of them sons—and though it gave Catherine pleasure to have near her the cousins and companions of her childhood their coming, heralding the 'Italian invasion' which was to bedevil her subsequent statecraft, served only to increase her unpopularity.

And the one man she would have wished to see, Ippolito, could not come to her. In the June of 1535 he was poisoned by Alessandro.

It was natural enough for Catherine to have in her service a certain amount of Italians who had accompanied her to France on her marriage. Outstanding among them were the Gondi. Antonio Gondi was a small banker and his wife a lady-in-waiting whom Catherine intended to be—and eventually was—nurse to her children. There was another banker, Birago. There was Ludovico di Gonzaga, younger brother of the Duke of Mantua who had been one of the suitors for Catherine's hand.

In course of time the names were to be changed. Gondi's eldest son became the Comte de Retz, Marshal of France; Birago became René de Biragues, the Chancellor; the Gonzagas became Ducs de Nevers.

As, for the proper understanding of Catherine, it was necessary to stress that Machiavelli had dedicated *The Prince* to her father and written it specifically as advice to her house, so, for the same reason, it should be emphasised that in these first miserable years of her marriage was begun the pattern that was completed at the crisis of her life and reputation, the massacre of St. Bartholomew.

Of the eight people who took the final decision for the massacre, only one —old heretic-hating Tavannes—was a full Frenchman. The other seven were Catherine herself, her two elder sons—aged twenty-two and twenty-one;

the twenty-two year old Duc de Guise, whose mother was Italian; and de Retz, Biragues and Nevers. The then Ambassador-extraordinary of Venice (who can hardly be accused of anti-Italian prejudice) reported: 'The Catholics are disgusted beyond measure as much as the Huguenots—not, as they say, at the deed itself so much as the manner of doing it. They call this way of proceeding, by absolute power without legal process, a tyrant's way, attributing it to the Queen-Mother as an Italian, a Florentine and a Medici, whose blood is impregnated with tyranny. For this reason she is detested to the highest degree and, on her account, so is the whole Italian nation.'

Two other Italians whose influence on Catherine was unbounded were the Ruggieri brothers, Cosimo and Lorenzo, sons of the Ruggiero, called 'the old' to distinguish him from his offspring, who had been physician, astrologer and mathematician to the Medici and, in conjunction with the mathematician, Bazile, had cast the horoscope of Catherine's nativity with such accuracy— including her peril during the siege of Florence and her marriage to a Prince of France—that it would have predisposed her to believe the truth of astrology had she not already naturally accepted it.

Even as a child, studying the fresco of *The Journey of the Magi* on the walls of the Medici chapel or the picture of *The Adoration of the Magi* by Botticelli in the Church of Sta. Maria Novella where also her forbears were depicted as the Kings, she began to consider the Magi as the particular protectors of her house and observed their feast, the Epiphany, with particular reverence. Quite apart from the universal belief in astrology, Catherine recognised it as an intrinsic part of the Christian religion, since Christ's birth was recognised, apart from a few shepherds in the immediate vicinity, only by three royal astrologers who, by the exercise of their art, had been star-led to a stable in Bethlehem.

On Cosimo Ruggieri, when they came to France, Catherine relied as she relied on no one else. On his part he devoted himself entirely to her, whereas his brother Lorenzo accommodated himself to a more general practice among the courtiers. Eventually she took no major decision without consulting him as to whether the stars ratified the advice of her counsellors or her own analysis of a political situation. Cosimo, on his side, impressed on her the importance of the classical wisdom: *Astra declinant, non necessitant,* the stars dispose but do not compel. Though it might be possible for an adept to discern the destiny of an individual, neither he nor anyone else could predict how several people, thrown together in a Council or some other body, would act, with their conflicting wills and differing destinies. Yet for herself, he continued to predict the apparently impossible—that she, childless wife of the King's second son, would become Queen of France and mother of ten children.

She did her best to remedy her sterility. She consulted several doctors, accepted indiscriminate prescriptions and submitted to every experiment, however distasteful, but with no result. Gossip attributed her barrenness to hereditary syphilis. No one had the courtesy to suggest that it might be her husband who was to blame.

It was not a matter of great moment except to her until on 12 August 1536 the Dauphin died of pleurisy, brought on by drinking a glass of water when he was overheated by violent exercise. The water had been given him by his cup-bearer, Count Sebastian Montecuculi, in answer to his request for it. The King, who idolised his eldest son, was so stricken with grief by his sudden and unexpected death that he accused Montecuculi of poisoning him and insisted on the Count being brought to trial. The motive was supposed to be that Montecuculi, who had come over in the Pope's train for the wedding and had stayed on, originally in the service of the Queen, was the secret agent of the Queen's brother, the Emperor Charles V, by whose orders and in whose interest he had been required to poison both the King and his heir.

The result of the trial and torture of the innocent Italian was placarded in Lyons, where the Court was, on 6 September 1536: 'Sentenced to be torn by horses Count Sebastian Montecuculi for having plotted to poison the King and having succeeded in poisoning the eldest son of the King by arsenic powder put by him into a vase of red clay in the Maison de Plat at Lyons.' As the news spread throughout France, it was enough for the populace that Montecuculi was an Italian and the death of the Dauphin made Catherine's husband heir to the throne for them to maintain that 'the Italian woman' was responsible for the poisoning. From that moment there were not wanting pamphleteers to suggest that almost any crime committed anywhere in France was in some way attributable to Catherine de' Medici.

The Dauphine

The idea that the Emperor had instigated the poisoning of the King derived
some credibility from the circumstance that Charles and Francis were at war
again. The Emperor, in pursuit of his ambition to rule all Europe, had
revived the old Imperial claim to the Arlate and was determined to be
crowned at Aix, Charlemagne's city, as King of Arles and Provence. By the
time of the Dauphin's death, his army of fifty thousand, mainly Germans and
Spaniards, had swept the French out of Piedmont, had captured Nice and
was preparing for a descent on Lyons.

The Grand Master of France, Anne de Montmorency, who was also the
Governor of Languedoc, was put in charge of the French forces and established himself in the neighbourhood of Avignon at the junction of the Rhône
and the Durance. With a force of 30,000, many of them Swiss mercenaries,
he thought Fabian tactics the safest and took a course so extreme that only
his great reputation and authority made it obeyed.

He gave orders that Provence was to be rendered impossible for a hostile
army to live there even if it could not be prevented from entering it. Towns,
villages, olive groves, vineyards, farms, were ruined. No bakehouse or mill
remained; hayricks and cornstacks were burned, wine-casks staved in, wells
filled up with corn 'to corrupt the water'. Grimly Montmorency stayed in his
lines (which an observer declared were like a well-governed city rather than a
newly-formed and heterogeneous camp of soldiers) and watched the destruction of France's fairest province in an agony of doubt as to his wisdom.

But he was justified. In less than two months, the Emperor recrossed the
Var, with a ruined army and a dimmed reputation. At first, on the frontier, he
had managed to find hidden stores which in the hurry of destruction had
been overlooked; but as he proceeded further into Provence and his lines of

Opposite: *Portrait by Titian of the Emperor Charles V, whom the French
suspected of instigating the death of the Dauphin.*

*Wood-engraving depicting Anne de Montmorency, one of the
most powerful noblemen in France, the great Constable of France, who was
Catherine's trusted friend and 'gossip'. Montmorency has also been
described as 'a Renaissance barbarian'.*

communication lengthened, the desolation became more absolute. His convoys from Toulon were intercepted by the hungry peasantry and the soldiers, eating unripe figs and grapes, went down with dysentery so fast that in less than a month a quarter of the army was disabled. An attempt to take Marseilles failed and retreat became inevitable.

Shortly after the Dauphin's death, Henry, the new Dauphin, arrived in Avignon, and was particularly welcomed by the young nobility, who disagreed with the Grand Master's tactics and were chafing at the continued inaction. They implored the prince to defy Montmorency and to lead them against the enemy. Dearly as Henry would have liked to do so, he was, in this matter, too wise to agree. For one thing, he had no wish to alienate his father and he knew that Francis implicitly trusted the Grand Master, who had fought with him at Pavia and shared his Spanish captivity. Also, now that he was allowed to be a soldier, Henry had found a calling in which his physical abilities could be used to give him confidence in himself and, making his own judgments, he willingly rendered to his commander the soldier's first duty of obedience.

The Dauphin's loyalty to the Grand Master at this juncture was reciprocated and marked the beginning of an unbreakable friendship which ended only in death.

One of its immediate consequences was to give Catherine another powerful friend. When her husband was in camp she wrote to Montmorency as 'My gossip' begging him to take good care of Henry 'because I have heard it said that he fell the other day and came very near injuring himself'. She signed herself 'Your good cousin and gossip, Catherine' asking for more news but bidding the Grand Master 'not to write to me any more ceremoniously.'

When the war ended, the Grand Master was created Constable of France and for three years was the unchallenged power in the country until he became enmeshed in the struggle between the two mistresses—Madame d'Etampes, the King's, and Diane de Poitiers, the Dauphin's.

It was sometime between 1538 and 1540 that the Sénéchale changed her rôle in Henry's life from mentor to mistress. Their liaison, lasting until his death, was unparalleled among royal amours till that of Louis XIV and Madame de Maintenon which it in many ways resembled. To the outsider, the character of it must remain a mystery. Diane was hard, grasping and unscrupulous. She was not particularly intelligent. She was not beautiful, as her authentic portraits—the sketch by Jean Clouet and the enamel by Limousin—show clearly enough, with her plain, plump face and pursed, discontented mouth. The idealised portrait by Primaticcio (who probably never saw her) and the bronze by Benvenuto Cellini are exercises in an Artemis. Henry, even in the first flush of attraction, could find no better word than *'honnête'* to describe Diane's face, and an observant courtier wrote: 'It is a grievous thing to see a young prince adore a faded face covered with wrinkles and a head fast turning grey and eyes which have grown dim and are sometimes red.'

Whatever the cause of Diane's influence, it was absolute.

> *De fosse creuse ou de tour bien murée*
> *N'a point besoin de ma foi la forteresse*
> *Dont je vous fis dame, reine et maîtresse,*
> *Pour ce qu'elle est d'éternelle durée.*

Henry wrote in one of his early poems to her; and 'dame, reine et maîtresse' she remained.

If Henry loved no one but Diane, Catherine loved no one but Henry. Her love for him was in fact so great that she faced the long martyrdom of jealousy with a quiet acquiescence. An ambassador noticed that, though at the beginning, she could not endure it, 'she has resigned herself and now bears it with patience at the urgent prayers of her husband'. And years later she wrote to her daughter that 'never did woman who loved her husband succeed in loving his mistress' but that 'if I made good cheer for her it was really him I was entertaining.'

The three years from 1539 to 1542, Catherine's twentieth to twenty-third year, were made additionally miserable by her continued failure to bear a child, combined with Diane's efforts to induce Henry to divorce her.

At this crisis, Margaret, Francis's sister, hastened to console her. 'My brother,' she wrote from Navarre, 'will never allow this repudiation as evil tongues pretend. But God will give you a royal line when you have reached the age at which women of the House of Medici are wont to have children. The King and I will rejoice with you then, in spite of these wretched backbiters.'

Catherine decided to face the crisis. The Venetian Ambassador reported to the Doge: 'She went to the King and with many tears told him she had heard it was His Majesty's intention to give his son another wife, and as it had not yet pleased God to give her the grace of children it was proper that as soon as His Majesty found it undesirable to wait longer, he should provide for the succession to so great a throne; and that for her part, considering the great obligation she was under to His Majesty, who had deigned to accept her as a daughter-in-law, she was much more disposed to endure this affliction than to attempt to oppose his will.'

For the good of France, she said, she would retire to a convent or remain in the royal service, whichever he pleased.

'*Ma fille,*' said the King, 'have no doubt, since God hath willed it, that you ought to be my daughter-in-law and the Dauphin's wife, and that I would not have it otherwise. It may be that it will please Him to grant the grace that you and I desire more than anything else in this world.'

The obstruction lay not with Catherine but with Henry. 'Nothing is commoner in surgical experience' as Balzac has put it, 'than such a malformation as the Prince's, which gave rise to a jest of the ladies of the Court, who would have made him Abbé de Saint-Victor, at a time when the French language was as free as the Latin tongue. After the Prince was operated on, Catherine had ten children.'

The birth of the eldest, a son (named, inevitably, Francis after his grandfather), took place the following year and was welcomed lyrically by the faithful Margaret of Navarre:

> *Un fils! Un fils! ô nom dont sur tous noms*
> *Très obligés à Dieu nous nous tenons!*
> *O fils heureux! joye d'un jeune père!*
> *Souverain bien de la contente mère!*
> *Heureuse foy, qui, après longue attente,*
> *Leur a donné le fruit de leur prétente!*

During the miserable years of waiting, Catherine naturally attached herself to the King's party, led by Francis, his sister (when she was not with her husband and daughter in Navarre), his mistress, Madame d'Etampes

Margaret, Queen of Navarre, greatly-loved sister of Francis I, authoress of the Heptameron, *and Catherine's unchanging friend.*

(who liked it to be known that she had been born on Diane's wedding-day) and the Constable, with his two favourite nephews, the Cardinal Odet and his younger brother—who was six weeks older than Catherine—Gaspard de Coligny.

The Dauphin's party, provocatively wearing Diane's colours of silver and black, were chiefly the Guises, the younger branch of the great Dukedom of Lorraine on the eastern borders of France. Of the sons of the first Duke of Guise—a title only fifteen years old—one was married to the daughter of Diane; one, Francis, who was a few months younger than Catherine, was a soldier; one, Charles, who was only seventeen, was already a Cardinal.

Francis was to become in due course the foremost soldier in Europe and Charles, as Cardinal of Lorraine, one of the most influential ecclesiastics. They were to mould the history of France; and the relationship between Catherine and their family was one of the keys to international politics for

Opposite: *The portrait of Catherine at the age of twenty-one always preserved by her own family; in front of the crown she is wearing the seven great pearls which the Pope gave her on her wedding, and which she in turn gave to Mary Queen of Scots.*

Below: *The three brothers Coligny: left to right, Odet, the Cardinal, Gaspard, the Admiral, and Francis (Andelot), Colonel-General of Infantry.*

decades. And, once more, these early days dictate the future and explain apparent paradoxes. Without any doubt, the Cardinal had the best brain in government circles and would have been Catherine's wisest counsellor, but she relentlessly hated him and opposed him. For it was the Cardinal, with all the insouciance of his seventeen years, who had originally suggested the divorce.

Similarly, when thirty years later Catherine had to make the terrible decision whether or not for the safety of the state to have Coligny assassinated, the victim was not someone remote from her personal life but one she had known well from her first days in France, her one-time partisan on whose behalf she was now writing to her cousin, Maria Salviati's son, in Florence, that Coligny and his brother were about to visit Italy, and that 'because they are gentlemen whom I hold in very high esteem, I have begged them, my cousin, to visit you and tell you all the news about me. I assure you that you will give me very great pleasure by showing them all the favour you can and I shall be as grateful to you as if you had shown it to me.'

The division between the rival parties at Court in these early years was, of course, anything but rigid and did not even suggest the definition that religious fanaticism was later to give them. Protestantism, in those circles, was nothing but a current literary fashion dictated by Margaret of Navarre, who was a correspondent of Erasmus and a patron of the young French lawyer, Jean Cauvin, (later to be better known as John Calvin), who worked out his new system in his *Institutes* while he was her guest in Navarre.

Margaret also suggested to the poet Clément Marot, one of the wilder spirits of the time, who had been successively *valet-de-chambre* to King Francis (who called him *'mon bien aimé varlet-de-chambre'*) and to her, that he should translate thirty of the Psalms of David into French verse. These translations became the rage of the court. King, Dauphin, Margaret, the Dauphine, the Constable and the courtiers and the cardinals—all had special favourites which they knew by heart and sang even when hunting. Humming Marot's psalms to some air or other—for they were set to dance tunes as well as the lugubrious chants which the humourless John Calvin circulated—became indeed a mark of fashion. Catherine's favourite, which though not identifiable with any particular original was appropriate enough to her circumstances, was that beginning:

Opposite: *Diane de Poitiers, mistress of Henry II, and the main cause of Catherine's misery.*

Overleaf: *Aerial view of the Château of Chambord, Francis I's most ambitious essay in stone.*

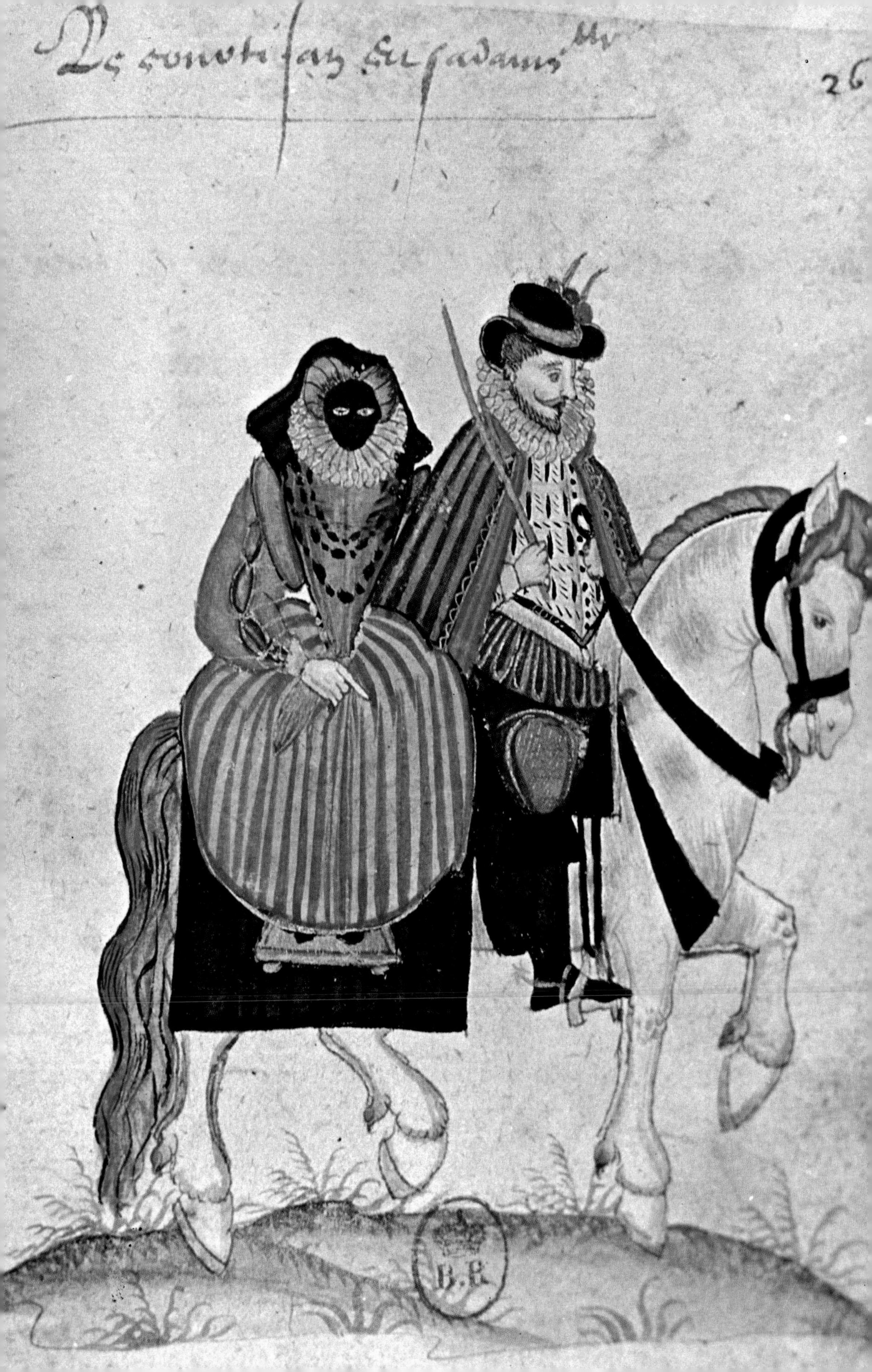
26
B.R.

Vers l'Eternel, des opprimés le Père,
Je m'en irai Lui montrant l'impropère
   Que l'on me fait.

When the Emperor visited France after the war had ended, the King presented him with a royally printed and bound copy of Marot's Psalms. This gesture alone would have been sufficient to show that there could be no thought in Francis's mind that Marot was inclined to heresy, for when the Lutheran propensities for destruction which had been manifested in the sack of Rome and were at that moment rife in England showed themselves in Paris by the mutilation of a famous statue of the Virgin and Child, Francis himself, bareheaded, led an expiatory procession through the capital and, at the conclusion of it, mounted the pulpit of Notre Dame and, in the presence of the Court, the Parlement of Paris and the Ambassadors, pledged himself to stamp out heresy.

It so happened that, because the Dauphin, Diane and the Guises came to be identified with the strict Catholic party, while Margaret's influence on her brother and his mistress was in the direction of unfettered theological discussion, Catherine, on the strength of belonging to her father-in-law's instead of her husband's set, has been credited with sympathy with Protestantism. Nothing could be more misleading. She might find consolation in singing Marot's Psalms. Being who she was, she was unlikely to regard the Pope with the reverent eyes of a pious provincial priest. Her lively mind enjoyed intellectual speculations almost as much as Margaret. And when Catherine in later years had to face Huguenotism as an armed revolutionary movement bent on the subversion of the state, she temporised and negotiated whenever *force majeure* made it politically necessary. But never, at any point, had she the slightest sympathy with Protestantism of any variety, and her enemies' assumption, based on her personal attachments as Dauphine, that she had such leanings added to her reputation for Machiavellian duplicity.

Catherine's Medicean background was of particular benefit to her in creating a bond of sympathy and understanding with her father-in-law in his passion for building. It was said of Francis that he roamed over France like a sower and châteaux sprang up in his steps. He was rebuilding the Louvre, transforming it from a prison-fortress into a 'logis de plaisance pour soi y loger'. On his return from his captivity in Madrid he had tried to exorcise the evil associations of the name by building, in the Bois de Boulogne, his Château de Madrid, a veritable *non pareil* of a palace. But his pride was

Opposite: *A lady and gentleman of the Valois court; a watercolour from*
'Habits de France' published in 1581.

Chambord in Touraine, 'the heart of the garden of France.' He had started building it in 1519. It was to be his great creation, the embodiment of his own personality and the epitome in stone of the art of the Rennaissance. Now, twenty years later, the architect, Pierre Nepveu, known as Le Trinqueau, was desperately trying to finish it in time for the reception of the Emperor. He did not succeed, but even so the immense palace was impressive enough, with its wonderful double-staircase, its unique lantern, its 365 chimneys and its superb terrace.

Chambord was all French, but for the other house of his heart, Fontaine-bleau, Francis turned to Italy. Fontainebleau had been merely a hunting-box, 'une âpre solitude'. Now, to turn it into a peer of his other palaces, Francis appointed an Italian master of works and summoned for the embellishment of it Titian and Girolamo della Robbia, Andrea del Sarto, Primaticcio, Michelangelo's pupil, Il Rosso and many more. Above all, Benvenuto Cellini, now in his thirties, came to serve the ageing King, who found him 'a man after my own heart' and gave him a lodging in the Petite Tour de Nesle in Paris. Here, accompanied by Margaret, Madame d'Etampes and Catherine, the King visited Cellini to be the first to see the great silver Jupiter which was the beginning of an Olympian series for the gallery at Fontainebleau.

The royal connoisseurs rightly adjudged the Jupiter the sculptor's masterpiece, but as time at last brought the King his greatest joy, Benvenuto received the Royal commission for something very different—'some red dolls, a cradle, a toy tournament and a doll's kitchen in silver'.

The Fountain Court of the Château de Fontainebleau; a drawing by the architect.

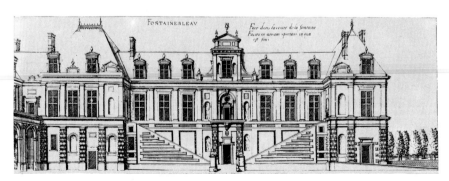

58

The Mother

The Dauphine's achievement of the status of motherhood in no way diminished Diane's power. If anything, it increased it, for the Dauphin not only installed his mistress as his wife's head-nurse, superintending the bringing of the children into the world and appointing the individual nurses, but insisted on granting her a considerable emolument 'on account of the good, praiseworthy and agreeable services' she rendered Catherine in this respect.

King Francis lived long enough to see two of his grandchildren, his name-sake Francis, who was born in the January of 1543 and Elisabeth, born in the April of 1545. Another girl, Claude, was born in the September of 1547—six months after King Francis's death and the Dauphin's accession to the throne as King Henry II.

Before the old King died, Catherine's position was weakened by the absence from court of her 'gossip', the Constable, who so openly reciprocated Madame d'Etampes's detestation of him that Francis had sadly allowed him to go into retirement with the explanation: 'I cannot find more than one fault in you and that is that you do not love those whom I love.'

The final severance came at the betrothal ceremony of Margaret's twelve-year-old daughter, Jeanne, a self-willed, obstinate child, whose most characteristic juvenile exploit had been to substitute foxes' heads for those of the priests in a piece of her mother's embroidery depicting the celebration of Mass.

When the King offered his arm to his small niece to conduct her to the altar, Jeanne, who was wearing a crown, a gold and silver robe heavy with jewels and an ermine cloak, affected to be so weighed down that she could not walk. Francis ordered the Constable to carry her, and Montmorency did not dare to disobey, although he considered it a menial task and tantamount to public disgrace. He exclaimed: 'C'est fait désormais de ma faveur. Adieu lui dis!' and was not seen at court again until the next reign.

Three generations of the Royal House of France.

Left: *Francis I, who reigned from 1515 to 1547 and died at the age of fifty-three.*

Centre: *Francis's son Henry II, Catherine's husband, who reigned from 1547 to 1559 and died at the age of forty.*

Right: *Henry's son Francis II, Catherine's eldest child, reigned from the July of 1559 to the December of 1560 and died at the age of sixteen.*

With the loss of the Constable's influence, it was some consolation to Catherine that, just after the birth of her daughter Elisabeth, she found another supporter, Gaspard de Saulx, Sieur de Tavannes, a small, ugly, devout, cynical soldier in his mid-thirties just back from the Italian wars, who came to her and offered to cut off Diane's nose. The offer, though appreciated, was refused, but Tavennes remained Catherine's life-long champion, counsellor and friend.

As the King, growing weaker, saw his son and Diane gaining in power, he became apprehensive for the future of his kingdom. On his death-bed he gave a solemn warning against Diane's *protégés*, the Guises. To Henry and Catherine he said: 'Beware the House of Guise! They will strip your children to their waistcoats and your poor subjects to their shirts.' But Henry would not, because of Diane; and Catherine could not, because of Henry, heed the warning.

When, in the April of 1547, Henry and Catherine became King and Queen of France, Diane, whom Henry created Duchesse de Valentinois, was more influential than ever and, despite the return of the Constable to power, the Guises took an increasing share of the government. The seal was set on their triumph the following year. In the August of 1548 the six-year-old Mary Queen of Scots arrived in France to be betrothed to the Dauphin Francis, seven weeks her senior.

Mary's mother was Mary of Guise, the elder sister of the Duke and the Cardinal. Her husband, King James V of Scotland, had died shortly after the child's birth, leaving her as Queen-Regent for the six-weeks-old Queen. Catherine herself was distantly related to her daughter-in-law-to-be—her uncle Albany's father had been the younger brother of King James III of Scotland—but she was under no illusion that the paramount influence on the growing child would be that of her Guise uncles.

Mary was brought up with the Royal children, sharing their lives but, by the King's command, always taking precedence of them all because she was already 'a crowned Queen'. She shared apartments with Elisabeth, but her future husband was her favourite playmate. 'The Dauphin loves Her Most Serene Highness, the little Queen of Scots,' an ambassador wrote. 'She is a very pretty little girl. Sometimes it happens that, with their arms round each other, they go away into a corner so that no one can hear their childish secrets.'

The children's *Gouverneur*, who was appointed just before King Francis I's death, was M. d'Humières, a leading noble of Picardy, a Chevalier of the Order of St. Michael who had served as Lieutenant-General in Saxony and Piedmont. He and his wife constantly received letters from Catherine when she was away from the children, going into such details as the suggestion that when her daughter Claude was ill—poor Claude with her twisted back and tubercular hip—she should be fed on 'toast soaked in water rather than anything else, since it is healthier for her than broth.'

On another occasion she instructed the d'Humières to move the children from the château to the pavilion which would be better for their health because it was not so near the water. One day she sent the tailor who made the dresses of the Constable's small daughters to make one for Elisabeth and bade Madame d'Humières 'take great care it is very well cut'. At the same time Francis the Dauphin who, at four, objected to still being dressed as a girl was to be granted 'his reasonable request' for breeches.

When Catherine was away from the capital, she asked for portraits of the children to be painted and sent to her, giving the specification that they were to be painted from the opposite side to that which the artist was accustomed to use 'so that she might see how they looked from that angle.'

The Professor of Greek at the Collège de France was appointed tutor to the Dauphin, while the three girls were entrusted to Jacques Amyot, a brilliant classical scholar who was translating Plutarch and who, in his student days had been rescued by Margaret of Navarre from near-starvation in a Paris garret. Catherine, however, insisted on herself overseeing the education of all the girls as they grew up and one passage which she dictated to Mary Queen of Scots for translation into Latin has an interest as much psychological as linguistic.

'The true greatness and excellence of a prince', it ran, 'does not consist in honours, in gold and silver and other luxuries but in prudence, wisdom and knowledge; and the more a prince wishes to differ from his subjects in his mode of life the further he should be removed from the foolish opinions of the vulgar crowd.'

In 1548, the year Mary came to France, Catherine gave birth to her second

Anonymous drawing of Catherine's second son, later Charles IX.

Jacques Amyot, tutor to the royal children.

son, Louis, a sickly child who died in 1550. That year her third son was born. As a compliment to the Emperor, who had just paid his visit to France, he was christened Charles-Maximilien and was to become known in history as King Charles IX, whose name was to be ever associated with the massacre of St. Bartholomew.

By the time the next child arrived, the September of 1551, the international situation had so changed that war was again in preparation between France and the Emperor and King Henry II had made at Chambord a treaty of alliance with England. To compliment his new ally, the boy-king Edward VI, he had his newly born son named Edward-Alexander. The Anglo-French accord, however, was so short-lived that, on the boy's confirmation, the name was changed to Henry; and it was as Henry—later to be King Henry III— that from the day of his birth till the day of her death he held Catherine's heart as no other human being was able to do. He was the most robust of her children and the only one who was completely unblemished. In him the Medici started to emerge. He resembled her far more than his father, and had her beautiful hands and complexion.

Next year, 1552, the King and the Constable led the French army to the eastern frontier to attack Metz, Toul and Verdun, three independent German bishoprics whose territory formed part of Lorraine. Catherine, who had been appointed Commissary-General, was taken ill at Joinville, the main seat of the Guises, with what appears to have been a dangerous attack of the measles. It was known as 'the purples' and its main symptom was an eruption of red patches all over the body, accompanied by a swelling of the tongue so great that speech was impossible. For some time her life was despaired of and the King refused to continue his march until she had recovered. Diane was even more concerned than Henry. She would not even leave Catherine's bed-side. She feared that, in the event of the Queen's death, 'the King might marry another woman and grow cold towards her.'

When Catherine was well again the King went on to Metz and she to Châlons which was the base of supplies for the army. She threw herself energetically into her new task. 'My gossip,' she wrote to the Constable, 'I have not lost any time in learning the office and duties of a Commissary of Provisions in which, if everybody does his duty and carries out his promises, I assure you that I shall soon become past-mistress, for from one hour to another I don't study anything else.'

For a Medici, this was surprisingly ingenuous. She was soon disillusioned. On 10 of June she was writing to her husband: 'We arranged yesterday another bargain for twenty thousand loaves a day. At the same time I assure you that everyone who has arrived recently from your camp say they have met a large number of waggons carrying bread, flour and wine—not only men who are in the state service but also volunteer merchants.'

The question was, what happened to them? A week later Catherine took the matter up with the Constable: 'I found it exceedingly strange, my gossip, that of all the horses and carts which have carried provisions, not a single one has arrived at the camp. And I cannot imagine where the provisions have been taken. As for understanding where the failure is, you must see, my gossip, that it can much more easily be discovered at camp than it can be here. Nevertheless, following your advice, I shall give orders that, from now on, provisions will be transported in the charge of those who will be responsible for them and will hand them over to the commissaries of provisions who are with you; from whom they will demand a receipt.'

When Catherine heard that the King, who insisted on sharing all the hardships of the campaign, even sleeping in the trenches with his soldiers, had fallen ill and was recuperating at Sedan, she immediately left Châlons for that city and herself nursed him till the campaign ended and, having watered his horses in the Rhine as a symbolic gesture, Henry returned to Paris.

At the end of the war another child was begotten, who was born in the May of 1553 and named Margaret after the great Margaret of Navarre who had died four years earlier. This 'Margot' too was in due course to be Queen of Navarre by her marriage to the elder Margaret's grandson, Henry; but, apart from their interest in scholarship and the arts, the two 'Marguerite des Marguerites', as they were known in their respective generations, had nothing in common. Margot was to be the bane of Catherine's life. Near the end of it, the old woman confessed: 'I see that God has left me this creature for the punishment of my sins through the afflictions she gives me. She is my curse in this world.' And Margot admitted: 'She brought me into the world and now she wishes to drive me out of it.' Throughout her life, Margot was to be the centre of plots and intrigues, with her nymphomania and her incestuous love for her elder brother, Henry, which turned to mortal hatred and made her used as a pawn in her endless feud with him her younger brother, Hercules.

Hercules, Catherine's last child to survive, was born in the May of 1554, ten months after Margot. No name could be more inappropriate to the frail, hunchbacked, double-nosed little creature and, after the death of Francis, the eldest boy, the youngest annexed his name.

Catherine's final child-bearing in 1556, when she was 37, produced twins, Victoire and Jeanne, of whom the one died at birth and the other seven weeks later.

Catherine in her child-bearing had not only found some happiness and

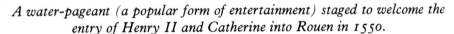

A water-pageant (a popular form of entertainment) staged to welcome the entry of Henry II and Catherine into Rouen in 1550.

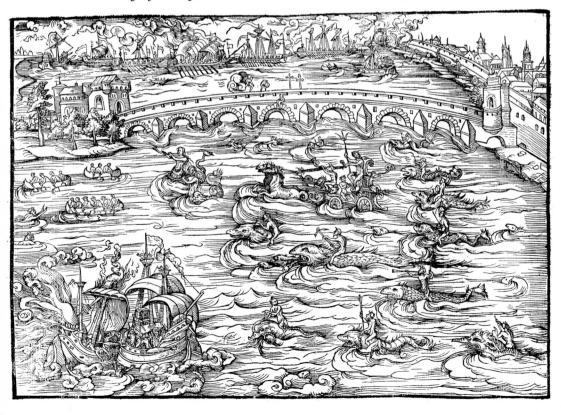

consolation in the present of slights and neglect, but had laid up for herself a future in which she would be able to exercise, both directly and vicariously that *affetto potentissimo* which an observant ambassador had noted in her, her passion for ruling—*un affetto di signoreggiare.* Her three eldest sons sat in turn on the throne of France and Henry was additionally King of Poland, while the youngest was the suitor of Queen Elizabeth of England and became the ruling Duke of Brabant. Of the three girls, Elisabeth married the King of Spain, Claude the Duke of Lorraine and Margot the King of Navarre. Her Lorraine grand-daughter, Christine, for whose education she became entirely responsible, married the Grand Duke of Tuscany and so returned to rule from the Medici Palace in Florence.

Catherine's own residence during the reign of Henry II was the château of Chaumont-sur-Loire, the least prepossessing of the royal houses, which still retained the air of a gloomy fortress. She had wanted the lovely Chenonceaux, the hunting-box at the edge of the forest of Amboise, originally an old mill worked by the waters of the Cher which Francis I had bought and, in twenty years, had transformed into a diminutive palace spanning the river on six arches. Catherine had often visited it on hunting expeditions with Francis and it had been assumed that she would become its châtelaine when he died. Henry, however, gave it to Diane.

Forced to content herself with Chaumont, Catherine made one addition to it. She built a tower, from the roof of which she and Ruggieri could observe the stars, while on the top floor was a laboratory where they could experiment with those medicinal concoctions, such as the mixture of cream and pigeon's blood for the complexion, which she was never tired of inflicting on her family and recommending to her correspondents—a life-long foible which lent point to Diane's gibe when she informed Mary Queen of Scots that the *palle* of the Medici arms were really apothecary's pills.

From a book on astrology printed by Nicholas la Rouge at Troyes in 1529.

Queen of France

Catherine's patience was at last rewarded. In the August of 1557, an army of combined German, Spanish, English and Netherlands forces was advancing on Paris. It was led by Philip II of Spain, the son of the Emperor Charles V who had abdicated in his favour and retired to spend his last years in a monastery. The Constable, with his nephew Coligny, was at St. Quentin, a town with crumbling walls defended mainly by a great marsh, which was one of the main bulwarks of Paris. The King was established at Compiègne, about thirty miles behind the permanent entrenched camp of the French army. Catherine was with him and on August 9 he sent her back to the capital to ask the Parlement for an additional subsidy for the war.

Next day the battle of St. Quentin was fought. Half the French army was killed; most of the rest in flight or captives. The Constable and Coligny and Marshal St. André were among the prisoners. All the French standards and all the artillery except two pieces were captured. Philip sent orders to Spain that, as the day was the Feast of St. Laurence, the victory should be commemorated by the building of a great palace, El Escorial, shaped like a gridiron, the instrument on which the Saint had been martyred.

Paris was stunned. Many believed that the enemy was already within the walls and packed their possessions and fled, some to Orléans, some to Bourges, some still further afield.

Catherine did not waver. She went to the Parlement and, in the word of the Venetian Ambassador 'she expressed herself with so much eloquence and feeling that she touched all hearts.' She persuaded them to continue resistance and to grant an additional subsidy of 300,000 francs (which, since other towns were accustomed to follow Paris's lead, meant a million and a half in gold) as well as the guarantee of a force of 60,000 men within a month. The Parlement remembered that 'the Italian woman' was, by birth, half-French and, at this crisis, was the voice of France. 'She spoke with so much eloquence and feeling that she touched all hearts and made well-nigh the

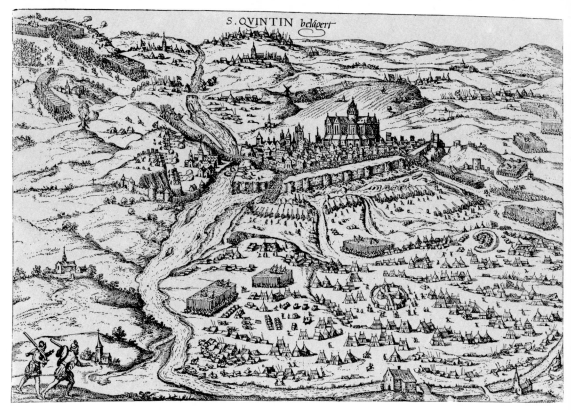

*The siege of St. Quentin in 1557; after a heroic defence, Admiral Coligny
and his brother Andelot were imprisoned by Huguenots for two years.*

whole Parlement shed tears of emotion. All over the city nothing was talked
about with such satisfaction.'

From this day, it was said, the King entirely changed his attitude to his
wife. It was Catherine, not Diane, whom, each evening, he visited to discuss
affairs of state. The outward and visible sign of the change was that now, for
the first time, François Clouet struck a medal with the King's head on one
side and Catherine's on the other.

Catherine's confidence was so greatly restored that she even permitted
herself the luxury of dropping the mask of rigid politeness to Diane which she
had so patiently and persistently worn; and the Court buzzed in astonishment
to learn that on a recent occasion, when Diane asked her conversationally
what book she was reading, Catherine replied: 'I am reading a history of
France and I am surprised to find how often courtesans have meddled in the
affairs of kings.'

When the war was in its last stages and the Duke of Guise had managed to
restore the country's morale by the capture of Calais, the last English
possession in France, Catherine accompanied Henry on a triumphal state

68

visit to the recovered territory and returned with him to Fontainebleau, whence she wrote to the Constable, still a prisoner in Spain: 'The King and all the children are very well and after Easter we shall leave here to attend the marriage of the Dauphin and the Queen of Scots in Paris where I wish it would please God you could be. I assure you that you are much longed for.'

The Constable, in honourable captivity, was negotiating a settlement, but it was not until a year later, the April of 1559, that the signing of the Treaty of Cateau-Cambrésis brought the war to and end.

Peace was an urgent necessity for financial reasons alone. Both Henry and Philip were bankrupt. But, as Sir John Neale has put it in his important *The Age of Catherine de' Medici*, 'Henry wanted peace so desperately that he was prepared to surrender almost anything. Money was not the only reason. He had an overwhelming desire to tackle a domestic problem, the urgency of which had been growing in recent years. That problem was heresy.' And no one in authority questioned that heresy was synonymous with secular subversion. Once the bond of religious unity was broken, every other rebellion would eventually follow. It menaced Philip no less than Henry and the Treaty of Cateau-Cambrésis contained a clause that 'the two princes, moved by the same zeal and sincere determination to employ all their powers on behalf of the Holy Catholic Church, would strive to restore its true unity and concord.'

Philip's most trusted adviser, the Duke of Alva, discussed the matter personally with the Constable and they agreed to give each other all the help they could 'for reformation and punishment in matters of religion in which every day in both realms increasing harm was done by the emissaries of Geneva.' And the theocratic republic of Geneva was—to quote Sir John Neale again—'making allowance for the differing scale of the world, in many ways like Moscow during those years when the Soviet State dreamed of world communist revolution.'

John Calvin had dedicated to Francis I the famous treatise *Institutio Christianae Religionis* which he had started to compose while the guest of Margaret. Francis admired its elegant Latinity but did not otherwise approve of the lucid, logical exposition of the 'Institutes' in which the young lawyer laid down the principles of a Reformed Church organised in opposition to the Catholic Church. Its rules of government, organisation and discipline and its rights in relation to the State were now being put into practice, under Calvin's personal instruction, in Geneva and its influence was spreading throughout Europe.

By a stroke of genius Calvin had combined the doctrine of an *élite* with a repudiation of personal responsibility. He taught that God had predestined

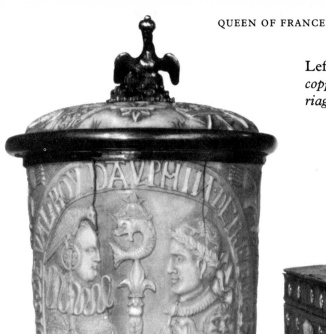

Above: Mary Queen of Scots' jewel-box.

each man before birth to salvation or damnation and that no heroic virtue a man might show or no vile crime he might commit could alter that pre-natal verdict. A man was an automaton with no moral choice. On the other hand, if he had a conviction, a 'lively sense' that had been elected to salvation, then he probably had been. In this case he would act morally, not because such conduct could affect his ultimate fate but because by so doing he would give the clearest presumptive evidence that he was indeed one of the Elect. Thus did Calvin counter the logical tendency to libertinism implicit in his doctrine by a pride-inspired rectitude.

Opposite: Mary Queen of Scots as Queen of France, wearing on her head the seven great pearls Catherine gave her when she married the Dauphin Francis.

The Elect—for despite the *caveat* that only God knew who they were no Calvinist really doubted that he was among them—were strictly organised. At the head were the ministers who conducted the *Prêches,* the preachings, the main Calvinist service when the Bible, interpreted according to the predispositions of the preacher or the current political needs of the sect, became a Divine organ of propaganda.

Each local church was ruled by three categories of officials—the minister, the elders who joined with him in making policy and administering discipline and the deacons who were concerned with social organisation. Effective control was thus in the hands of carefully selected laymen—the elders and the deacons.

Minister and elders, acting together in committee, formed a Consistory. Above the Consistory came the Colloquy, made up of neighbouring Consistories, and above the Colloquy was the Provincial Synod, drawn from a wider geographical area. Crowning the edifice was the National Synod which welded all the Calvinist churches in each country into a single unit, looking to Geneva as their head. Consistory, Colloquy and Synod, each at its own level, exercised a rigid disciplinary control over the lives of the ordinary members of the new church.

The first National Synod in France was held in Paris a month after the proclamation of peace—in the May of 1559—and though outwardly it was only a matter of seventy-two men secretly meeting in a lodging-house, it was an event of incalculable importance. The implications and the consequences of it dominated French politics for the rest of Catherine's life.

The rapid spread of Calvinism in France was due in great part to the structure of the Catholic Church in the country. By a concordat with the Papacy in the first years of the reign of Francis I the King had the right of nomination to bishoprics and abbeys, with the result that every bishop was appointed for political and not for spiritual reasons. At least half the benefices were given for Court services and the rest to please influential local magnates. The gift of them was considered only in terms of revenue so that priesthood was no longer regarded as an evangelical vocation but merely as a qualification to hold a benefice. It was estimated that not one in ten of the lesser clergy could read and this ignorance, combined with the low spiritual quality of those in orders, had produced a situation in which, according to one con-

Opposite: *French school painting of Catherine's husband, King Henry II, on horseback.*

Overleaf: *King Henry II touching for scrofula; illustration taken from a Book of Hours.*

temporary observer, there was not one in fifty parishes in Brittany which had a resident rector, while in Bordeaux there were middle-aged men who had never attended Mass or understood the Faith.

Calvinism, as a new (and in its origins a specifically French) creed, was theologically poles apart from the German Lutheranism which had manifested itself in the sack of Rome, but it had in common with it the realisation that the essential prelude to the destruction of Catholicism was the destruction of the Mass and everything connected with it. Luther had taught: 'I affirm that all brothels, murders, robberies, crimes, adulteries are less wicked than the abomination of the Popish Mass. When the Mass is overthrown I think we shall have overthrown the Papacy. It is on the Mass as on a rock that the Papacy wholly rests. Everything will of necessity collapse when their abominable Mass collapses.'

And now in Paris streets, the Huguenots (as the French Protestants, for some reason not certainly known, came to be called) put up placards calling the Pope 'and all his vermin of cardinals, bishops, monks and priests, the sayers of Mass, as well as all who consent thereto, false prophets, damnable deceivers, apostates, wolves, false shepherds, idolators, seducers, liars, execrable blasphemers, murderers of souls, renouncers of Jesus Christ, traitors, thieves, robbers of the honour of God and more detestable than devils.'

This was more easily understood than the theological niceties of the godly and it was not long before a fanatical *canaille* merited the description: 'It is easy to be a Huguenot these days, for all that is necessary is to rob churches, to slander the Pope, to give the Host to dogs, to grease boots with Holy Oil and to drag the image of the Blessed Virgin through the mud.'

The King, by establishing in various centres special courts for dealing with heresy, did what he could to prevent the spread of it; but persecution only strengthened it and by 1559 there were, it was estimated, at least two thousand separate Huguenot churches in France—a secret, disciplined network, strongest in centres of international trade like Lyons, so near to Geneva, in the east; and in Normandy and Brittany in the north, with their commercial links with Protestant England and the Netherlands; and in the south in Languedoc with its proximity to Navarre.

Henry had made his own attitude to Huguenots clear enough when he

Previous page: *Anonymous seventeenth-century painting of John Calvin in his study.*

Opposite: *The Château of Chaumont, which Catherine gave to Diane de Poitiers in exchange for Chenonceaux, after the death of Henry II.*

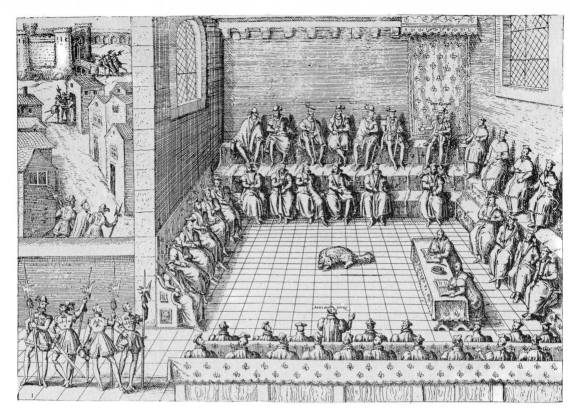

The Mercuriale, *an assembly of Parliament called on 20 June 1559;*
through the window can be seen the arrest of the Huguenot Anne du Bourg.

announced that 'were he able to set his affairs in order he would make the
streets run with the blood of this artisan *canaille*'. And now that Cateau-
Cambrésis had set affairs in order, he summoned a *mercuriale*, a meeting
called two or three times a year to consider 'the morals and conversation' of
officials and of members of the Parlement.

On 20 June 1559 a *mercuriale* met for the specific purpose of discussing the
petition of the Huguenots, agreed on in their National Synod the previous
month, they they should be allowed to hold their *Prêches* in public. The
mercuriale was opened by the King, attended by all the chief functionaries of
church and state and each member of it was asked in turn for his opinion.
According to the English Ambassador's report to Queen Elizabeth, 'out
of the one hundred and twenty presidents and councillors present only
fourteen Councillors and one President were really against the policy of very
strict repression.' This was generally regarded as a diplomatic exaggeration,
though there was certainly a considerable amount of plain speaking which
drew from the King a curt: 'I see there are some good men here and some evil
men. We shall protect the good and make an end of the evil.' This was

The execution of Anne du Bourg on 21 December 1559; an edict by Francis II in November had introduced the death-penalty for heresy.

interpreted by some to mean that stricter measures to repress heresy were imminent.

At the moment, however, the matter which took precedence of everything else was the celebration in honour of the royal marriage which was to cement the Treaty of Cateau-Cambrésis. The fourteen-year-old Elisabeth, 'la Fille de France', was to become the bride of Philip of Spain whose wife, Mary Queen of England, had died seven months earlier with the word 'Calais'—so she said—written on her heart.

Philip had fallen in love with François Clouet's portrait of Elisabeth in her young loveliness, with her dazzling eyes, her olive skin and her black hair which seemed, in the words of Brantôme 'like a shade unto her complexion' and at their first meeting she gazed at him with such intensity that he, acutely conscious of his thirty-three years, asked her if she was trying to discover if he had any grey hairs. Whatever she was looking for she found, and the marriage was to result in deep mutual love. But Philip did not himself come to Paris for the ceremony. For dynastic and diplomatic reasons connected with precedence, he sent the Duke of Alva as his proxy, much to the disappointment of Henry who, always proud of his physical prowess, had hoped

79

Left: *Philip II of Spain, son of the Emperor Charles V*. Right: *Catherine's daughter Elisabeth, who became Philip's third wife.*

to exhibit it before Philip himself in a great tournament he had arranged as the climax of the festivities.

The lists were set up in the rue Saint-Antoine adjoining the ancient palace of Les Tournelles, on the eastern outskirts of the city between the Bastille and the river. Here, on Friday 30 June 1559, was held the 'Tournament of the Queens', the last event before Elisabeth's departure for Toledo. Catherine presided at it, as Queen of France, with Elisabeth the new Queen of Spain, and Mary Queen of Scots on each side of her. Henry was jousting in his armour of black and silver, Diane's colours, but it was to his wife that, at the end of the tournament, he sent a message that 'he would try one more bout for the love of her.'

The news froze Catherine's heart. Ten years earlier, Ruggieri had predicted that Henry at the age of forty would be fatally wounded in a duel and only a week ago the prediction had been renewed. Henry himself had heard it and dismissed it with a Caesarian remark about death. He had paid no attention to Catherine's pleas to abandon the joust altogether and, when the tournament was over without any injury to him, her relief sharpened the deadly fear she felt for its resumption or one more bout.

Quite apart from Catherine's fears, there was an inexplicable tension in the atmosphere. As the King had ridden into the lists, a boy had called out: 'Sire! do not tilt!' and when seized and examined by the officials he was unable to explain his impulse. When the King announced his intention of continuing, the Marshal de Vielleville, who was Master of the Ceremonies, besought him: 'Sire, you have shown enough of your skill. Let me ride in your place' and, as Henry remained adamant, the Marshal risked his favour by 'Sire, for three nights I have dreamt of calamity.' Strangest of all, the King's opponent himself begged to be excused the bout.

That young man was Gabriel de Lorges, Comte de Montgoméry, the Captain of the King's Scottish Guard, owner of large estates in Normandy and a dedicated Calvinist. He had already broken two lances with the King and both times had nearly unseated him. It was for this reason that Henry, wounded at least in his pride and conscious of Spanish eyes—in particular Alva's—upon him, insisted on the further bout.

The English Ambassador, who was a spectator, described the outcome: 'When the trumpet sounded young Mr. de Montgomery gave him such a counter-buff as, first lighting on the King's head and taking away his pannage (whereupon there was a great plume of feathers), which was fastened to his headpiece with iron, did break his lance, and with the rest of the lance hitting the King's face, he drove a splinter right over his eye on the right side, the force of which stroke was so vehement that he had much ado to keep himself on horseback.'

The King reeled, sagged in his saddle and was saved from falling to the ground by the grooms who rushed forward. When they took off his helmet his whole face was covered with blood. The Constable and the Cardinal of Lorraine rushed to his side, accompanied by Catherine who forbade Diane to follow. The Dauphin who had fainted was carried into Les Tournelles after his father.

Once in the palace, Henry insisted on trying to walk up the staircase, but had to be helped by the Constable and the Cardinal. In his room he groped dazedly for his bed, climbed into it as if it were a saddle and pitched forward again into unconsciousness. Catherine, finding that the hastily-summoned surgeons were unable to agree from which side the splinters had entered the brain, gave orders for the immediate execution of four condemned criminals that their heads might be dissected.

Eventually Henry bore, with his almost incredible fortitude, the extraction

The fatal tournament at which Henry II was, either by accident or design, fatally wounded by the Huguenot Montgoméry, and Catherine was left a widow.

of five splinters from his temple and eye and as his strength and will were no less than his courage and as he had not, as was expected, died immediately, hopes began to rise for his recovery. On the third day, he showed some improvement. He was conscious and asked for Montgoméry. When told that the young man had fled from Paris immediately, he said: 'He must be brought back at all costs. What has he to fear? This accident happened not through his fault but by an unlucky chance.'

So it was left, though Montgoméry's subsequent conduct, which included leading Huguenot forces against the Crown, betraying his Norman fortresses to English Protestant invaders and adopting as his device a broken lance, made his innocence extremely improbable and Catherine at least regarded him as deliberately her husband's murderer.

On the fourth day, the King as he continued to make some progress, summoned all his remaining strength to dictate a letter to the Pope, pledging himself, if he recovered, to 'punish, chastise and extirpate those who hold these new doctrines, sparing none of no matter what quality or dignity, so that I shall purge my kingdom if it is humanly possible.'

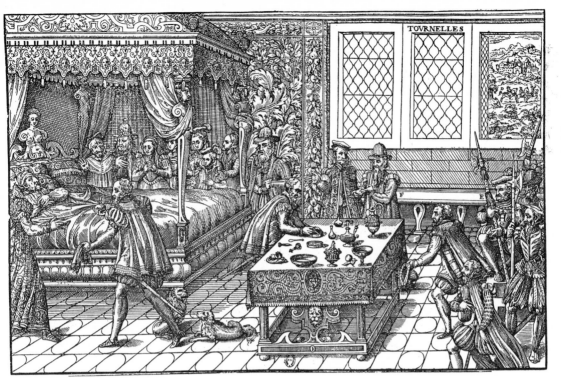

The deathbed of Henry II, eleven days after the tournament. Facing across the bed are the Cardinal of Lorraine, the Constable, and Catherine at the head, and the Dauphin leaning forward at the foot.

It was his last effort. On the eighth day, Henry called for the Dauphin, who had been wandering about the palace like a lost soul, banging his head against walls and moaning: 'My God, how can I live if my father dies?', and taking his hand in his said: 'My son, you are about to lose your father, but not his blessing. I pray God that He make you happier than I have been.'

On July 10 the King died and when the news reached Geneva, the city went *en fête* and Calvin composed special prayers of thanksgiving for the occasion.

The Widow

Catherine was prostrate with grief. For the first two days she remained on the floor of the death-chamber, inarticulate, sobbing uncontrollably. Gradually she mastered herself, donned an austerely-cut black dress and widow's peak, determined to wear nothing but mourning for the rest of her life, and braced herself to receive the condolences of the foreign ambassadors. But they found her voice so weak and stifled with emotion that they could not hear what she said. Even a week later Mary Queen of Scots wrote to her mother in Scotland: 'She is still so unhappy and plunged into such deep grief that I fear her misery will bring on a serious illness.'

The motto which she had adopted when she came to France as Henry's bride: *J'apporte la lumière et la sérénité* she changed to *Lachrymae hinc, hinc dolor* with a coat of arms of tears falling on a heap of quicklime and the legend *Ardorem extincta testantur vivere flamma*—the glow lingers though the flame is gone.

To the end of her life, Friday remained a day to be dreaded. Nothing good could ever happen on the day Henry was wounded—'a wound which brought to me principally but also to the whole kingdom so much evil.' That his death had come to him in the exercise of that physical prowess he so rejoiced in because there alone he could savour uncomplicated achievement, was a bitter irony. When she had been with him on hunting expeditions and he had applauded her daring, which matched his, she had found consolation in times of misery. It was an avenue to their understanding and she had never

Opposite: *Catherine in her Chamber of Mourning after her widowing; enamel by Jean III Pénicaud and Pierre Raymond le Vieux.*

Overleaf: *Aerial view of the Château of Chenonceaux, Catherine's favourite, and repossessed by her from Diane de Poitiers after Henry II's death.*

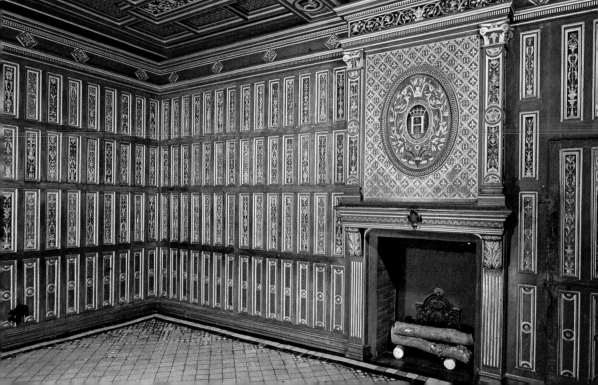

forgotten the care he had shown her after one of her dangerous falls. Diane might fancy herself, because of her name, as the classical goddess of the chase, but it was Catherine who had the greater right to the title.

Catherine sent for Germain Pilon, the sculptor whose bust of Henry both he and she had preferred to any other, and ordered him to make a *gisant*—a dead figure—of the King, as well as to design an urn to hold his embalmed heart. She also sent orders to Diane immediately to return all the jewels Henry had given her, to retire to her château of Anet and to give up Chenonceaux in exchange for Chambord. Now that Henry was dead, Diane was not worth a second thought even of hate. Then in her room on the first floor of the Louvre, in which everything—windows, doors, floor, furniture—was covered with unrelieved black, 'cut off from the light of the sun and the moon', Catherine continued her mourning.

According to custom the widow of the King of France was expected to remain exiled from life for forty days, but Catherine realised that an observance of protocol would amount to a posthumous betrayal of Henry. Her own life had now only one purpose—the carrying out of his wishes. She was charged to see that his sons ruled, in fact as well as in name, a France restored to its former greatness and united in its loyalty to the Catholic Church. In the circumstances, the task might have daunted the wisest and most experienced of kings and the measure of Catherine's greatness is that this widow of forty, with five sickly, neurotic and untrustworthy children as her instruments, should by the time of her death thirty years later have all but achieved the impossible. The depth of her mourning was profound enough for her to be able to defy convention and discard the official signs of it so that she might immediately take into her own hands the tangled threads of affairs.

She discovered that the Crown was over forty million *livres* in debt and that the royal income, much of which never reached the Treasury, was no more than twelve million. Direct taxation—the *taille*—was so heavy that in many places, particularly in Normandy, peasants had left their lands and fled to join roving bands of the discontented.

The whole royal pay-roll, from high officials to common soldiers, was hopelessly in arrears, in many cases for years. Consequently officials recouped themselves from the unfortunate people in their power by official exactions added to the ordinary taxation. The great number of officials made matters worse, for both Francis I and Henry II had created many new and

Opposite: *Rooms in the Château of Blois:* Top left: *Catherine's bedroom.* Top right: *Chimney-piece in the 'Salle d'Honneur' decorated with the emblems of King Francis I and Queen Claude.* Bottom: *Catherine's study.*

unnecessary posts because the sale of them was an easy way of raising ready money for the wars.

The lesser nobility—*les gentilshommes*—though theoretically exempt from direct taxes did not escape forced loans. Their rank made them particularly vulnerable to the raging inflation which had drastically reduced the value of money while rentals remained fixed. By law the *gentilshommes* were forbidden to engage in trade, while their rank demanded a continuous expenditure on the education of their children and the maintenance of a certain standard in dress in an age when a courtier was expected to have at least thirty changes of raiment. The coming of peace, so essential for the economy as a whole, finally ruined them, for war was the only trade they knew or were allowed to practise.

In these circumstances, it was not surprising that the leaders of the rebellious Huguenots were almost exclusively members of the lesser nobility like the Sieur de Montgoméry. Entitled and accustomed to carry swords, they became official protectors of the local congregations in loyal Catholic areas where attempts at interference with the '*Prêches*' were likely. They were—to use an anachronistic but intelligible phrase—the Storm-Troopers of the Godly, and it was a short step from such 'protection' to organised insurrection.

Such an insurrection was at the moment being organised. The leading spirit was Godefroy du Barri, Seigneur de la Renaudie, who had been convicted of forgery and had fled to Geneva, where he had managed to recruit a mixed company of students, discontented artisans, discharged soldiers, land-younger sons and pillage-prone mercenaries. With these he had returned cautiously to France where he continued to gain recruits from similar sources. Just before Henry II's death he obtained a pardon and the restitution of his own estates in Périgord, which gave him an advantageous position from which to continue his plans. The death of Henry II was a godsend for the conspirators (if, indeed, Montgoméry's action was not part of the plot) and it was decided to kidnap the new King and to deliver him into the care of the Princes of the Blood who, constitutionally, were the guardians of a sovereign who was under age.

How much, at this point, Catherine knew of the plot is impossible to guess, but it was the news that the Princes of the Blood, the Bourbons, (who alone shared with the Valois the blood of Hugh Capet, founder of the French Monarchy) were on their way to Paris to claim their hereditary right, that made her break her mourning to rush to the side of her son who was at Fontainebleau.

Of the three Bourbon brothers, the eldest was Antony, King of Navarre in the right of his wife, Jeanne, whose masterfulness had steadily increased since the day the Constable had had to carry her to the altar. It was said that

Bust of Henry II by Germain Pilon on Henry's tomb in the Chapel of the Valois at Saint-Denis.

there was nothing feminine about her except her sex. Antony himself was a poor creature, blown by every wind of opinion, unable to make up his mind on anything or keep faith with anyone. With his sandy hair, his nondescript beard, his vacant eyes and his variegated ear-rings, he had the air of a creature born to blend with its surroundings and was appropriately nick-named 'Caillette'—the little quail whose coat changes colour and is also symbolic of the lustfulness which was his main positive characteristic. He was also known as 'L'Echangeur'.

His youngest brother, Louis Prince of Condé, was—except for his amorous proclivities—a very different matter. A sharp-featured little hunchback, he had a buccaneering temperament combined with considerable military skill. He was prepared for any enterprise which might lead to his aggrandisement and he nursed the secret ambition to become King Louis XIII.

The third brother, between the others in age—they were all in their late thirties—was Charles, Cardinal of Bourbon, who asked nothing but an undisturbed life of luxury and in pursuit of it was prepared to eschew politics of any sort. He had recently officiated at the wedding of Francis and Mary Queen of Scots. Catherine had taken his measure and she, as well as everyone at Court, knew that 'she could twist him round her little finger.'

What no one knew, at that point, was that Condé was the real head of La Renaudie's conspiracy—the *Chef Muet*, the Silent Leader who, La Renaudie explained to his followers, was unable to declare himself until 'the Day'. Then he would come forward and because of his eminence safeguard the revolution. Until then he himself must be safeguarded by their silence. The rank-and-file must face possible torture and death rather than betray the secret of his existence.

For Catherine the mere presence of Navarre and Condé, urging their hereditary claims, was menace enough. She decided to get rid of them immediately, sending Antony to Toledo to take Elisabeth to her husband and Louis to Brussels to discuss some details of the recent Treaty. Meanwhile arrangements could be made for proclaiming the King of age on his sixteenth birthday in January and the intervening six months occupied by a prolonged

The wing of the Château of Blois constructed by Francis I's predecessor, Louis XII, who lived a simple, even bourgeois, life at Blois in contrast to the splendours of court-life there in Catherine's day.

hunting-party during which the Court would be perpetually on the move and she always by her son's side.

So from place to place they went—Fontainebleau, Saint-Germain, Meudon, Dampierre, Nanteuil, Bar, Marchenois, Blois, Amboise—with Catherine riding, as she had with Henry in the days after her near-fatal fall, *à la planchette*, with a foot-rest she had invented, a velvet sling on which sitting sideways she could rest both feet, supporting one knee in a hollow cut in the saddle. (Her enemies said the reason for it was that it displayed her attractive legs to advantage.) The purpose of the prolonged peripateticism of the Court was also misconstrued. 'The King will hunt for ten or fifteen days', wrote the Spanish Ambassador, 'to escape the importunities of captains or others who are owed much but paid nothing.'

The feverish hunting was, from one point of view, in pursuit of health. Francis, already troubled by an infection of the ear which was soon to kill him, was undergoing an uncomfortable adolescence. His face was a mass of

The Bourbon Princes of the Blood. Left: *Antony, King of Navarre*, right: *his youngest brother Louis, Prince of Condé.*

blotches and pimples and his physicians had suggested that his violent exercise had only the effect of disseminating poison in his blood. They recommended that he should remain in the soft climate of Touraine and take frequent aromatic baths. This did not please him, but Catherine insisted on having a special bath-house built in the grounds of the royal château at Blois.

Francis's intellect was hardly more healthy than his body. He could not, even if he would, have grasped the meaning of government or understood the problems which confronted the Crown. There was an undercurrent of relief in his immediate proclamation that all state documents were to contain the formula: 'This being the good pleasure of the Queen my Lady Mother, and I also approving of the things which are in accord with her advice, I am content and I command that . . .'.

The actual ruling of the country continued in the hands of the two Guise brothers. Francis, the Duke of Guise, now forty and the victorious hero of the recent wars, was Lieutenant-General of the Kingdom; Charles, Cardinal of Lorraine, who was thirty-five, controlled the administration, both lay and ecclesiastical and, as Archbishop of Rheims, crowned the young king. Though Catherine still could not overcome her personal dislike for him, she appreciated his ability and, though he was a physical coward, for which she additionally despised him, she was forced to admit that in the moral courage he now displayed in facing the disastrous situation he was not unworthy of his house. He liked men to think well of him and yet he carried through unflinchingly measures which were bound to make him the most unpopular man in France. 'I know I am hated', he said to her, 'and I regret it; but after all I am hated because I defend the King's interests.'

He inaugurated a programme of drastic economy, which included the suppression of 100,000 *livres* for the postal service, the reduction of the army and the suspension of pensions to the great nobles, of salaries to the magistrates and of accounts to the Court tradesmen, as well as the revocation of all grants from the royal domain made during the reign of Henry II. Having thus made himself new enemies in all parts of society to add to the Huguenots' ceaseless attacks, the Cardinal made a collection of twenty-two pamphlets of more than ordinary scurrility, not for the purpose of punishing the authors but as fuel for his amused cynicism. He laughed at the anagrams men made of his name—'Charles de Lorraine' transformed into 'Renard, lasche le roi' or 'Hardi larron se cêle'. Even the popular poem addressed to him beginning

Tigre enragé! Vipère venimeuse!
Sepulchre d'abomination! Spectâcle de malheur!

could ironically be construed as a compliment. No one who knew him would

Catherine, as Queen-Regent, consulting the Cardinal of Lorraine and the Duke of Guise on the eve of the conspiracy of Amboise.

Right: *Francis, Duke of Guise, showing the scar which gave him the nickname 'Le Balafré'.*

ever associate him with a tiger! He dismissed the attacks and patiently continued to mend the economic ruin. The bankers seemed as intractable as the Huguenots, but he managed to reduce their rate of interest from 16% to 8·3%.

La Renaudie's plans continued apace. Armed risings were planned to take place simultaneously in Normandy, Brittany, Gascony, Champagne and the Limousin. Meanwhile the main force, composed mostly of disbanded soldiers who were interested only in pay and pillage, was to make its way in separate, scattered groups to Nantes at the month of the Loire, so that they would be in a position to attack, both by land and by water, whichever of the Touraine châteaux the King happened to be using.

They planned to seize the King and deliver him into the care of Antony of Navarre as Regent; either to murder the Cardinal and the Duke out of hand or to put them on trial for treason; to summon a States-General; and thereafter to reorganise the government of the country in independent cantons on the Swiss model. 'It is a great folly that the country should be governed by a single sovereign', wrote La Renaudie, who in the January of 1560 visited Geneva to consult Calvin and to raise more recruits. The first independent canton to be created was La Renaudie's own district of Périgueux.

As the enterprise enlarged, allies were sought. The German Lutherans and

95

the Anabaptists of the Netherlands were asked for help. Elizabeth of England, who had made a secret understanding with Antony of Navarre within two months of King Henry II's death, was so unexpectedly generous with money that more than one historian has construed the conspiracy as, in essentials, an English plot. The Queen was understandably incensed that the new King and Queen of France were quartering the arms of England with those of France and Scotland. Unfortunately for the conspirator, the matter was discussed indiscreetly enough for it to come to the ears of some English Catholics, who promptly sent word of it to the Cardinal of Lorraine.

The Cardinal was also warned by one of his personal friends among the German princes and by the Archbishop of Arras in the Netherlands but it was not until 17 February 1560 (which incidentally was the birthday of both the Guise brothers) that a Calvinist lawyer from Paris with whom La Renaudie had lodged gave the Cardinal full details of the plot. The Duke gave immediate orders for the Court to leave Blois, which was not defensible, for Amboise, which could if necessary withstand a siege. When they arrived there the castle gate leading into the park was walled up; a company of musketeers was stationed behind the main gate of the town; patrols were sent out to scour the countryside for five or six miles around and captains on whom Guise could rely absolutely were sent to command the garrisons of neighbouring towns.

La Renaudie's main force had now moved up-river from Nantes to Tours about twenty-five miles from Amboise and it was there and at that time that, according to the President of the *Cour des Aides*, the word 'Huguenot' came into being. 'This appellation', he wrote, 'began to be used in the city of Tours, a few days before the conspiracy, because of the gate of the city named after King Hugh, near which those of the New Religion were wont to go to say their prayers. Taken up by the courtiers, the name became universally adopted.'

The move to Amboise signified, among other things, Catherine's accession to power. The Cardinal asked her advice. If, for the last six months, the Guises had been content to influence the King through the Queen, their niece, they now needed the wisdom of the Queen-Mother to help them to meet the crises. Guise bowed to Medici.

Amboise possessed a symbolic appropriateness for the emergence of Catherine as a ruler. It was in its chapel dedicated to St. Hubert, patron saint of hunters, that her parents had been married and the young King Francis I had presided over the unequalled festivities, including the moon-

Opposite: *Contemporary wood-cut of Catherine; she used a special saddle of her own invention, designed (her enemies said) to exhibit her shapely legs.*

CINA DE MEDICI OLIE
HENRICO II RE DI FRACIA

light *'bal aux flambeaux'* when the Loire reflected the flames of a thousand torches, as the *élite* of Florence 'all dressed in crimson velvet' danced on the terrace. For the first three years of his reign, Francis I had lived at Amboise and there Leonardo da Vinci had died in his arms. The meeting of French and Italian culture was memorialised by the first *'jardin à l'italienne en "carreaux de broderie"'* where now Catherine walked with the Cardinal of Lorraine discussing the future of the kingdom.

She advised the immediate summoning of a special council to draw up the terms of an edict which might divide the insurgents. To it Condé must certainly be commanded to come and be given the post of Captain of the King's Bodyguard, which would both immobilise him and keep him under discreet surveillance. The Constable was too ill to attend, but it was essential to have his nephew, the Admiral Gaspard de Coligny, officially on account of his rank, though in his imprisonment after the defeat of St. Quentin, he had been converted to Calvinism and, though he tried to keep it a secret, would probably speak from the Huguenot point-of-view.

The Edict issued as a result of the conference stated that 'the King, by the advice of his honoured mother and his council and not wishing that the first year of his reign should seem to posterity bloody and full of the death of our poor subjects, however much they may have deserved death' ordered the release of all people arrested and imprisoned on the grounds of their religion, except the actual preachers. Calvinists were permitted to worship in private, though not in public; but Calvinism itself was condemned in the strongest possible terms and all loyal subjects of the King were called upon to live in future as good Catholics.

Catherine's olive-branch of toleration, however, had little effect, if only because religion was a pretext for rather than the cause of the unrest. As a Catholic diarist in Paris noted, there was in it 'more *malcontentment* than *Huguenoterie.*' Yet many of those whom the royal patrols captured in the woods and countryside round Amboise at the beginning of March were merely poor artisans, docile as sheep, quoting Biblical texts and talking of an appeal to the King. Fifty-six of them were brought into the courtyard of the castle and questioned. They said that thirty-thousand gentlemen from their province of Poitou were following them to present a petition to the King. The King, with his mother beside him, addressed them from a window, ordered his guard to distribute money among them and told them to go home.

Guise then sent the Duke of Nemours to investigate the Château de Noyzé which was occupied by one of Coligny's cousins, the Baron de Castelnau, in charge of a large contingent of Gascons. The search revealed a great hoard of munitions. Castelnau and fifteen other noblemen were arrested and taken to Amboise for questioning. Guise was convinced that they constituted the effective leadership of the rebellion and that with them in custody all that remained was to round up the now leaderless bands.

The rebellion, however, was by no means crushed. At dawn on March 17 some boatmen on the Loire noticed a band of two hundred horsemen wearing the white scarves which marked them as Condé's followers approaching Amboise on the road from Orléans in the north. The boatmen reported it to the Castle, where the news was quite unexpected, for all the information that had been gained from the various prisoners pointed to attacks from the south. Orléans was, certainly, a Huguenot-dominated town, but this picked troop seemed out of the pattern. Before Guise could summon a sufficient force, the horsemen had galloped through the faubourg and were attacking the main gate. Eventually Guise, uncertain whether or not the troop was an advance guard of the main force, thought it prudent to provide himself with more men than were needed merely to defeat the two hundred and mustered everyone within reach, a sufficient number to sally out of a side gate, attack the rebels in the flank and easily disperse them.

Next day, however, they returned, reinforced by La Renaudie himself and a large force which had been taking cover in a wood a few miles away. La Renaudie demanded a safe-conduct so that he might approach the King with a petition. When this was refused he asked if he might speak with the Prince of Condé but was told that the Prince was too occupied with his duties as Commander of the King's Bodyguard.

Narrative wood-cut of the conspiracy of Amboise (La Renaudie bottom left).

La Renaudie hesitated. Considering the odds, an attack on the castle was impossible. It was even dangerous to continue the parley, in case the royal troops should close in on him. He retreated to the countryside, managing to avoid several ambushes. Eventually he ran into a large royalist force. In the ensuing skirmish he was killed and his body was brought to Amboise where it was spread-eagled on the bridge bearing a placard to identify him as the author of the conspiracy.

Until the attack on Amboise—though it could hardly be dignified by the name of attack and was rather a 'Tumult', as it was often designated—no blood had been shed. But now that the existence of an armed insurrection against the King had been established beyond a doubt, severity became a necessity of government. Summary trials were held and the thirtieth of March appointed for the execution of fifty-seven of the leading Huguenots.

The event was staged as a species of *auto-da-fé*. Notices were sent to all the towns in the neighbourhood ordering official attendance. Preachers announced it in every pulpit in Nantes, in Tours, in Orléans and in Paris. In Amboise itself three stands were erected against the curtain-wall of the castle, facing the Square. The centre stand, more elaborate than the others, was for the royal family and the ambassadors, the others for the civic officials, the courtiers and their guests. On the other three sides of the Square, in the centre of which a scaffold had been built, tiers of benches were constructed for the less important spectators. Windows were procurable at the exorbitant cost of ten *livres*.

The town could not accommodate the influx of sightseers. A crowd of more than ten thousand spent the previous night in the fields and at dawn scrambled for any vantage point, from hill-tops to roof-tops, from which the scaffold might be seen.

The day of execution opened with special masses offered in the Castle chapel and all the churches of the town. Then the privileged spectators took their places and the fifty-seven condemned men were led into the Square, escorted by a company of the King's Scottish Guard and accompanied by many Dominicans who, even at this last hour, were endeavouring to bring them back to the Catholic faith. The Duke of Guise, splendidly apparelled as Governor-General of the Realm, was on horseback between two Marshals of France and his captains, beneath the royal stand.

The King and Queen took their places. Catherine sat next to Francis, with the Cardinal of Lorraine on her left. On the other side of the King, the Prince of Condé was placed between Mary Queen of Scots and young Charles of Orléans, Catherine's second son. The Papal Nuncio stood behind the King.

At the appearance of Condé, all the prisoners bowed to him and, bravely enough, the little hunchback returned their courtesy. At that moment, he was careless of discovery, although he was convinced that they had no intention of betraying him as their *Chef Muet* and that for them to have ignored him as a Prince of the Blood known to favour Huguenotism would have been in itself suspicious.

As the first victim mounted the steps of the scaffold, the other fifty-six sang one of Marot's Psalms. So it continued throughout the day, the volume of sound gradually diminishing until only a single voice was left, that of Castelnau.

Condé turned to the Papal Nuncio and said: 'You must admit, Monseigneur, that if the gentlemen of France know how to plot, they also know how to die.'

The crowd grew restive and called for mercy for Castelnau. But there was none. The old Baron's head fell like the rest and the spectators dispersed.

Next day the Court left for Chenonceaux. It was necessary, Catherine said, 'to get rid of the horror of blood.'

The execution of the Amboise conspirators on 15 March 1560; La Renaudie is marked A, Castelnau B, Villemong C. Villemong has dipped his hands in the blood of his companions; anonymous engraving.

The Queen-Mother

The 'Tumult of Amboise' may be a mere detail in the history of France and unknown outside it, but in the life of Catherine de' Medici it assumes the importance of a landmark. It marks the beginning of her exercise of personal power. It defines the religious position she never forsook—for herself a conventional but rigid Catholicism and toleration of the beliefs of others provided they were not expressed divisively in open schismatic worship. It is the opening of the second phase of pamphleteering attacks on her (her conduct as Queen had killed the early hatred and in Paris, at least, she now had a popularity she never lost there) and the Huguenot pamphlets so increased in numbers and viciousness that even today the effect of them can be felt. Most English writers on Catherine assume the truth of them and are, in any case, biased towards the Huguenots, as England's allies in the 'religious' wars.

Catherine's own consistent attitude to the scurrilities was epitomised, some years later, in her reaction to one of the worst. *A Life of the Queen-Mother by a Huguenot,* popularly known as *The Life of St. Catherine,* became a best-seller. According to a contemporary, 'the Queen-Mother has it read aloud to her and laughs till she can hardly hold herself. She says that if only they had given her notice beforehand she would have told them of many things of which they were ignorant and reminded them of some they had forgotten, which would have greatly increased the bulk of their book.' He added, piously: 'Thus does she dissimulate *à la Florentine* the evil talent she has hatched to thwart the Huguenots.'

The Venetian Ambassador confirmed Catherine's *insouciance*: 'She is perfectly well aware that all the evils of the kingdom are imputed to her and that she is detested. But she does not care a fig either for the ill-will or for the accusations people pile upon her.'

Catherine's attitude, however, cannot be attributed to her 'Medicean' qualities. Rather it reverses them, for if there was one thing for which the

Medici were notable it was the desire to make a good impression—the foundation-stone of 'Machiavellianism'. To suggest that duplicity was used to make a bad impression is to carry illogicality to extremes. The reason for Catherine's attitude is much more likely to have been the circumstance defined by an eighteenth-century English wit: 'The consciousness of innocence is of the greatest prejudice to you. What is it makes you negligent

Michel de l' Hôpital, the Chancellor of France, who supported a policy of toleration and made many necessary legal reforms.

of forms and careless of the world's opinion? Why, the consciousness of your own innocence. What makes you thoughtless in your conduct and apt to run into a thousand little imprudences? Why, the consciousness of your own innocence. If you would only make a *faux pas,* you can't conceive how cautious you would grow!'

It may certainly be argued that an inability to estimate the impression her actions might make on the mob, conditioned by propaganda, was a weakness in her. Had she heeded it, her reputation in history might be nearer Queen Victoria than Jezebel. As it is, there has emerged the 'enigma' of Catherine de' Medici, which is nothing but an impossible attempt to reconcile the real woman with the vicious caricature of Huguenot revolutionary propaganda. As Balzac so rightly said: 'When once calumnies are undermined by facts, everything is explained to the glory of this wonderful woman.' There is no enigma except how, against such odds, Catherine managed to achieve so much.

The affair of Amboise marks the beginning of this phenomenon. That she and the Court officially witnessed the executions was represented as a casual appearance on the battlements after dinner to gratify a decadent blood lust. That the boys Francis and Charles were there was cited as an early example of Catherine's endeavours to corrupt her children. That the Queen-Mother reproved the young Duchess of Guise for a show of emotion was held to demonstrate how flint-hearted Catherine was and how much she herself was enjoying the spectacle of death.

An essential of rulership is the ability to face the consequences of one's acts. It would have been easy enough for Catherine to have had the executions carried out privately. But the scale of the intended revolution demanded public punishment and that, in turn, required the presence of the Crown. For herself, she had been long schooled into the appearance of grim impassivity; and Francis, although he would be nauseated and disturbed, had to learn that a King must know how to endure unpleasant things without flinching. But Charles, who was only ten, she would have spared if she could. Charles, however, as Duke of Orléans, had his own household and was within the orbit of the Court. He could not be allowed to be absent, even though the effect of the executions on his curious, unstable nature, already apt to be excited by the sight of blood during a hunt, might be dangerous. Yet she could shield him no longer, as she could the younger children, who were safe in the nursery.

Catherine's original intention in coming to Touraine was to spend some weeks hunting, after which the Court would make a journey to Toulouse by way of Bordeaux and spend the following winter in Languedoc and Provence. But the situation no longer permitted it. She was determined to understand, as far as she could, the root causes of unrest and to disentangle, if it were possible, the religious from the political. Before she left the country-side of the Loire she issued from Romorantin an edict which transferred cases of heresy from the King's courts to the bishops' courts and which provided summary justice for illegal armed assemblies. The religious question was to be debated by calling a conference of all the faiths, at which the question of a vernacular translation of the Bible was to be considered. This was at the suggestion of the Cardinal of Lorraine who, as a skilled theologian, was perfectly aware that it could produce nothing but uproar, as the two wings of the Reformers, the Lutherans and the Calvinists, disagreed with each other more violently than either did with the Catholics.

Both Catherine and the Cardinal agreed on the appointment of a new Chancellor of France, the fifty-three-year-old Michael de l'Hôpital, an Auvergnat lawyer whom Ronsard celebrated in a classical ode, comparing him to the great lawyers of Greece and Rome. L'Hôpital was a man of out-standing integrity, who 'carried the lilies of France in his heart' and could be relied on to carry out a policy of reconciliation without the surrender of the Catholic faith.

On the new Chancellor's advice, the King summoned to Fontainebleau in August an Assembly of Notables which Catherine opened by begging the great company—the Cardinals of Lorraine and Bourbon, the Duke of Guise, the Constable, the Chancellor, the Admiral, Marshals and Bishops, the Knights of the Order of St. Michel and the royal secretaries—to counsel the King her son in such a way that 'his sceptre may be preserved, his subjects eased and the malcontents contented, if it be possible.'

There were two notable absentees, in spite of their promise to attend—the Princes of the Blood, Navarre and Condé; but Coligny, speaking for them in fact, if not in name, presented a petition which reminded the King that the office of King had been ordained by God and prayed him that 'following the example of good kings like David, Hezekiah and Josiah' he would restore in the kingdom 'the true and right service of God and exterminate all abuses.' It also called on the Queen-Mother to follow the example of Esther, to have pity on the chosen people and to deliver them: 'Therefore, Sovereign Princess, we supplicate you, by the affection you owe to Jesus Christ to establish His true service and drive out all others.' To this end they asked for temples—Huguenot churches—to be established in every town and village in France.

The Cardinal of Lorraine said curtly that to grant such 'temples' would be to approve of idolatry and thus to merit damnation; but he added in a more conciliatory tone that those who attended heretic services unarmed or who merely stayed away from Mass ought not to be persecuted, as hitherto, since, from a severely practical point-of-view, such persecution had been a conspicuous failure in eradicating heresy.

The Assembly unanimously agreed that the whole matter should be referred to a States General, which was summoned to meet on December 10 at Orléans. This was announced on 31 August 1560, the Assembly's last day at Fontainebleau. As no States-General had been called for almost eighty years and the understood policy of whoever ruled France was that, if possible, it should never meet, the edict was regarded as a concession as great as it was unexpected.

But before the Assembly dispersed, the entire situation had changed radically. The Duke of Guise had been keeping a critical eye on one of Condé's partisans and, as he set out to return to Béarn, had him arrested on suspicion. His valise was filled with letters to Condé which, when examined, revealed the existence of a plot more widespread and dangerous than that of La Renaudie. Poitiers, Tours, Orléans and Lyons were to be seized by the Huguenots, who would then advance on the Court with forces gathered from all parts of the southern provinces. The Princes of the Blood were to assume the government and the Guise brothers were to be executed.

After studying the letters, the Cardinal, though it was late at night, went immediately to Catherine. Together they went to the King's room and asked him to summon the Constable and the Chancellor, who had long been in bed. They discussed the matter till one in the morning and then ordered the arrest of the powerful Seigneur de Maligny, Vidame de Chartres, who was the most deeply compromised. The Vidame had just visited Geneva where he had not only raised a regiment of soldiers but had also obtained Calvin's official blessing on the insurrection, confirmed by the sending of his most able lieutenant, Theodore Beza, as adviser to the King of Navarre.

The Vidame was to capture Lyons, the financial capital of France, which, situated at the cross-roads of the trade-routes, with the constant comings and goings of merchants and the couriers of foreign banks, afforded an ideal base for a seditious operation. Once in Huguenot hands it was to be made a canton on the Swiss model as the ally as well as the geographical neighbour of Geneva. Its seizure was planned for September 5.

This left so little time that the Spanish Ambassador was immediately, in the dawn, sent to Madrid to inform King Philip what had happened and to beg him to be ready, in case of need, to send assistance. At the same time, Catherine sent to her daughter Elisabeth a letter which reflects her attitude to the providential discovery of the plot: 'You will see the reason for this letter by what the Ambassador will tell you about it, which is the reason why I do not repeat it. I will only say that God has helped us and I shall put things again in such a state, if it pleases Him to aid us, that we could not have a

greater occasion to thank and serve Him as we ought to according to the grace
He has shown towards us of allowing us to discover everything. For it seems
that it is really a miracle, the way in which we found out everything and God is
certainly showing us how much He loves us and all the Kingdom. He will
maintain you also, but I pray you never to forget to be grateful to Him and to
serve Him as you ought.'

Few, if any, other letters of Catherine so reveal the heart of her.

On the night of September 4 the royal garrison of Lyons, warned by
Guise, suddenly struck while the rebels' final preparations were being made.
After a short but bitter fight the Vidame's men were defeated and rounded
up, though he himself managed to escape. At the same time moves were made
against the rebels in other disaffected districts. Guise issued instructions to
his various lieutenants: 'Take care so well to chastise those who have played
the devil that it will be an example. It should be easy to discover those who
have contributed money. Do not hold your hand in making them pay, for if

*The armour of Francis II,
Catherine's eldest son.*

*Charles, Cardinal of Lorraine;
attributed to Jean de Gourmont.*

this could in part defray our expenses it would be no mean service. As to those you find in arms, after you have punished the leaders according to military regulations, you can send the rank-and-file to the galleys where the King has great need of convicts.'

The immediate results of the crushing of the new rebellion was that the King of Navarre and the Prince of Condé could now be treated openly as rebels and, Princes of the Blood though they were, measures could be taken against them. The King sent a message to Navarre ordering him to come to Court and bring his brother with him, warning him: 'If you refuse to obey, I am capable of teaching you that I am King.' The message was his own. After the midnight scare at Fontainebleau, he had no need of anyone's prompting.

Catherine, however, took a different view. For one thing, her practicality considered that the Bourbons were at the moment less of a menace than they had ever been. Now that their plans were known and countered they were virtually powerless. In the second place, she was not satisfied that the King of Navarre was really implicated. About his brother there was no doubt at all, but Antony was such an unreliable fool that it was quite possible that Condé in his desire to become King Louis XIII had thought it wiser not to take him into his full confidence. In consequence Catherine sent to assure Navarre that he personally was not suspected and that all that was required was for him to bring Condé to Court to explain himself and to ask formally for any pardon he might seem to require. The Cardinal de Bourbon added his assurances to those of the Queen-Mother and urged his brothers to come to Court.

Eventually they came. They arrived in Orléans on October 30 and were taken to the Hôtel Groslot where the Court was temporarily in residence.

The King greeted them icily and announced that Condé would be tried immediately by the Council.

'I am answerable to no jurisdiction but that of my peers' said Condé. 'The Council has no standing in this.'

'You still defy me, then?' said the King. 'You shall have time in prison to repent it.'

Catherine, realising that the arrest of Condé would not only dishonour her assurances but that it would be, as she saw it, the stupidity of stupidities by precipitating a new and dangerous situation from which withdrawal would be impossible, laid her hand on her son's arm and said: 'My son, this needs more thought and anger is a bad counsellor.'

Francis shook off her hand, shouted 'I have myself decided on this arrest long ago' and called to the officers of the guard to take the Prince of Condé into custody.

Condé turned to the Cardinal de Bourbon, and said: 'With your assurance of safety, you have delivered your own brother to death'. Both the Cardinal and the King of Navarre threw themselves on their knees and implored mercy for their brother; but the King was adamant and the Prince was led away to the prison of Orléans until special apartments had been prepared for him in the château of Amboise in that part of the castle where doors and windows had been walled up and iron gratings added at the time of La Renaudie's threat, seven months ago.

A commission of magistrates visited Amboise to settle the preliminaries of Condé's trial, but the Prince persistently refused to have anything to do with them. He stood to his right to trial by his peers.

In the middle of November the King decided to go on a hunt until the official opening of the States-General on December 10. On November 17, however, he fell ill. The abscess in his ear had been giving more trouble than usual. The weather was bitter—the Loire was frozen over—and his physicians diagnosed nothing more than a bad cold in the head. Francis was ordered to bed for a week. But his condition grew worse. His headaches became so excruciating that he found the least noise unbearable. A lump formed behind his ear.

The sickroom was closed to all but the family. Catherine and the Guise brothers took turns to sit by the boy who, they were convinced, was dying. To prevent the news leaking out, the ambassadorial service was suspended. And Catherine, determined to know the worst, rode through the bitter weather to Chaumont, which Diane was not yet occupying but where Ruggieri still watched the stars.

There were with him others of what might be termed her astrological council—the French Ogier Ferrier and the Italian Gabriale Simeoni as well as the famous Luc Gauric, who stood so high in the favour of the Pope that he had been given a bishopric, and the greatest of them all, the Jew Michel Nostradamus, who had published a book of rhymed prophecies which he had dedicated to King Henry II, the 'first monarch of the universe', assuring him that 'there was nothing whatever in these writings to militate against the true Catholic Faith while consulting the astronomical calculations to the best of my knowledge.'

Henry and Catherine had met Nostradamus in 1555 when, as a result of his prophecies, they had invited him to Court to cast the horoscopes of the royal children. They had allowed him to occupy the Paris mansion of the Bishop of Sens where, for a short time he had become the rage of the capital and gifts to him of jewels, plate and money from grateful or hopeful clients partly compensated for what he considered Henry II's meanness in rewarding his dedication with no more than 130 *écus* in a velvet purse, to which Catherine had added a hundred crowns. Before long, however, the prophet returned to his home in Salon in Provence, midway between Avignon and Marseilles, with the promise that he would always advise Catherine by letter and, if she sent for him urgently, come to her.

In the present crisis she had sent for him urgently to join the others at Chaumont because she needed his power of magic, based on his undoubted gift of second sight.

When Catherine entered the laboratory at Chaumont, she found already traced on the floor the magic circle in which she was to stand. Opposite her was a mirror at the corners of which were written in pigeons' blood the four Jewish names of God—Yahve, Elohim, Mitratron and Adonai. Nostradamus started a lilting incantation and the mirror clouded over. When it cleared, Francis was staring at her as if from an adjoining room. He walked round it once and vanished. His brother Charles followed him and made fourteen turns of the room—which meant, the astrologers explained, that he would reign for fourteen years. Charles was followed by her favourite Henry, whose regnal span was fifteen. But in place of her youngest son, Hercules, whom she was expecting to see next, there appeared the figure of Antony of Navarre's young son, Henry.

Catherine's cry of 'No! No!' was involuntary, but she mastered herself as Nostradamus blew on the mirror and the unwelcome vision vanished. She returned to Orléans with her resolution strengthened. If the line of Valois

was destined to die out, at least she would see to it that while her sons lived they ruled. Also, it was possible to prolong her posterity by marrying Margot to young Henry of Navarre when the time was appropriate. But at the moment there was an immediate duty. When, in a few days, Charles became King Charles IX, it was essential that she, not Antony of Navarre, Premier Prince of the Blood, became Regent. How long Francis would live no one could tell. The stars were unhelpful in that particular and the doctors were divided in their opinions, but she feared that a week was the limit.

She summoned Antony of Navarre immediately and bade him listen while one of her secretaries read out precedents from the past establishing the right to the Regency of the mother of a minor, notwithstanding the Salic Law which disallowed inheritance through a female. She then insisted that in any case the recent conduct of the Princes of the Blood in fomenting two plots against the Throne, completely disqualified him for the Regency to which his status conventionally entitled him and asked him formally to renounce his claim to it. In return she promised him the life of his brother Condé and the Lieutenant-Generalship of the Kingdom. Antony agreed.

On the afternoon of December 5, he gave her in writing his resignation of the Seal to her. At midnight the King died.

The Cardinal of Lorraine had been uninterruptedly at the boy's bedside, not as a statesman but as a priest. He asked Francis to say, as his dying prayer: 'Lord! pardon my sins and do not impute to me, Thy servant, the sins committed by my ministers under my name and authority.' Then he gave him his last absolution.

Opposite: *Catherine consulting Nostradamus about her children.*

Below: *The Hôtel Groslot, which was used as a royal residence when the King visited Orleans, and where Francis II died.*

The Regent

Once more Catherine poured out her heart to Elisabeth in Spain: 'Do not let yourself be troubled for me. I assure you that I shall not fail to govern myself in such a manner that God will be satisfied with me, for it is always my chief aim to have His honour before my eyes in everything and to uphold my authority not for myself but to preserve the realm for the good of your brothers whom I love, as I love you all who are your father's children. And therefore, my daughter, my darling, commend yourself to God, for you have seen me as happy as you are now, thinking of no other tribulation except to be loved by the King, your father, who honoured me more than I deserved; but I loved him, so that I was always afraid for him, as you well know; and God took him from me: and, not content with that, has now also taken your brother, whom I loved, and left me with three small sons in a realm altogether divided, having no one whom I can trust because there is no one who is disinterested. And therefore, my darling, think of me . . . '

There was, however, one person she trusted—her old 'Gossip', the Constable, who, at her request, old as he was, had ridden into Orléans at the head of his *corps d'élite* to take military control of the city in the name of the new King Charles IX and his mother, the Regent.

A week after Francis's death, the 438 Deputies to the States-General met in the large wooden hall which had been built in Orléans to accommodate them. Among the members of the Third Estate was a hard core of Huguenots who had already received their instructions from Geneva as to what policy to pursue. Calvin, who had exulted: 'Behold the Lord our God has awakened and removed that boy!', laid down as the first essential step the dispossession of Catherine and the establishment of a Regency in Huguenot hands. 'The principal point', he had instructed Coligny, 'because it is the one on which everything else depends is to establish a Council to govern. Unless the King of Navarre acts promptly, a mistake may be made which it will be difficult to rectify. For him to admit that a woman, and a foreign Italian woman at that,

Tortorel's engraving of the Assembly of the 'Three States' at Orleans on 15 January 1561. Letters indicate: A, King Charles IX; B, Catherine; C, Henry of Anjou; D, Margot; E, Antony of Navarre.

should be allowed to rule would cover him with dishonour. It is essential to insist on the establishment of a Council.'

Catherine, meeting some of the deputies on their arrival and being plied with a demand for a Council of Regency as if it were a lesson learned by rote —as indeed it was—determined to keep Antony of Navarre true to his promise by fulfilling her part of the bargain and releasing Condé, who, swearing that he would never go to Mass again, departed for his estates in Picardy.

In the debate on religion in the States-General, the Orator of the Third Estate, following the Geneva line, inveighed against the avarice, idleness and ignorance of the clergy. The Orator of the Nobility urged that Huguenots should be allowed the right of public assembly. The Orator of the Clergy counter-attacked by asking that anyone who presented a petition on behalf of heretics should himself be declared a heretic.

This brought Coligny angrily to his feet. He was in a difficult position. So far he had managed to keep his Calvinism a secret from the Court and particularly from his uncle, the Constable, who supposed that his support of the Huguenots was merely political and a natural consequence of the rivalry between their house and the house of Lorraine. On this assumption, the Constable had even approved of it, though he was as stern and unbending a Catholic as the Guises. He never missed Mass. Every morning, whether at home or on horseback, hunting or with his troops, he told his beads—a circumstance which gave rise to the *mot* : 'Beware the Constable's rosary!', for, according to Brantôme, he never put his rosary out of his hand even when he was giving his troops such orders as: 'Round up the Huguenots who want another Church than the King's! Burn their villages down! Start a blaze a mile wide!' Coligny dreaded the consequence of the old man's discovery that there was a practising Calvinist in the family. Above all, he dreaded it being made public in the States-General by the indiscretion of some foolish Huguenot deputy.

So now the Admiral demanded an apology for the suggestion that because he was prepared to support the just demands of a persecuted minority, therefore he shared their beliefs.

The Orator replied that he was merely enunciating a general principle and had made no personal reference.

'Yet it will be understood everywhere', said Coligny, 'that I was intended.'

'Then I hasten to explain', said the Orator, 'that no such thing was in my mind. Indeed I was only speaking from my brief authorised by my Estate.'

Coligny bowed, glanced at his uncle and sat down, apparently satisfied.

The conclusion of the religious discussion was satisfactory enough for the Huguenot element. Though public worship was not permitted, Catherine renewed the earlier Edict of Toleration and Calvin wrote: 'The concessions which the Queen makes out of necessity will have great results. Our church will progress rapidly far and wide.'

On the other hand, Philip of Spain (whose experience of heresy while he was King of England had extinguished any spark of sympathy he might once have had for the policy of toleration) sent a special embassy to Orléans to implore his mother-in-law 'never to permit the innovations which had sprung up in France to make further progress and never to favour in the least degree any who were less firm in the Faith than they should be . . . '

Had Catherine been able to dissolve the States-General immediately the political and the religious debates were over, she might have been able to congratulate herself on a successful outcome. Unfortunately there was still the financial question to face. During the last twelve years, forty-two alienations of the Royal Domain had been made and the patrimony of the Crown had virtually ceased to exist. The Chancellor, on the Queen's behalf, asked for a subsidy from each Estate so that by repurchasing its one-time property the Crown should recover its independence.

No subsidy was forthcoming. The three Orders agreed on a unanimous

The interior of a Protestant church during a Huguenot 'Prêche'.

recommendation that the Crown should furnish its own endowment by reducing its expenses.

Catherine, not of a banking family for nothing, worked feverishly. She suppressed certain offices, reduced her domestic staff, took a third from the state pensions and a quarter from the official salaries and abolished one of the departments of government. In ten days she had saved nearly two and a half million *livres*. An admiring observer was moved to remark that 'the greatest of subsidies is the drastic economy which the Court imposes on itself in all things.'

The States-General, however, took a different view. The Deputies considered that if Catherine could save 2,300,000 *livres* in ten days, she could,

115

over several months, work wonders. On the last day of January they dispersed without granting her a *sou*.

She saw immediately that the key to the financial situation was held by the religious. Ruling would be impossible without accommodation. The question was the extent of the accommodation, and the way in which it should be arranged. With no adviser who was not *parti-pris* and with no precedent to consult, she wavered. It was at this time that a Venetian envoy complained: 'When she wishes she gives an answer which, while it seems quite decided and definite, actually contains no decision at all.' And an exasperated Spaniard wrote: 'She changes her mind three times a day.' At one time she even considered inviting Calvin to Fontainebleau but was saved from this excess of ecumenism by Coligny.

The Admiral, on account of the past as much as the present, was the obvious person for Catherine to turn to. In the circumstances, indeed, he was the only one. The unyielding orthodoxy of the Constable and the Guise brothers made it impossible for them to suggest compromise and the Chancellor, l'Hôpital, though a man of the middle-road, was as yet too new in office for Catherine to have any confidence in him. Antony of Navarre was worse than useless.

To Coligny it was a providential opportunity, though he used it a little too obviously by laying himself out to capture the ten-year-old King's affection and was so far successful in his assiduity in charming Charles that the boy started to call him 'Father'.

Catherine showed herself not unaware of the dangers of this situation by insisting on sleeping in the King's room, and surrounding him more carefully than ever with servants and tutors on whom she could rely both to instruct him and to make their reports to her. But, having thus safeguarded her personal ascendancy, she allowed Coligny and his sympathisers the utmost latitude. Coligny engaged a Calvinist chaplain and held *prêches* in his apartment of the palace. As Easter approached, he became bolder and the Spanish Ambassador reported to King Philip: 'Whereas formerly the Admiral held his preaching with closed doors, on Palm Sunday he held it with open ones. They began their ceremonies like those of Geneva, singing Psalms so loudly that the whole courtyard was filled with the sound.'

A week later, on Easter Day, 6 April 1561, came the inevitable answer to the provocation. The Cardinal of Lorraine had left Court to attend to his Lenten duties in his own diocese, but the Duke of Guise and the Constable, in spite of the hereditary family rivalry, had been drawn together by what, in their passionate, if simple, Catholicism, they regarded as an attack on their Faith. Throughout Lent each morning at dawn they, with one of the Marshals of France, Saint-André, had heard Mass in the little chapel in the *basse-cour*.

This German Protestant print of a Catholic church compares it with the Protestant church on page 115, which supposedly represents simplicity.

That Easter Day they received Holy Communion as a pledge of loyalty and dedication and, at breakfast together at the Constable's table, they constituted themselves a Triumvirate to defend the Faith.

This action was the real turning-point in the history of the time, for, as Sir John Neale has expressed it, 'a party existed, menacing in its power, whose object was to defend the Catholic faith, apart from the King and if need be against him.'

Catherine did not become fully aware of this new turn of events till a month later. On their way to Rheims where, on May 15, the Cardinal of Lorraine crowned Charles IX—as he had crowned Henry II and Francis II—Catherine asked the Duke of Guise whether it was true that he had formed a league to support religion, the King and her authority. Guise admitted it.

Catherine then asked: 'If my son and I should adopt the new religion, which' —she said with great emphasis—'we have no thought in the world of doing, would you and your confederates renounce your allegiance to us?'

'Yes.'

'You would renounce your allegiance?' She was incredulous.

'Yes. But, as you have said, it is impossible and as long as "the Most Christian King" remains the "Eldest Son of the Church" we would all give our lives for you.'

The forming of a new party owing its primary allegiance to the Church and prepared to defend it, if necessary, even against the Crown made imperative the success of Catherine's plan for a consultative religious assembly which would reconcile the heretical sects with Catholicism. The summer of 1561 was devoted to preparing for the conference, which was to be held in the great Dominican monastery at Poissy, a few miles from Saint-Germain where the court took up residence. Calvin's representative, Theodore Beza, with fourteen ministers and theologians from Geneva, were invited to attend, as well as a score of delegates from the Huguenot churches in France and a sprinkling of Lutherans from Germany.

Catherine's hope was that there might be agreement on measures for the reform of the Church and the finding of a formula which could be accepted by all sides as a definition of Holy Communion. The decisions could then be put forward by the Cardinal of Lorraine at the great Ecumenical Council of Trent which, at the moment, was dealing with the same problems on behalf of the Pope.

One historian has written that 'there was no other sovereign in Europe then, or for many generations afterwards, who could have conceived the idea and perhaps no other act of Catherine's so strongly brings out the ability and breadth of view which she brought to the service of France.'

What she lacked was the one quality which would have made her realise that success in such an undertaking was impossible. 'I do not believe', said the Venetian Ambassador after a conversation with her, 'that Her Majesty understands what the word "dogma" means.'

It was easy enough to agree on such things as the need for a decent clergy, an end to nepotism and a proper method of appointment of bishops. Every one, from the Pope downwards, was agreed on reform. But when it came to finding a formula which could be adopted by the different faiths to define the dogma behind the Mass, success was impossible. How impossible may be gauged by remembering that the precise differences which the Colloquy of Poissy failed to solve in 1561 brought the Catholic Church to the edge of schism in 1971.

The Catholics believed that when, at Holy Communion, the celebrant pronounced over the bread and the wine Christ's words: 'This is My Body:

this is My Blood', the bread and the wine became His Body and His Blood. The Lutherans believed that they became His Body and His Blood while at the same time remaining bread and wine. The Calvinists and the Anabaptists believed that no change took place but that the elements remained bread and wine. It is obvious that no formula can be found to reconcile these mutually exclusive interpretations. Had the matter been a mere philosophic exercise, it would have been of little consequence, but as all the parties agreed that this was the core of the Christian religion and that Holy Communion was a necessity for survival after death, (according to Christ's words: 'Except ye eat the flesh of the Son of Man and drink His blood, ye have no life in you: whoso eateth My flesh and drinketh My blood hath eternal life and I will raise him up at the last day'), there was, literally, nothing in life of equal importance. And, as the antithetical beliefs issued in action, the Catholic saw in the Calvinist who did not pay respect to the bread which by consecration had become the Body, a blaspheming atheist, so the Calvinist regarded the Catholic who prostrated himself before that was nothing but bread as a pernicious idolater.

Consequently when Beza opened the great debate at Poissy by outlining the Calvinist position and asserting that 'Christ's Body is as far distant from the bread and the wine as the highest Heaven is distant from the earth', there was a roar of dissent; and when the Cardinal of Lorraine answered him by a reasoned defence of the traditional doctrine all the Catholics sprang to their feet and shouted at the King: 'Sire, this is the true Faith, this is the

Theodore Beza, Calvin's chief representative.

The Colloquy of Poissy on 9 December 1561. In the front row facing the reader from left to right are Antony of Navarre, Henry of Anjou, Charles IX, Catherine, Margot, and Jeanne Queen of Navarre.

pure doctrine of the Church; we are all prepared to subscribe to this and if need be to seal it with out blood.'

The General of the Jesuits addressed himself directly to Catherine, accusing her of compassing the ruin of the realm by tolerating the Huguenot 'wolves, foxes, serpents and assassins'. His reproaches, according to an observer, 'brought tears to her eyes'.

A committee consisting of three bishops, three Catholic theologians and five leading Calvinist ministers continued to work on the elusive formula and on October 4 managed to produce a definition of Holy Communion which they all signed and submitted to the conference. It was unanimously and angrily rejected and the Colloquy of Poissy broke up, leaving the two parties even more bitterly, because more logically, at odds than when it assembled. Its only practical result was that the King of Navarre was so disturbed by the cogency of the Catholic arguments that he not only returned to the Church but openly joined the Triumvirate and, accompanied by the Constable, the Marshal de Saint-André and the Duke of Guise, rode in public procession

The Council of Trent was held in 1563 to discuss Catholic policy towards Huguenots; the Cardinal of Lorraine attended to represent France.

through Paris to hear Mass at St. Genevieve. Henceforth the Huguenots had another nickname for him—Judas.

The Guise brothers decided to relinquish any active part in the struggle. The Cardinal of Lorraine was only too glad to lay down his administrative burden and go to Rome to take his place at the closing sessions of the Council of Trent. With the return of their widowed niece, Mary Queen of Scots, to Scotland just before the Colloquy of Poissy met, the Guises' personal interest in court circles waned. The Duke of Guise wanted time to attend to his own estates in Lorraine. The brothers left Court with all their adherents in a great company of more than six hundred horse.

Before they left, they made an attempt to persuade the ten-year-old Henry, Catherine's favourite child, to accompany them. The Duke of Nemours, one of Guise's closest friends, found an opportunity to ask the boy if it was true that he had become a Huguenot. Henry replied: 'No, I am of my mother's religion.' Nemours then realised that two of Catherine's waiting-women were behind a tapestry and, taking Henry to the other side of the room, said in a low voice: 'There is a great deal of trouble in the kingdom and you are not safe here because the King of Navarre and the Prince of Condé want to seize the Throne from your family and you will be killed. If you like, I'll take you to Lorraine, where you'll be safe.' Henry reiterated that he had no wish to leave his mother. Nemours replied: 'Then remember this, before we leave, say to the Duke of Guise: "My cousin, if you can't take me with you now, I beg of you to come when I need you".'

Guise's son, Henry, who was the same age as Henry of Anjou and his dominant playfellow, also suggested that a visit to Lorraine would be a great adventure and, once there, Anjou, as Heir to the Throne, would be entertained and petted as he never had been even by his mother; and the Duke of Guise said that it was not too soon for the Heir to see something of the country he might one day have to rule. But Anjou remained uninterested and when the Guises left Court on 20 October 1561 and Nemours was injudicious enough to say to him: 'Remember what I have told you!' Catherine, overhearing, easily extracted from her son the whole story.

Her anger was measureless. Of all the Guise interferences, this was the most bitterly resented and its final results the most disastrous. The seeds of Catherine's ultimate failure were sown here. The relationship between the two boys, her overloved son, Henry of Valois, and Henry of Guise were to dominate events for the rest of her life, yet not till the very end of it, over a quarter of a century and seven civil wars later, did she realise, brokenheartedly, that had she trusted the younger Guise rather than her son the terrible turmoil of the interim would have been avoided. Yet it was, of course, humanly impossible for her, especially in view of what can only be called her mania for her favourite child. To her personal hatred of the Guises, which had started when the Cardinal of Lorraine had suggested her divorce and increased when her Guise daughter-in-law, Mary Queen of Scots, lessened her influence on her eldest son, was now added the unpardonable attempt to kidnap the boy who was the apple of her eye.

The unpopularity of the Guises, fostered by the Huguenot propaganda, made her instinctive attitude easy enough to rationalise. 'All this trouble has been for no other reason than the hate which the entire realm has for the Cardinal of Lorraine and the Duke of Guise. So I have made up my mind to look to the safety of your brothers and my own safety', she wrote to Elisabeth in Spain, 'and not to mix any longer their quarrels with mine. The reason why they are disliked is because of the stupidities *(sottises)* they have perpetrated on all sides, trying to make people believe I was not a good Christian in order to make them suspect me and saying that it was because I wasn't a good Christian that I didn't trust them.'

She explained that she wanted Elisabeth to see that her husband, Philip, understood this, 'in case they send something secretly to make him believe that they have been put out of power because of religion.'

What Philip feared most, however, was that in the Huguenot-dominated atmosphere of the Court, the King himself might become infected with heresy. From his ambassador the Spanish King knew that Catherine had taken Charles to hear Beza preach, that she had given him a copy of Marot's Psalms, that Coligny was laying himself out to gain influence over him and, most dangerous of all, that the boy's tutor had been changed.

When Catherine gave Charles the volume of Marot, which as far as she was concerned was evocative of nostalgia rather than theology—she may well have given him her own copy—she realised the possibility of misunderstanding and forbade him to show it to anyone. The King, however, immediately showed it to Cypierre, his tutor, to whom he was greatly attached. Cypierre took it away from him and having told him, as a general principle, that men should not obey women went to report it to the Constable who, in his turn, remonstrated with Catherine.

In the ensuing altercation with her 'Gossip' Catherine became so enraged that she dismissed Cypierre and in his place appointed a Huguenot tutor, reinforced by Condé's mother-in-law and another extreme Calvinist, Madame de Crussol, as ladies-in-waiting.

The result was not what the Queen had intended. Charles stopped calling Coligny 'father', went to Mass regularly and ostentatiously, and on one occasion knocked at the door of the Queen of Navarre's apartments where one of Beza's *prêches* was in progress and when on the fourth knock it was opened shouted: 'Don't make any mistake about it; if you keep on with your *prêches* you will every one of you be burnt.'

If Charles was so immediately contra-suggestive, so was his brother Henry. The Guise attempt to inveigle Anjou to Lorraine made him an energetic supporter of the Calvinists. His sister Margot, then aged eight, recorded in after years one of the results of the change: 'He often urged me to change my religion, often threw my prayer-books in the fire and instead of them gave me Psalms and Huguenot prayers, compelling me to carry them. I answered his threats by tears, because I was very young. He answered that he could have me whipped or killed if he wanted. I answered him that he could have me whipped or even have be killed if he chose to, but that I would suffer everything that could be done to me rather than damn my soul.'

Not only the Valois children were involved in the religious controversy. It affected also the boy Henry of Navarre, whom Catherine, after she had seen his image in Nostradamus's mirror as the successor to her own Henry, had determined to marry to Margot and so keep the throne of France in the family at least in the female line. To initiate discussions on this point, as well as because his formidable mother, Jeanne, was a leading Huguenot, she had invited the Queen of Navarre to the conference.

Jeanne, who was now twenty-four, had a secondary reason for accepting the invitation. She was anxious to find out for herself what was happening to her husband, Antony, who had long lost any love he may have felt for her and who, she had heard by rumour, had been ensnared by the Queen-Mother's 'Flying Squadron'. Catherine had extended the principle of Francis I's *Petite Bande* from pleasure to politics and formed an *Escadron Volante* of young beauties, mostly daughters of the smaller landed gentry, whom she could use to discover the secrets of her enemies. She had already managed to immobilise Condé with the golden-haired, blue-eyed Isabelle de Limeuil, and now she provided his brother with a fifteen-year-old charmer known as 'la belle Rouet' who enslaved Antony so completely that he was willing to divorce Jeanne if necessary.

On arrival at Saint-Germain, Jeanne wrote to Calvin that 'the King of Navarre has grown so deluded and enervated mentally and bodily by indolence and luxury that he has allowed the Guises, aided by the Constable, to regain the upper hand, to his great shame and the calamity of France. Calvin replied by assuring her that he would pray for Antony's early death. 'Take courage, Madame, that you may overcome by the strength and goodness of Him in Whom and by Whom all things can turn into blessing and consolation.' Calvin was not alone in seeing possible death as an ally. Catherine wishes that 'God would take the Queen of Navarre so that her husband might marry again without delay.' The intended second wife was not, of course, 'la belle Rouet'—she had no purpose but to loosen him from Jeanne—but the widowed Mary Queen of Scots, which would indeed have been a political masterstroke.

In the meantime Catherine remained on as courteous terms with Jeanne as their different temperaments permitted and only once did her control break. On one occasion when she complained of feeling unwell, the Queen of Navarre, with her accustomed candour, retorted that, considering the amount of melons the Queen-Mother indulged in, it was not surprising. Catherined snapped: 'It's not the fruits of the garden that hurt me. It's the Fruits of the Spirit.'

Antony, now firm in the Catholic faith, insisted that his wife should renounce her Calvinism. Publicly, according to an observer, 'finding her about to step into a litter and attend a *Prêche* he took her by the hand and led her back commanding sternly that she should no more attend the Huguenot

Queens of Navarre. Clouet's portraits of Margot as a child (left) and her mother-in-law Jeanne d'Albret, queen in her own right.

services but outwardly conform in all things to the worship of the Roman Church.'

Jeanne replied: 'Never will I be present at Mass or any Papist ceremony.' and young Henry ran to his mother's side and shouted at his father: 'Nothing will make me go to Mass either!'

'If you ever dare to do so', said Jeanne, 'I shall disinherit you, so that you will never be King of Navarre.'

This reminder that it was only by marriage to her that Antony was King of Navarre considerably exacerbated the situation. Antony boxed his son's ears as hard as he could and ordered his physician, a Sicilian Jesuit named Lauro, to thrash him. He then appointed Lauro the boy's official tutor and took him away from Jeanne's care, ordering her to return to Pau with their other child Catherine.

Instead of going back to Béarn, however, Jeanne set out for Paris, where, with her brother-in-law Condé, she installed herself in the Hôtel de la rue Grenelle which she made 'a school for the study of the Reformed Religion.'

Husband and wife never met again.

Catherine refused to abandon her efforts for a *modus vivendi* among the churches. On 17 January 1562 she promulgated a new Edict 'in order to keep our subjects in peace until such time as God shall give us grace to reunite them in one fold.' It provided that the Huguenots should immediately return all the churches they had seized and all the ornaments and other property they had moved from them. They were forbidden to build places of worship of their own in towns or cities, but, on the other hand, they were for the first time given complete freedom of public worship in the suburbs outside the walls of the cities in which they lived and the magistrates were to see to it that they were not to be interfered with going to or coming from their worship. People of both religions were forbidden to irritate each other by the use of inflammatory language, especially in sermons. No Calvinist synod or

Jeanne d'Albret, Queen of Navarre, preaches to a group of Huguenots in the countryside; engraving after a painting on glass.

consistory was to be held without permission of the Crown and a royal officer was to be allowed to attend all assemblies if he so wished. No one of either religion was to carry any arms except the sword and dagger usual with gentlemen.

Pragmatically, in the circumstances, 'the Edict of January', as it was called, could hardly have been bettered. Essentially it was a police measure to prevent public disturbances in the crowded streets of cities, but however utilitarian the apparent motive, the measure conferred official status and legal recognition on Huguenotism. The ancient principle, 'un roi, un loi, une foi', was abandoned in favour of the existence of two rival religions in one state, a step which undermined the traditional social order itself.

It provoked an immediate Catholic protest. Priests refused to read the Edict from their pulpits and, instead, preached sermons likening Catherine to Jezebel introducing idolatry into the kingdom. A forest of placards appeared in Paris calling for the forcible extermination of heresy. Copies of the Edict, printed for nation-wide distribution, were seized and burnt. A deputation went to Saint-Germain to inform Catherine that 'they would lay down their lives rather than consent to such a disgrace' and to warn her that 'society would be entirely violated and dissolved, unity of faith being the bond of states.' And the Parlement of Paris refused to ratify the Edict.

For five weeks dispute and deadlock continued. Then Catherine lost her temper. 'The which Lady', noted a diarist, 'in her wrath and rage took horse at Saint-Germain and rode post-haste to Paris. And in sooth it was hard work to keep her from riding straight into the Council Chamber that she might the better demonstrate her absolute will and see the Edict safely registered. By no means cooled from her anger, she entered the room where sat the Presidents and all the Councillors and began to plead and grew shrill with them as women do when they are irritated. And when they had patiently listened, they tried to remonstrate with her and to prove the harm the Edict would do to King and kingdom, to the dishonour of God; wherefore, they said, they could not receive or register it. All of which the aforesaid lady refused to hear and, persevering in her threats, ordered them to accept it.'

As it was impossible, by law, to delay acceptance indefinitely and as Condé and Jeanne de Navarre from their Hôtel were organising Huguenot disturbances in the city, the Parlement surrendered. But the surrender was under protest and conditional. It was a temporary measure 'pending the King's coming of age.'

Catherine, additionally disappointed by the comparison of her near-failure with the Parlement and her triumph when she had first faced that body as the emissary of her husband ten years ago, was exhausted. She resolved to recuperate for a few weeks in her beloved Fontainebleau where she could meet the spring by the lake of swans and in the forest as well as on the lovely terraces. She would 'enjoy the benefits of time', and let the consequences of the Edict of January sort themselves out. On the way to Fontainebleau she paused at her château of Montceaux-en-Brie and there she learnt of the first result of her Edict—the massacre at Vassy.

On March 1, the Duke of Guise set out from Joinville, where he had been visiting his mother, for his estates in Nanteuil. On the way he stopped to hear Mass at Vassy, a town in Champagne which had once been under the Guise jurisdiction. Here the Huguenots were at least a thousand strong and were defying the new Edict by worshipping openly in the centre of the town in a large barn less than a hundred yards from the parish church. As soon as Mass started, the sound of the Psalms at the Prêche, sung with deliberate intensity, made the hearing of it impossible. Guise, after enduring the calculated noise for a quarter of an hour, sent his personal squire to ask the minister to discontinue the service until Mass was over. The minister returned the message that as the Duke was only a man whereas he was proclaiming the word of God, he would not dream of obeying him. As the squire was returning with the message, several of the Duke's men-at-arms who were not at Mass were drawn by curiosity to the open door of the barn. The Calvinists, alarmed by the sight of armed men, yelled 'Papist Idolaters!' and closed the door. The Guisards battered it open again and were greeted by a volley of stones.

Guise, as soon as he was told of the situation, left the church and hurried to the scene of pandemonium where he ordered his own followers to restrain their enthusiasm and the Huguenots to withdraw from their illegal gathering. They were forbidden by the Edict, he pointed out, to assemble in the centre of the town, though they were perfectly free to do so in the suburbs half-a-mile away.

As he was speaking a well-aimed stone hit him in the face. He was not seriously hurt, but the wound re-opened the famous scar which he had originally received at the siege of Boulogne and which gave him his nickname *Le Balafré* and he started to bleed profusely. At the sight of it, his men could no longer be restrained and attacked the Huguenots. Some they killed, some they wounded so badly that death ensued in a week or two, some they maimed for life.

The minister, who had torn off his gown in his effort to escape, was nevertheless recognised and brought to the Duke who asked him the reason for his breaking of the law.

'Sir,' answered the man, 'I have done nothing but preach the gospel of Jesus Christ.'

'*Mordieu*', answered Guise, 'did Our Lord preach sedition? You are the cause of the death of these people and you shall be hanged for it.' And he ordered the gibbet to be made from the benches of the barn and erected by the door of it. Then the Duke and his escort rode on their way, leaving about thirty dead and a hundred wounded.

The 'massacre of Vassy' was a godsend to Huguenot propaganda. Condé immediately issued a call to arms and sent a message to all Huguenots in the provinces: 'We wish you to take note of the horrible cruelty which M. de Guise has shown to our poor church at Vassy. We must be prepared to take arms to protect our lives against the violence of these brigands.' In response, Hugenot congregations everywhere started to arm and to endeavour to gain control of the towns in which they were situated.

Condé also sent Beza to Montceaux to demand from Catherine official vengeance. He refrained from going himself because he considered it impolitic to advertise the split in the Bourbon family. His brother, Navarre, as titular head of the Triumvirate and the Queen's chief adviser did not shrink from answering the protest. When Beza demanded that Guise should be punished, Antony 'mocked him in pungent and contemptuous words' and pointed out that the Huguenots at Vassy had quite obviously disobeyed the law and had been properly punished for starting the riot by throwing stones.

Catherine, trying to calm the situation, informed Beza that she had ordered a full legal enquiry into the happenings at Vassy and that, pending its findings, she was forbidding Guise to enter Paris. Could not the Huguenots show a similar restraint?

Beza promised to do his best, but events were out of his control. Huguenots were parading through the streets of Paris chanting the Lamentations of Jeremiah; Catholics were making bonfires in the streets to burn all Huguenot books, including Protestant translations of the Bible. One of the Calvinist ministers started to organise a wholesale massacre of Catholics and wrote to inform Geneva that he felt called by God to follow 'the examples of Gideon and Judith' by doing this meritorious deed. The missive was intercepted and taken to the Duke of Guise who had arrived at Nanteuil and was undecided whether to go to Montceaux as Catherine had ordered him or join the rest of the Triumvirate in Paris as she had forbidden him.

At this critical moment Guise was particularly anxious not to act illegally. Despite the absurd rumours, the wild exaggerations and the partisan hatred which had turned Vassy already into a fantastic legend, he knew he had nothing to fear from an impartial inquiry and both his loyalty to the Crown and his own traditions made him wish to go to Catherine at Montceaux. But the intercepted letter tipped the balance and convinced him that his duty to the Faith demanded his presence in the capital.

With fifteen hundred of his men who had sworn to die in his service, he entered Paris on Monday, 16 March, to a clamorous welcome, a triumphal ovation which exceeded even those he had been accustomed to receive after his military triumphs. 'Le Balafré', with his young son and heir, Henry, who had pleaded to be allowed to be with him, riding at his side, was once again the hero of the Parisians. The chief of the municipality, the Provost of the Merchants, came to greet him with the offer of twenty thousand soldiers and two millions in gold for the defence of Catholicism.

Guise, still straining to observe strict neutrality, replied that the Queen-Mother as Regent and the King of Navarre as Lieutenant-General of the Realm could, as the properly constituted authority in the state, be trusted to take whatever measures were necessary. Then, from his headquarters at his family Hôtel, he sent a message to Condé at Jeanne of Navarre's Hôtel, urging him to keep the peace.

Condé's reply was to flee the capital while Paris was at church at the Palm

Huguenot destruction of churches, rifling of tombs and murder of monks were commonplaces of a campaign by the Baron d'Andrets.

Horribles cruautez des Huguenots
en France.

La rage des malings ne laiſſe etre en repos
Les os ſacrez des ſainčts aux ſepulchres enclos,
Orebelles mutins, en meſpriſants les loix!
Leurs corps enſeueliz par pluſieurs ans paſſez
Brulétu as en cendre, & puis en l'air iectez,
N'ayant aucun reſpect aux Seigneurs ny aux Roys.

Sunday ceremonies of March 22. He established himself at Meaux, twenty
miles from Paris, urgently summoning his uncle, Admiral Coligny, to come
to him with men and money. The Admiral arrived at Meaux at the head of a
large body of men, 'all mounted'—the main strength of the Huguenots lay
always in their preponderance of cavalry—on March 27. They decided to
proceed in force to Fontainebleau, where the Court had now arrived, and
capture the King. Civil war was now seen to be inevitable and in any civil
war the trump cards are the King and the capital. Condé had lost the capital
where, he admitted, the Huguenots had as much chance against the Catholics
'as a gnat against an elephant'. He would however make sure of the King and
he could make the *coup* under cover of legality, because Catherine had
written to him: 'I see so many things which vex me that if it were not for my
faith in God and my conviction that you will help me to keep this kingdom
safe and will serve my son the King in spite of those who wish for universal
ruin, I should be yet more vexed; but I hope that we shall still remedy all
things with your good counsel and help.'

But Guise struck first. On the same afternoon that Coligny joined Condé at
Meaux—March 27—the Triumvirate arrived at Fontainebleau to escort the
royal family, willingly or unwillingly, to Paris. Catherine stormed, argued,
wept, but to no avail. 'The Catholic lords', wrote the Papal Nuncio to Rome,
'speaking to the Queen offered to pledge themselves to maintain and to
increase her authority. But they gave her to understand that she, on her part,
must abandon her attempts at conciliation because matters had now come to
such a pass that either one party or the other must be victorious. They ended
by declaring that if she refused to act on their advice and if the King, her son,
thought of changing his religion, they would not hesitate to change their
King.'

In the circumstances there was nothing Catherine could say. Forced to the
point, she had to drop her diplomatic pretence of favouring heresy. At the
same time her personal dislike of the Guises reinforced her fear of being, in
effect, the prisoner of the Triumvirate and she put every obstacle she could
in the way of a removal to Paris. Antony of Navarre, superintending preparations for the journey, had to threaten to thrash the domestics who refused to
dismantle the Royal bedchamber 'because of the Queen'. But it was done at
last and Charles, sobbing bitterly, was lifted into one litter while his mother,
trying to maintain her composure, was handed by Guise into another.

'You understand, Madame,' he said, 'that this is for your benefit.'

Her mouth worked, but no words would come.

'A benefit is a benefit,' said Guise, in his most matter-of-fact tone, 'whether
it is bestowed by affection or by force.'

One effect of the crisis on Catherine was to make her see more clearly the extent to which her diplomatic approaches to the Huguenots had been mis-interpreted abroad. She wrote hastily to her ambassador in Madrid: 'I am anxious that all the Lords should write to the King of Spain about my feeling for religion, not that I need any testimony before God or man in regard to my faith or my good works, but because of the lies that have been told about me. For I have never changed in deed, will or habits the religion which I have held for forty-three years and in which I have been baptized and brought up. And no one should be surprised that I am annoyed, for this slander has lasted too long for mortal patience; and when one has a clear conscience it wounds one sorely that those who have none should talk so boldly of this matter. Show this letter to the Duke of Alva and to the King.'

Catherine in this year 1562 saw the subject of a special report by an Envoy-Extraordinary of Venice which brings her vividly to life. 'Her intelligence', he wrote, 'is all alive—she is affable, capable in affairs, diplomatic above all things. She never lets the King out of her sight nor allows anyone but herself to sleep in his room. She knows that there is a feeling against her because she is a Florentine, but she holds everything in the hollow of her hand—including the royal seals. In the Council Chamber she lets others speak first, but her opinion is the final court of appeal. In her way of life, materially speaking, she shows very little rule. Her appetite is enormous and she is already a stout woman, but she is assiduous in taking exercise, walking a great deal, riding hard, hunting with the King, her son, pushing him into tangled thickets and following him with an intrepid courage such as one rarely sees. While she is walking or eating she always talks about affairs with somebody or other. She turns her mind not only to things political but to so many others that I don't know how she can face all these manifold interests, and she can undertake six important buildings at the very moment all these other thoughts are preoccu-pying her mind.'

Uppermost among the things on her mind at the moment was the action of Condé who, having failed to gain the King or the capital, had in desperation proclaimed himself as Protector of the Royal family and the Huguenots as the legitimate defenders of the Throne against the Triumvirate and the Catholics. To justify his attitude, the Prince published in Germany and the Netherlands the Queen's letters to him.

Catherine immediately denounced him as a madman, a slanderer and a man with a grudge, explaining that as he had asked her permission to bear arms to ensure the safety of the throne, she had granted it on condition that he would disarm whenever she ordered. This, however, when she sent a messenger to him to entreat him, as he loved her, to lay down his arms, he not only refused to do, thus breaking his word, but wronged her afresh by saying that it was she who made him resort to arms in the first place. 'I would give my life,' she said, 'to see the realm at peace as I so earnestly wish and as I pray God it will be.'

But peace was at an end, for it was now impossible for the Huguenots to pretend with any likelihood of being generally believed that they were the official party of the Crown. Nor dared they remain inactive. Their one hope was to capture the rich and populous city of Orléans and turn it into a Huguenot capital. On April 1, Condé with two thousand horse, rode through the gates which had been opened for them by their co-religionists. A week later, the Huguenot leaders drew up an Act of Association declaring the Prince of Condé to be their leader and the lawful Protector of the Crown. They proclaimed as their objects the rescuing of the King from the control of the Triumvirate, the enforcement of the Edict of January and 'the maintenance of the honour of God and His true service'—that is to say, Calvinism. The bond was signed by 'about four thousand gentlemen of the best and most ancient houses in France.'

Prominent among the signatories were the Admiral, Gaspard de Coligny, and his younger brother, Andelot, Colonel-General of the Infantry; the Vidame de Chartres, who had made the earlier attempt to seize Lyons, and the Sieur de Montgoméry, who had killed King Henry II in the tournament; as well as two whose names were to be better known in the future—Jean, Sieur de Genlis and Francis, Comte de la Rochefoucauld.

Condé and Coligny had by now realised that their one chance of victory lay in foreign Protestant aid. They sent the Vidame and Montgoméry to England to negotiate with Queen Elizabeth the Treaty of Hampton Court by which England was to be given Le Havre, Dieppe and Rouen as well as, eventually, Calais, in return for 6000 English troops and 140,000 crowns to pay 7000 German Lutheran mercenaries. Having secured this, Coligny despatched his brother Andelot, accompanied by Beza, to Heidelberg to procure the German *reiters* and *lansquenets* by the additional bribe of the sack of Paris. The rebels' main concern was now to keep Catherine and the Triumvirate immobilised by discussions until the invaders arrived.

Catherine continued working feverishly for peace. Twice a meeting was arranged between her and Condé but each time he failed to honour his word. On June 2 the Prince again signified his willingness to meet her at Tours, but when she arrived there he refused to join her on the ground that she had brought too large an escort. Eventually, on June 9, they met on a bare, wind-swept plain not far from Tours. In spite of a steady rain-storm, Condé refused to enter the barn in which the discussions were to have been held. He would not even dismount and the Queen, with Antony of Navarre at her side, rode to meet him in the space between the ranks of their attendants—a hundred horsemen each, the Royal detachment in crimson, the Huguenots wearing the white surcoats which had become their distinguishing badge.

'My dear cousin', said Catherine, 'why do your men look like a lot of millers?'

'To show that they are well able to beat your donkeys, Madame', answered Condé.

Pleasantries were succeeded by two hours of exasperating argument which from the beginning were pointless because Coligny, who had refused to accompany Condé, had vetoed the acceptance of any terms until he had approved them.

When the abortive conversation was abandoned, the gentlemen of both sides streamed into the open space to greet each other affectionately for the last time, miserably aware that a civil war 'of religion' was now inevitable. One of the Huguenot nobles described the scene: 'I had a dozen friends on the other side, each of whom was as dear to me as a brother, and there were many others in the same situation, so that, man after man asking permission from his officer, the two lines of crimson cloaks and white cloaks were soon mingled together in friendly talk and when they separated it was with tears in their eyes.'

But Catherine still refused to abandon hope. She was ill, so lame from a fall from her horse that she could not walk without a stick and she had a thick cold which made her so hoarse as to be almost inaudible, but she arranged another meeting, this time in Huguenot-held country at Beaugency, south of Orléans. There, on Midsummer Day, Coligny with fifteen of his leading followers drew up and signed a document undertaking that, if the members of the Triumvirate would leave Court and retire to their own estates, the rebels on their part would obey Catherine's commands and would put Condé into her hands as a pledge of good faith.

The Catholics immediately agreed and within three days the Constable, the Duke of Guise and Marshal de Saint-André had made preparations to return to their own châteaux. The following day Condé requested that the Admiral might visit the Queen-Regent in camp to kiss hands. She not only agreed but when Coligny arrived she 'kissed him on the mouth as is the custom of the Queens of France with the great officers of the King.'

The Admiral now promised that the Huguenot leaders would also retire to their estates, provided she would re-enact the Edict of January, which had been rescinded owing to the troubles. The Queen agreed and set off with Navarre for the Royal headquarters. She was surprised that Condé did not, as he had undertaken to, accompany them, but she accepted his excuse that Coligny needed him to return with him for consultation in the Huguenot camp.

It was not until two days later that she understood the reason.

On July 1, Coligny put into operation his real plan which was nothing less than a night-surprise of the Royal forces, lulled into a false sense of security by the promises he had never had any intention of keeping. At nightfall, after public prayers, the whole Huguenot army set out 'stirred by a high and buoyant courage', the Admiral riding at its head with a *corps d'élite* of eight hundred cavalry. Through the night it marched, the white surcoats of the men as they rustled through the cornfields, suggesting a gathering of ghosts. But at dawn they found they were still miles from the Royal camp and that

The capture by Huguenot troops of the town of Montbrison in July 1562;
engraving on copper by Tortorel and Périssin, now in the museum of the
Société de l'Histoire du Protestantisme français.

surprise was quite impossible. The guides had lost their way in the dark.

The fiasco had one inevitable result. It was no longer possible for Catherine, even though she would have 'given her soul for peace', to try to pretend that the Huguenot insurrection was anything but what it was—an armed rebellion against the Crown. Within a week, Coligny was deprived of his post as Admiral of France, which was given to his cousin, a younger son of the Constable, and on July 27 all who were in arms at Orléans or elsewhere were proclaimed guilty of rebellion.

Catherine's fundamental attitude was expressed, as was usual with her, in her letters to her daughter Elisabeth. 'Everything that is done on one side and the other is nothing but a desire to rule and to take from me under cover and colour of religion what power I have.' She believed there was not, on either side, 'sanctity or religion but only private passions, vengeance and personal hatred.'

Whereas Coligny was relying on foreign Protestant intervention, Catherine's overpowering dread was that Spain might intervene on the Catholic side. To her ambassador in Madrid she confessed the fear that 'my son, the Catholic King might, under pretence of aiding me to save the kingdom, make himself the tutor of my son; which would be the very greatest of all misfortunes and the total ruin of this state' and asks that King Philip may be told that she has summoned 6000 Swiss so that 'knowing this fact you can take away from the King any desire to come to my aid.'

There was one other factor in the situation which, in all probability, the Queen did not allow for—Coligny's hatred for Guise which far exceeded even her own dislike of the Duke. When Catherine had first come to France, Guise and Coligny were inseparable friends. They were the same age. They were, wrote Brantôme, 'both in the latter years of the reign of Francis I and well on into that of Henry II, such great comrades, friends and confederates that they were wont to dress in the same livery and attire and be on the same side in tourneys, mimic fights, running at the ring and masquerades, committing more extravagant follies than all the rest.' These were the terms of their relationship when she had first known them—those early days when she had given Coligny an introduction to her cousin in Florence—and such impressions die hard, nor was she in a position to study, even had she had the desire to do so, the course of their gradual severance.

As they had been inseparable at Court so in the wars they at first fought side by side. Coligny was Colonel-General of the infantry when Guise, leading the cavalry, received his spectacular wound at Boulogne. Each rivalled the other's reputation, but if Coligny was as good a soldier as Guise, he was far less popular. Though both were haughty and intolerant, Gaspard lacked Francis's compensating charm. Also Coligny, the weaker character, was naturally the more obstinate, subject to sudden bursts of irrational anger and prone to sharpen any difference of opinion by importing a personal bitterness.

The first open rift between the friends came when Guise was given general supervision of all military operations and Coligny was made Lieutenant-General for the continuing Boulogne campaign. Relying on his somewhat vague and undefined powers, Guise claimed the right to preside at a duel between two of his captains. Coligny denied his competence to interfere. A point of procedure was apt to assume altogether disproportionate importance for Coligny who had drawn up the official code of conduct for the army, the *Ordinances,* which were known by his name and which, in their meticulous attention to detail, were a monument to his obsessive dislike of disorder. The King, Henry II, had given the *Ordinances* his royal approval and, now appealed to, upheld Coligny against Guise. Guise then complained to Diane de Poitiers and was mortified to discover that, on this occasion at least, her royal lover was impervious to her influence.

Though from this moment Guise and Coligny continued to grow apart, when Guise went to the defence of Metz Coligny, who had just been appointed Admiral of France, wrote to him: 'I could wish nothing better than to have the good fortune to be near if the Emperor comes to besiege you.' And none was louder than the new Admiral in praise of Guise's epic defence of the city.

They were supporting each other again at the battle of Renty, fought not long after the raising of the siege of Metz, when Guise was unable to drive his cavalry charge home because an enemy party, sheltered by a wood, were commanding the battlefield. Coligny put himself at the head of a thousand infantry and cleared them from their shelter. This was the turning-point of the battle and the result was a complete victory.

After the action, Guise said: 'We have delivered the finest charge ever made!'

'Yes', answered Coligny, 'you supported me very well.'

'*Mordieu*', said Guise, 'would you rob me of my honour?'

'I have no desire to' said Coligny.

'Nor could you, even if you desired', said Guise.

In the next campaign they were in different theatres of war. Guise was sent to Italy, Coligny to the north where he was charged with the defence of Saint-Quentin, which he held against impossible odds for seventeen days while Guise, summoned in panic, made his memorable forced march across Europe to his rescue. Inevitably the Duke was too late and by the time he arrived the Admiral was a prisoner in the Flemish castle of Léclusse. All Guise could do to right the balance of the war was to capture Calais and thereby win an acclamation all the greater because it in part avenged Coligny's defeat.

The two years' imprisonment in a foreign fortress which the Admiral had now to endure was the watershed of his life. He spent much time reading Calvin's *Institutes* and corresponded with Calvin himself who wrote to him inviting his conversion 'seeing that God hath given you the opportunity to profit in His school of adversity, as though He wished to speak to you privately in your ear.'

The Admiral returning from his captivity four months before the death of Henry II quickly discovered how greatly things had changed during his enforced absence. He found that he had to bear the stigma of all unsuccessful generals and that his own reputation was at its nadir while Guise's was at its zenith. He realised that no return to power or influence was possible except in the shadow of Guise or in open opposition to him. And opposition was now possible because during his two lost years the Huguenot movement had not only grown strong but was starting to attract aristocrats and gentlemen who had been ruined by the wars or disappointed by lack of advancement. They needed a leader and, as Condé, still the *chef muet*, was his nephew by marriage, the Admiral saw himself as the power behind the throne in any successful revolution as well as a possible leader if he became, as Condé was, a seceret Huguenot.

At the little town of Valleville, near his château of Châtillon-sur-Loing where he was building a vast new wing to house the paintings and sculptures he had commissioned to celebrate the history of his family, he attended a Huguenot service, begged the congregation to forgive him the weakness which had hitherto prevented him joining them and, accepted by the minister, fell on his knees and gave thanks that he was now one of the Elect.

The sincerity of Coligny's conversion to Calvinism will always be a matter of debate, but the political necessity of it for him at that moment was unquestionable. In his own person he now united 'the Huguenot of State' with the 'Huguenot of Religion' and became the unquestioned leader of a new force capable of displacing Guise. And to Guise the Admiral's apostasy—as he saw it—was the final and unpardonable action which turned his one-time affection into hatred. He never saw Coligny again, refusing to be at any conference he attended. For to all the Guises their religion was the deepest thing in their natures. Their worldly ambition might be inordinate, but it stopped short at compromising their Faith.

Once the actual fighting started, the Royal forces easily regained the towns and districts of which the Huguenots by their swift local actions after the

Opposite: *School of Clouet portrait of Gaspard de Coligny, Admiral of France.*

SPARD·DE·COLLIGNY·SEIGN^{EVR}·DE·CHATILLON—
MIRAL·DE·FRANCE·

publication of the Edict of January had gained control. Within a fortnight they had recovered Blois, Angers, Tours and the whole course of the lower Loire, with Anjou, Berry, Poitou and Saintonge. Only Rouen, Orléans and Lyons, with a few lesser and unimportant places remained in rebel hands. These Coligny determined to hold at all costs, Rouen as the key to Paris for the English troops which were already arriving at Le Havre, Lyons as the gateway for the German mercenaries and Orléans as the central Calvinist stronghold. The Admiral and Condé took charge of Orléans, while Montgoméry was instructed to hold Rouen, which was in his own countryside.

The original plan of the Triumvirate had been to isolate and reduce Orléans as the best way of quickly ending the rebellion. It was Catherine who dissuaded them. 'What is Orléans?' she stormed at Navarre. 'There are Huguenots there, but nothing else. But Rouen—that is the door to the heart of France! Once the English hold it they will hold Paris. And, if we give them time to fortify it, they can make it impregnable.' Guise, who realised that, quite apart from her personal desire to capture the killer of her husband, she was tactically right, supported her; and the whole army, with Catherine herself riding at the head of it, set out for Rouen.

The siege presented many difficulties. Protected on one side by the Seine and on the other by a hill with an almost inaccessible fortress on the summit, Rouen could be counted on for a stubborn resistance. The autumn was one of the worst on record. The unceasing rain made the camp a morass. Epidemics broke out. The morale of the Royal troops was at vanishing point. Catherine did her best to rally them by her presence, surveying operations from advanced posts and exposing herself to enemy fire with an indifference to danger which made Guise remonstrate with her.

'Why should I spare myself when I have as much courage as you?' she retorted.

She insisted on accompanying Navarre when he rode up under the walls to reconnoitre the actual battlements of the fortress. He was wounded in the left shoulder by a stray bullet and she superintended his return to his tent where the surgeons pronounced the wound not to be serious.

Nevertheless, the news that their General had been wounded depressed the troops, especially as the rumour spread that he was dying and next day Guise and the Constable experienced some difficulty in getting the men into action.

Once more Catherine saved the day. She made a great oration to the army asking if they wished to leave her young son Charles, their king, to the mercy of the English invaders. The English had been driven out of France, the last stroke being that of the Duke of Guise in capturing Calais five years ago. Now traitors had let those hereditary enemies back again. Were they to stay?

The whole army rose to her. They saw a bulky, middle-aged, 'olive-skinned' woman after whom, in satirical affection, they had named the largest of their cannon. But the voice they heard was the voice of Joan of Arc.

Amid cries of jubilation, the Queen ordered ten thousand cannon-shots to be fired at the walls of the rebel city to be followed by an immediate assault. The masonry of Rouen could not withstand such a cannonade. A wide breach was made and, on that day, Monday 26 October, the fortress fell. But one thing Catherine was cheated of. Montgoméry managed to escape to Le Havre in a small boat and from there fled in panic to the safety of England.

Antony of Navarre in spite of his wound insisted on accompanying Catherine on the triumphal entry into Rouen, but he fainted in his litter and had to be carried, dying, back to camp. His wife, Jeanne, who was now safely back in her Pyrenean kingdom, would not have come to him even had she known of his plight. 'I have shut my heart for ever against my husband', she announced, and devote all the energy of love to the strict fulfilment of my duty.' So the Premier Prince of the Blood died, at the age of thirty-four, between his mistress, La Belle Rouet, and his son, the boy Henry of Navarre, who had inherited too much of his blood to be entirely happy—much as he loved his mother—at the prospect of being sent back to Béarn to imbibe the pure milk of the Calvinist word. Characteristically, *l'Echangeur* was attended in his last hours by both a Dominican friar and a Huguenot preacher and assured each of them that he died in that particular faith.

Condé received the news of his brother's death on November 17 when he was less than twenty miles from Paris at the head of his army. His first thought was how he might turn it to his political advantage by claiming that he was now Premier Prince of the Blood because the new head of his house, the sybaritic Cardinal de Bourbon, was in Holy Orders and at the same time to ask Catherine to give him dead Antony's post as Lieutenant-General of France.

Catherine saw in the possibility of his temporising one last chance to avert the full ferocity of war. She offered to meet him at Charenton, five miles from Paris. Condé agreed but, in his accustomed manner, failed to appear. He pleaded illness. The meeting was postponed. Again he was absent. Eventually Coligny took his place and assured the Queen-Mother that their only reason for resorting to arms was regard for the honour of God. When Catherine replied that the presence of thousands of English and German troops on French soil suggested a less simple explanation, the Admiral undertook to see that they were sent home as soon as the religious issue was settled.

Negotiations continued which Condé, waiving his dynastic pretensions, at last joined and by December 4 peace seemed assured. Huguenotism was to to be confined to those places where it had been allowed before the outbreak of hostilities, though it was to be forbidden in Paris itself and in frontier-towns. It was, in fact, a reaffirmation of the Edict of January, guaranteeing complete freedom of conscience with limited freedom of public expression. At the last moment Coligny wrecked the conference by proposing that the King should declare the Hugenot forces part of the Royal army and pay not only them but the German mercenaries as well.

The Admiral's anxiety was comprehensible, as the Germans, not content with their already considerable booty, had threatened to hold him and his estates as security for their promised pay. His one hope was to make a dash to Le Havre where the necessary English gold was awaiting distribution. Three days after the final failure of negotiations, Condé and Coligny set off for the coast and at the same time the Constable and Guise left Paris with the Royal army to deny them access to it. On 19 December battle was joined at Dreux on the shallow little Eure river on the borders of Normandy. At first the Huguenots, who, in the vital cavalry arm, outnumbered the Royal army by two to one, were sweepingly successful. The Constable was wounded and taken prisoner; the Marshal de Saint-André was killed. As the main army fled in disorder from the field, Condé and Coligny, resting for a moment in their pursuit near the village of Blainville, were congratulated on the famous victory. But Coligny pointed to a wood, partly screened by a rise in the gound, on the right of the battlefield. 'Wait, *Messieurs*,' he said, 'until that cloud bursts.' He knew his enemy.

There Guise, fighting as a simple captain, had waited throughout the battle with a *corps d'élite* of 350 cavalry. Nothing would induce him to move. When the Constable had been taken prisoner, one of his sons implored the Duke to go to his rescue, but Guise had refused with: 'It is not yet time.'

The time—the moment for which he had waited—came as the Huguenots, exultant in victory, broke ranks in wild pursuit of pillage. He gave the order to charge and joined the few surviving Catholics still in the field, rallying them with: 'Now, my friends, the day is ours!' With his right, he seized the rebel artillery and routed their infantry. With his centre he drove back the loose bands of Huguenot cavalry on Condé and Coligny. With his left he temporarily cut off the rest. The German *reiters* rushed to the rear for safety and in the confusion Condé was taken prisoner. Coligny, taking advantage of a pause while Guise accepted the surrender of 2000 German *lansquenets*, managed to draw off the rest of his force in small units which did not reform until after dark several miles away.

Guise made his headquarters at Blainville and in a tiny cottage he and his cousin (Guise's mother was Condé's aunt), exhausted, shared the one bed and the one blanket.

To Coligny this defeat at the hands of Guise was the final culmination of his hatred and drove him to the action which turned the civil wars into a blood-feud and led inexorably to the massacre of St. Bartholomew nine-and-a-half years later. The Admiral sent for one of his spies, Jean Poltrot, Sieur de Méré, who was attached to Guise's forces. Poltrot, a 'poverty-stricken, yellow-complexioned, bony little man' in his early twenties, was a cousin of La Renaudie, the Amboise conspirator, and was eager to avenge him. He was, wrote one who knew him, 'ambitious and devoted to the interests of the Huguenots.' When, after the victory of Dreux, Guise moved against Orléans, whose fall would have brought the rebellion to an end, Coligny set Poltrot to assassinate the Duke.

On February 18 Guise gave the order for the general assault on Orléans the following day. Riding back to the Château de Vaslins, his headquarters, after inspecting the fortifications, he 'doffed his coat of mail, the which he had not done since the beginning of the siege.' Poltrot, noticing this, rode on ahead and, hiding behind the hedge of a narrow lane leading to the château, shot the Duke in the back as he passed. Guise fell to the ground senseless

A narrative engraving showing the murder of Francis Duke of Guise by Jean Poltrot as Guise returned from Orleans to his Château of Vaslins on 18 February 1563; by Tortorel and Périssin.

but not dead and Poltrot, thanks to the swift horse Coligny had provided, was beyond reach of pursuit before Guise's page, who was walking in front of his master, could return with help from the château.

Catherine was at Blois when she received the news. She immediately offered 2000 *écus* for the name of the murderer and double the sum for his capture. She sent her own surgeons post haste to Guise and a letter to the Duchess: 'Although they have assured me that the blow is not fatal, I am so troubled that I do not know what to do. But I will make use of all the credit and power I have in the world to avenge it and I am sure God will forgive me whatever I do.' Next day she herself set off for Orléans, thirty-five miles away, and arrived at the Château de Vaslins shortly after Poltrot, who had lost his way in the dark and had been captured. She herself decided to question him.

'He told me voluntarily and without any pressing', she reported to her sister-in-law, the Duchess of Savoy, 'that the Admiral had given him a hundred *écus* to do this evil deed, and that he did not want to do it but that Beza and another preacher had persuaded him and assured him that, if he did it, he would go straight to Heaven. Hearing that, he determined to carry out the deed. In addition he said that I should do well to keep a strict watch over my children and to take great care of my own person because the Admiral hated me very much. So you see, Madame, that that righteous man who protests he has no motive but religion, wishes to do away with all of us. I see that during this war he will in the end kill my children and strip us of all our best people.'

Coligny necessarily denied Poltrot's accusation. When news of the crime arrived in camp, 'thanks were given to God solemnly and with great rejoicing', the Admiral publicly announced that he considered it 'the greatest of blessings to my family and to France', he admitted that Poltrot had told him of his intention to murder Guise and the he had done nothing to dissuade him, but he insisted that the hundred *écus* he had paid the assassin were merely his wages for spying and the swift horse an aid to a quicker delivery of the news he had gleaned in the course of it.

On Ash Wednesday, February 24, Guise died, protesting with almost his last breath that he was not responsible for the bloodshed at Vassy which had been used as a pretext for the Huguenot rebellion and imploring Catherine to arrange a religious peace as quickly as possible so that she might lead a united France against the foreign invaders.

The next day she wrote: 'God has seen fit to strike me again and, with me, the poor country; for by the most miserable of deaths He has taken from me the one man who stood out alone and devoted himself to the King. M. de Guise was the greatest captain in our realm and one of the greatest and

worthiest ministers the King could ever be served by. The wickedness of
this act, which may be said to be one of the most unfortunate ever committed
in France, is added to the execrable evils already wrought by the mercenaries.
I do not know how things will go without M. de Guise, because the Constable
is a prisoner in Orléans and we have no man to command our army, except
the Marshal de Brissac and he is not physically able to do it. Nevertheless,
I must make him believe that he is. Meanwhile it is I who will have to take
command and play the captain.'

*Francis Duke of Guise as painted by an anonymous artist of the school of
Clouet, who has been careful to minimise the famous scar.*

The Peacemaker

Catherine took immediate steps towards peace. The fortunate circumstance that both the Constable and Condé were prisoners of the opposing sides made accommodation the easier. And the fact that Antony of Navarre and Francis of Guise were both dead meant that she could now offer Condé the Lieutenant-Generalship of France—a bargaining-counter which was unlikely to fail. An additional advantage of the moment was that the implacable Coligny was still absent in Normandy and so unable to interfere with any arrangement.

A conference between the Queen, the Prince and the Constable in a barge moored on the Loire outside Orléans resulted in an agreement which was, with symbolic appropriateness, promulgated at Amboise. The new edict—'the Peace of Amboise'—was essentially a repetition of the Edict of January with slightly less favourable terms for the Huguenots, in that only the greater nobility were given the right of free exercise of Calvinism, while the lesser had to obtain permission from their overlords and were not allowed to entertain local congregations.

On Thursday 18 March, the day before the proclamation of the Peace of Amboise, Paris witnessed two spectacles—the execution of Poltrot and the entry into the city of the body of Guise, accompanied by his family, to lie in state in Notre Dame.

Four days earlier the Governor of Paris, Coligny's cousin and a secret sympathiser with Huguenotism, had promised the assassin that, if he would withdraw his charges against the Admiral, a rescue would be arranged. Poltrot, in his prison unaware that the hysterical state of the Parisians at the death of their idol would render such a thing quite impossible especially on the day when his body was brought back to them, naturally assented and, in his public examination of March 15, had retracted his accusation of Coligny as the inspirer of the murder. Early that morning of the execution he had repeated the denial, still thinking that his rescue would be accomplished on

*The peace conference between Catherine and the Prince of Condé, on l'Isle
aux Boeufs in the Loire near Orleans, on 13 March 1563.*

the way to the Place de Grève. But, arrived there to undergo the terrible death of being torn apart by wild horses driven in opposite directions, he knew that his hope was illusory and, with his last breath, he reaffirmed on the oath of a man on the edge of Eternity all his charges against Coligny.

At the head of Guise's funeral cortège rode the new Duke, Henry, who was now thirteen. He tried to ride as proudly as if his father were still horsed at his side and the Parisians rose to the boy even more vociferously than they had to father and son at the last, memorable entry. Henry's face was set and he was dry-eyed. He had taken his vow. A fortnight earlier when his father's coffin was still resting in the Royal chapel at Blois, he had turned sobbing to his uncle Aumale and said: 'God damn me for ever in Hell if I let Coligny live. I am right, am I not?'

'By the Body of God' answered Aumale, 'if I had found you of any other mind I should have killed you where you stand.'

The Guises' first move was to indict the Admiral before the Parlement of Paris. Coligny ignored it and set out to appeal directly to the Royal Council which was at St. Germain, but Catherine sent Condé to intercept him with the command to remain strictly within his own estates until the foreign war was over and she had driven the English from Normandy. Only then would she determine the question of his guilt or innocence.

She then busied herself with the preparations for the siege of Le Havre which was held by an English garrison, six thousand strong, and ordered sixteen new cannon so that as at Rouen 'we can give the town a furious battery with thirty or forty pieces'. She also got large supplies of ammunition from the Guise country of Lorraine and, with Condé as the new Lieutenant-General and the Constable in command of the army which contained some loyal Huguenots as well as Catholics symbolising the regained unity, she set off for the north. On the eve of victory, at the end of July, she brought the young King down the river to wait close by so that he could accept the surrender and make with her a triumphal entry into the reconquered town. To enhance the dramatic significance of the event she had Charles, who was now thirteen and a half, by virtue of a forgotten precedent which allowed a sovereign in certain circumstances to be considered of age before he was fourteen, declare his majority before the Parlement of Rouen on August 17. Next day, to show that he was indeed God's anointed, he touched for 'King's Evil' and healed many sick persons.

One of his first acts now that he was theoretically free of his mother's regency was to hear the renewed appeal of the Guise family. One Sunday after Mass the widow, the mother, the son, the brothers of the murdered man, all dressed in deep mourning, threw themselves on their knees before the King and asked for his authority to prosecute Coligny. Charles promised

Anonymous engraving depicting the execution of the murderer Jean Poltrot; for killing the Duke of Guise he suffered the penalty for high treason, which was to be torn asunder by wild horses.

with tears in his eyes that something should be done and appointed a tribunal of members of the local Parlement and members of the Grand Council in equal numbers to adjudicate. Once again the Admiral refused to acknowledge the court and, to break the deadlock, the King reserved the case to himself and promised to study it himself for three months at the end of which he would pronounce judgment.

'The King my son', said Catherine proudly, 'on his own account and without the least prompting from anyone made so good a decision that his whole Council welcomed it'. She then, as soon as she had recovered from a slight illness which, according to her habit, she refused to take seriously but which alarmed her family, set about reordering the realm.

The wretched condition of France, the continuing turmoil and feuds, murder and pillage, anarchy and chaos which continued in various localities in spite of the 'Peace', the ruined countryside denuded by the German mercenaries, the chronic economic instability, the swarms of unemployed and unemployable, all called for Catherine's concentrated ability. She applied herself to every aspect of the problem, from including in the peace-treaty with England a commercial agreement for freedom of trade between the two nations, cancelling most of the fees and exactions imposed on their merchants, to practical conveniences like ordering that the year should start on January 1 instead of at Easter; from the setting up of commercial tribunals to the simplification of trials.

She became convinced that the conventional channels through which the Crown kept in touch with the country—the *grands seigneurs*, the provincial officials and the local *parlements*—had become silted up. It was of the utmost importance to clear them. She dictated a memorandum to Charles bidding him receive all deputations from the provinces 'taking care to speak to them every time they present themselves in your room. I have seen your father and grandfather do this and when there was nothing else to talk about, they even went so far as to chat to them about their own household affairs.' It was most important and she was scrupulous to observe the custom herself; but still it was not enough. She decided to go on a two years' Progress, with the King and the Court, throughout the country. The terminus of the journey of pacification could be the Spanish border where she could meet Elisabeth and discuss the international situation with Philip and Alva.

Before she started Catherine decided it would be good policy to entertain the greater part of the nobility at Court, on the principle she had learnt from Francis I—that 'two things are necessary to live in peace with the French and make them love their king: to amuse them and to occupy them with some athletic exercise'. She gave a series of magnificent fêtes at Fontainebleau. The Constable opened proceedings with a great supper, to be followed next day by the Cardinal de Bourbon whose hospitality, as might be expected from his devoted *expertise* in such matters, far surpassed it. Two days later Catherine herself gave a royal banquet, followed by an Italian comedy acted in the ballroom of the château. Then the King's younger brother, Henry of Anjou, was the host, making at 12 his début in that rôle and providing after dinner a tournament where twelve gentlemen fought on foot with javelins and swords. Finally Charles staged a great fête and a masked tournament in which a castle defended by devils commanded by giants was assaulted by four Marshals of France on horseback, leading a troop of young courtiers. This was followed by jousts on more orthodox lines, though much of the old spirit seemed to have gone out of tournaments. The shadow of the unforgotten and unforgettable fatality was too deep.

Further to dull the edge of that searing memory, Catherine decided to destroy the old palace of Les Tournelles where her husband had been killed and to lay out on the banks of the Seine a magnificent garden. At the begin-

The session of the parlement of Rouen on 14 August 1563, where Charles IX was proclaimed to be of age.

ning of 1564 she began the construction of a new palace, the Tuileries, which was to be connected with the Louvre by a splendid gallery. Meanwhile she continued work on the Louvre itself to complete the great quadrangle designed by Pierre Lescot who had worked upon the building under her father-in-law and her husband. When she returned from the two-year Progress, there would be a new beauty to welcome her.

At last, on the afternoon of Monday 13 March 1564 the amazing procession, nearly a thousand strong, set off from Fontainebleau. The only notable absentees were the Guises and Coligny who, by the King's judgment, had been confined to their own estates and bound over to keep the peace for three years. Catherine, with the three children who accompanied her, the King, Henry of Anjou and Margot, shared the great royal coach, though each child had its own retinue and Catherine varied her method of travel by using a litter when she wanted to deal with state-correspondence along the way and her horse when she preferred exercise. She was getting uncomfortably stout. When she ordered new horses now, she specified: 'Above all they must be strong. I have worn out so many.'

Condé, as Lieutenant-General of France and Prince of the Blood followed immediately behind the royal party with his own Household. The whole cavalcade—it needed 8,000 horses—included Councillors; ambassadors; secretaries; the *Flying Squadron*; the Provost of the Household with his staff, concerned with billetting the company in the towns and villages at which they broke their journey; the Gentlemen of the Household, the Pages of Honour, the Swiss Guard and the Scottish Guard; the Grooms of the

Stable, the falconers and the huntsmen; the supply wagons with the gold and silver plate for the State Banquets; decorations, triumphal arches and ingenious gewgaws for State Entries, barges for water-picnics and aquatic entertainments; and, last of all, a travelling menagerie.

Easter, which fell that year at the beginning of April, was celebrated at Troyes, where a treaty was signed formally ending the war with England. The prolonged festivities which accompanied them were marred as far as Condé was concerned by Isabelle de Limeuil, the young mistress whom Catherine had selected for him from the *Flying Squadron*, being taken with labour pains during a State Ball and presenting him in the ante-room with 'a fine, splendid boy'. Any paternal pride he might have felt was nullified by his realisation that, by so doing, she had broken the first and inflexible rule of the *Escadron*. Catherine immediately immured her in a convent where she could repent her indiscretion at leisure while the Progress rolled on.

On May Day, at Bar-le-Duc, Catherine attended the baptism of her first grandson, the child of her second daughter, Claude, and her husband, the Duke of Lorraine, whom she had married at the same time Francis II had married Mary Queen of Scots. The King stood godfather to his little nephew and Pierre Ronsard excelled himself with his elegant complimentary verses.

At Mâcon the Progress was met by the Queen of Navarre returning from Calvin's funeral at Geneva, accompanied by twelve Calvinist ministers and her son Henry who, after a year under her tutelage, was regretting his father's death more than he thought possible and was overjoyed at the prospect of meeting the Court once more. Jeanne was in a particularly serious mood and insisted on discussing at length the question agitating the godly of Mâcon—whether Huguenot children should walk side by side with Catholic children in secular processions. Catherine, who found the point unworthy of the dialectical energy devoted to it, was not sorry when the Queen continued her way to her own kingdom, leaving your Henry of Navarre in the care of his uncle Condé.

Religious tensions, however, in that countryside so near Geneva, continued. At Lyons there were alternative rumours: a Huguenot rising, culminating in the murder of the Court, was imminent, or, on the other hand, Catherine was about to make new concessions to the Calvinists. Catherine laughed at the one and contradicted the other by prohibiting *Prêches* within ten miles of the Progress.

Opposite: *A young woman of Paris.*

Overleaf: *In this anonymous painting of a court ball in Henry III's reign, Catherine is seated with her back to the reader.*

They were obliged to flee precipitately from Lyons by a virulent outbreak of the plague. The English Ambassador reported: 'The dead are left lying in the streets throughout the day and at night they are thrown into the river because the people cannot dig graves. Almost as many are dying of hunger and lack of care as of the plague.'

When they reached Valence, death assumed a more personal guise. News awaited them there that Elisabeth had given birth to still-born twins. Catherine, bitterly disappointed that there would be no Spanish children for her to see at the end of the journey, wrote a long and cheerful letter to the Queen, reminding her that she was young and would surely have better luck next time. To dispel the gloom which the news shed over the rest of the family, she gave orders for more masques and entertainments by the way and surprised the Court by appearing dressed as a Turkish lady. She even played a practical joke for—as far as anyone could discover—the sole purpose of amusing her daughter of Spain. She suddenly deserted the Progress, leaving a note for Condé to say that she was on the way to Barcelona. When a highly alarmed Royal Council was convened to deal with the crisis, she was there to explain that she only wanted to see the effect on them of her absence and recorded the episode at length to her ambassador in Madrid with the instruction: 'Tell the story to my daughter the Queen that she may laugh over it.'

Catherine's short interlude of irresponsibility in the Mediterranean world of mimosa and palms and pepper-trees which brought her a breath of Italy was not without its effect on her youngest daughter. Margot started playing an amused game of her own. One day she would appear dressed in rich crimson brocade, glittering with jewels, her hair pyramided into careful ringlets. No sooner had the ladies of the court ransacked their travelling wardrobes to emulate her as nearly as possible than she would change to a simple white frock more becoming to her age, with her hair 'strewn loosely and naturally' down her back, looking 'très première communion'. She would take bets with Henry of Anjou, whose detached, cynical mind and exquisite body were more and more exercising their spell on her, as to which of her ladies would be the first to follow her various fashions.

On October 17, in the perfect aftermath of summer, they all arrived at Salon where the notables of the town, after presenting an address of welcome which managed to suggest that the King had showed singular wisdom in visiting so historic a town, were told curtly by Charles: 'We came to see Nostradamus'. This was true and Catherine went immediately to the astrologer's alchemical laboratory—which, after all, gave the little town

Opposite: A Huguenot 'Prêche' at Lyons in 1564; Beza, who is preaching, was apt to ignore the warning of the hour-glass attached to the pulpit.

whatever fame it had—for a long private talk. She returned to the question of the succession. Was Nostradamus quite certain that the mirror at Chaumont could not have lied? Was it certain that Henry of Navarre would succeed Henry of Anjou on the throne of France? Nostradamus replied that, considering the circumstances of the magical enquiry, an error was extremely improbable, but that as young Navarre was available he could check the matter by examining the moles on his body.

Henry was sent for and asked to take his clothes off. As this was the conventional preliminary, to which in the last year he had become accustomed, to a beating by his tutor for failing to satisfy his mother's educational standards, he rushed out of the room defying capture.

The Progress of Catherine and the Court sets out from Fontainebleau on 13 March 1564 on the journey to visit her daughter Elisabeth, Queen of Spain.

When he woke next morning he found Nostradamus bending over him, explaining gently the reason for the original request and Henry without a protest allowed his physical prognostications to be expertly examined and assessed. The verdict confirmed that of the Chaumont mirror. Sadly Catherine accepted it and decided that, if she failed to betroth Margot to Don Carlos, Philip of Spain's son and heir, (which was one of the secret objects of her journey), the girl might as well marry Henry of Navarre. The winter which came on early proved intensely cold. 'The bitter weather' wrote Margot in her diary, 'froze the rivers all through France; and by like means it cooled men's minds and hearts'. It was not her climate. But Charles loved it and, in after years, his keenest memory of the whole Progress was the deep snowfall at Carcassonne which gave him the opportunity to captain victoriously one of the sides in a prolonged snowfight against the combined forces of Henry of Anjou and Henry of Navarre.

It was springtime when, in Bordeaux, Catherine received the news that Elisabeth had been delayed in her journey to the frontier. The Queen-Mother had managed to accustom herself to the substitution of the Duke of Alva for King Philip, though she had continued to hope against hope that her son-in-law would change his mind. But her daughter's delay filled her with foreboding that the whole project, for which she had journeyed a thousand miles, was in danger of collapse. She asked the Spanish Ambassador for a reason. He could give none except that a rumour was circulating at the Spanish court that the Queen of Navarre had been invited to the conference. Between laughter at the absurdity and tears of vexation at the malice of the suggestion, Catherine exploded: 'Who thinks me such a fool?' The Ambassador apologetically explained that both the King and the Duke of Alva were still so displeased with what they considered the over-tolerant attitude of the Edict of Amboise that any rumour suggesting an accommodation with heretics on the Queen-Mother's part was likely to be believed.

'They fear, Madame,' he said, 'that when you wish to take steps to counter the danger it may be too late.'

'In that case', answered Catherine, 'speed is the more necessary so that the Duke may be made aware of the true situation and of the difficulties I have to face.'

The Spaniards moved at last but it was high summer before Catherine could embrace her daughter. 'Their Majesties of France', a chronicler recorded, 'having heard that the Queen of Spain was to cross the river which separates the two Kingdoms on the south, dined full early and straightway after dinner they set out for the said river, adjoining which they caused leafy bowers to be builded, about two leagues distant from St. Jean de Luz; where they being come, waited some two hours for her approach in a heat so des-

Elisabeth, Queen of Spain, Catherine's eldest and favourite daughter.

perate that five or six soldiers died, suffocated in their armour. At last, towards two o'clock, the Court of the Queen was beheld drawing near. Then the Queen-Mother, seized with a great joy, crossed the river and found herself face to face with her whom she had so long desired. Their salutations and embraces ended, they seated themselves in the boat and came to greet the King who was waiting for them on shore. And when the boat landed, His Majesty came aboard with the Princes of his house, and they made their salutations to the Queen without exchanging any kisses. And the troops gave forth a cannonade as furious as 'twas possible to hear, at which the Spaniards were amazed. These ceremonies over, they all mounted on horseback and so came to sleep for the night at St. Jean de Luz.'

'They arrived here', wrote Alva that night to King Philip, 'and the Queen-Mother wished to put the Queen of Spain on her right hand, but the Queen refused and turned red whenever her mother insisted. Madame Marguerite was waiting for her sister in the street at the door of the house in which she was to lodge.'

In the five years since Elisabeth had left her home and family, she had not only matured physically and blossomed into even greater beauty, but her grasp of statesmanship had been perfected by her husband's tuition. The 'Fille de France' was now in truth Queen of Spain. Despite the voluminous and didactic correspondence Catherine had maintained with her during the separating years, she was now Philip's wife rather than Catherine's daughter and had come to share her husband's dislike and fear of her mother's tolerance of heresy. There was disappointment in the Queen-Mother's tone as she said: 'How Spanish you have become, my dearest.'

Elisabeth, slightly irritated that her mother should confuse the political with the personal, answered: 'I admit it. It is my duty to be so. But I am still your daughter, the same whom you and my father sent to Spain.'

Catherine kissed her and afterwards spoke of state-affairs only to Alva, whose long dissentations on how France should best meet the challenge of Calvinism were unsatisfactory. 'I believe' wrote Alva to Philip, 'that the Queen-Mother is so imbued with the idea of coaxing both parties that nothing will turn her from this policy, from which the destruction of the Catholic religion and of the Throne and of her son, the King, must inevitably follow.'

The Queen-Mother and the Duke met, one blazing afternoon at the end of June, in the long pillared gallery of the palace she was occupying in Bayonne, where the deep shadows gave coolness and they themselves— she in her habitual black dress, he equally sombrely-suited—seemed like moving shadows as they slowly paced back and forwards.

She opened the conversation talking 'at incredible speed, touching one subject after another,' till he was unable to control a movement of irritation and bluntly raised the religious issue. With continuing volubility Catherine outlined events in France since the Peace of Amboise and asked him if he thought she should have acted in some other way.

'At the moment I see no need of it and my master would certainly not advise it unless the situation becomes more dangerous.' Catherine pressed him for his own opinion. He gave it slowly and with emphasis: 'It is absolutely necessary for you to cure these religious disorders with the greatest possible speed. Sooner or later, whatever you may wish and however wisely you may rule, the wretched Huguenots will make another insurrection. This will compel you to take up arms again and this time it may be under unfavourable conditions or perhaps even too late.'

'So what do you advise?'

'First, deprive them of their leaders. Condé's life is already forfeit for repeated treason; Coligny's for both rebellion and murder. Let the Guises have their way with him and the law take its course. Remember the proverb, Madame: "The head of one salmon is worth more than the heads of a thousand frogs.'' Without the Prince and the Admiral there may well be no insurrection.'

'And the second step?'

'Revoke the Edict, banish the seditious preachers and outlaw the whole evil sect. The King agrees with me in this.'

'Why should it concern Spain?'

'The cause is common to us all. The disease is spreading like the plague. Already England has gone and much of the Empire. The Low Countries are about to rise. My master does not wish to lose his crown and, it may be, his life.'

Catherine objected that religion was not the only issue. Political expediency had its part to play in governance.

'Unfortunately,' said Alva. The Spanish fanatic looked with hardly-hidden distaste at the Florentine diplomat. 'When I spoke of these things with the late King your husband, His Majesty was of my mind in the matter. If all good Catholics would unite to do what should be done, there would not remain one soul to break bread with that blasphemous brood.'

'You can rest assured' said Catherine, 'that I am not unmindful of my husband's counsel and you can tell your master of the zeal and goodwill we bear towards the Faith and of our desire to do all things that will further the true service of God.'

The deadlock on religious policy frustrated Catherine's hopes to arrange marriages between Margot and Don Carlos and between Henry of Anjou and a Princess of Portugal, since Philip refused to discuss such arrangements until he had his mother-in-law's firm promise to stamp Calvinism out of France.

The French prepared to return home. The final farewells, according to the Spanish Ambassador, 'were more heart-rending than words can express.' There were floods of tears in which Charles, though the Constable told him sternly: 'Kings do not cry', could not help joining. He left his sister on the river-bank. But Catherine crossed the river.

'My daughter the Queen', she wrote, 'parted from us on the third of July. I went on the same day to sleep at Irun that I might have the joy of seeing her as long as I could. We talked of nothing but caresses and good cheer, for in truth the chief reason for the meeting was to have this consolation—to see the Queen my daughter.'

Only the more perceptive realised this simple aspect of the Conference of Bayonne—that, as one Spanish Cardinal put it, 'it was nothing more than a meeting of a mother and a daughter'—and no one except, perhaps, Catherine and Philip realised that in spite of its apparent dynastic and political importance it had accomplished in those respects exactly nothing. There were to be no new marriages; there was to be no renewal of persecution. But to the Huguenots the mere fact of the meeting was treated as evidence of the Queen-Mother's determination to destroy them by the importation of Spanish troops and from that moment they began to make plans for a new insurrection.

Catherine's first action on her return was to convene an Assembly of Notables at Moulins at which the Chancellor, l'Hôpital, could announce the various reforms in the administrative and legal system and she herself could reconcile the Guises with Coligny. To this end she arranged that the Admiral should have rooms in the same house as the Cardinal of Lorraine and told them that she would hold each responsible for the safety of the other. After the King had pronounced his long-awaited verdict and found Coligny not guilty she ordered an official reconciliation between the families. The Duchess, masking the hatred in her heart, obeyed and, in the royal presence, embraced the Admiral. She was followed by the Cardinal of Lorraine after he had protested: 'Such accords can last only so long as the power to impose them exists and in course of time they will not prevent my brothers or my nephews killing the Admiral wherever they may find him.' As if to emphasise this, his younger brother Aumale said: 'Would to God that the Admiral and I could be locked in a room and let him who survives come out' and refused to give the formal kiss of peace, while Henry, the young Duke, now fifteen and taller than anyone else in the room, stood immovably apart looking with loathing at Coligny and with contempt at the King.

'By God', shouted Charles, 'you shall obey my orders!'

'In the matter of duty to parents', retorted Guise, 'your writ does not run.' And, making the curtest of bows, he walked slowly from the room as if daring anyone to stop him. No one tried.

Quarrels continued. The Cardinal of Lorraine, accused by the Admiral's brother d'Andelot, the Captain-General, of an attempt to have him murdered, demanded punishment for the slander. The Duchess of Guise and the Queen of Navarre, according to an ambassadorial report, 'blackguarded each other like two fish-wives in the presence of the Queen-Mother'. The Admiral and the Cardinal of Bourbon had such high words in the King's presence that Coligny's two brothers had to take him by the arm and lead him away, saying: 'Don't quarrel with a Prince of the Blood' and Condé, when he heard of the scene, was so furious with his brother the Cardinal that he refused to speak to him for a week. There was a wild scene in the Council when the Cardinal of Lorraine attacked the tolerationist attitude of the Chancellor l'Hôpital, all

Opposite: *François Clouet's oil-painting of Charles IX, King of France, as a young man.*

the more bitter because of their former friendship and admiration for each other.

Immediately the Assembly of Moulins was over and its findings promulgated in an Edict, Coligny, now publicly exculpated, retired to the privacy of Châtillon where, in easy secrecy, he began with Condé and Montgoméry to organise a new rebellion in which the first step was the capture of the King.

The Admiral also kept in touch with the Low Countries, where his cousins, the brothers the Count of Hoorn and Baron Montigny, with Hoorn's particular friend, the Count of Egmont, and with the German Prince, William of Orange (who was disappointed at not having been made Governor of the Netherlands), were waiting for an appropriate moment to raise a revolt against their sovereign, King Philip of Spain. In the June of 1566, Montigny went to Madrid to give an official account of affairs in the province to Philip and, travelling through France, was able to visit Coligny without—because of their cousinship—arousing any political suspicions. He assured the Admiral that the Dutch rebellion would not be long delayed.

It took place in Antwerp on August 15, the Feast of the Assumption of Our Lady, and the signal for it was what had become the key-action for heresy all over Europe—the despoiling of the churches. When the procession to the Cathedral was over and the great mediaeval image of Our Lady had been placed on one of the side-altars, the Prince of Orange, who was Governor of Antwerp, deliberately and ostentatiously left the city to allow the despoilers uninterruptedly to have their way. The image of Our Lady was taken outside by a mob of students and youths from the gutter, aided by prostitutes, and rolled in the mud. The great crucifix above the High Altar—one of the marvels of mediaeval art—was dragged to the ground by ropes and, with hatchets and hammers, chopped into a thousand pieces. The Host was taken from the pyx and put into the mouth of a parrot. The images of the saints were roped together, covered with pieces of armour and tilted against. An Englishman who was present described the iconoclasts as 'criminals and hirelings' and put their number at about a hundred. 'The very harlots, the appurtenances of thieves and drunkards, catching up the wax candles from the altars, held them to light the men that were at work.' When the great cathedral, the pride not only of Antwerp but of Flanders, was thoroughly despoiled and its priceless contents destroyed, the rioters proceeded to the other churches of the city and treated them in the same fashion. Before dawn thirty churches had been sacked. From Antwerp the movement spread from city to city until in the provinces of Flanders alone four hundred churches were gutted.

Philip, when he received the news in Madrid, was for once unable to mask his feelings. 'It shall cost them dear', he said. 'I swear it on the soul of my father.' He sent Alva with a force of 20,000 to restore order and set up a

Court of Inquiry. The Duke marched over the Alps and through Burgundy, Lorraine and Luxembourg to Brussels. Such an iron discipline did he enforce that no acts of violence or depredation were committed on the difficult and hazardous five-weeks march, which became the wonder of contemporaries. Nor did the army depart from its direct route but confined itself strictly to those territories which had made diplomatic arrangements for its passage.

Catherine, lest the Spaniards should stray over the borders of France during their march, had acceded to the demands of Condé and Coligny (made for their own reasons) and invoked the treaty with the Swiss cantons which was, quite rightly, regarded as the corner-stone of French military independence, laid by Francis I. By this treaty, which had been renewed by Henry II, Francis II and Charles IX, the Swiss were bound to provide, whenever asked, not less than six or more than sixteen thousand infantry to be paid by France. But the six thousand now supplied were soon seen to be unnecessary to repel the Spaniards who had behaved so impeccably and Alva's swift success in putting down the Dutch rebellion meant that Coligny, who had because of it to hasten his preparations for the French uprising, realised to his intense annoyance that he was hoist with his own petard. The Swiss could be used to keep order against the Huguenots. He went to Catherine and asked that they might now be sent home.

Catherine, with the utmost courtesy and apparent sympathy, disagreed. Foreseeing the collapse of his carefully prepared plans, the Admiral appealed to his uncle. But the Constable merely said testily: 'They've been paid, so they must be used.' There seemed at the moment, however, nothing to use them for and Coligny was additionally exasperated when Catherine arranged a special review of them to amuse the King.

Having failed to deprive the Crown of one of its defences, Coligny and Condé lost no time in making their final plans. The date of the rising was fixed for the end of September and the Huguenots were bidden to make their way to the place of assembly 'four by four, three by three, two by two so that their movements might escape notice.' As soon as the King was seized, Condé was to take over the government, the Cardinal of Lorraine was to be banished, certain key-towns, including Orléans and Saint-Denis, were to be occupied and the Swiss were to be cut to pieces.

Secrecy was so carefully observed that Catherine discounted the inevitable rumours and even a circumstantial report that a troop of 1,500 horse had been seen near Châtillon. She did indeed send a courier to Châtillon to make a first-hand report, but, as Coligny had ample warning through his spies, nothing was found but the Admiral dressed as a labourer, contentedly tending his vines. Catherine reported to Elisabeth: 'There had been some talk without foundation that those of "the Religion" mean to make a stir, but, thank God, we are as peaceful as ever we could wish.'

But on the morning of Monday September 22 some cavalry were seen in a little wood where the King was to hunt next day and in the afternoon a messenger arrived from Alva in Brussels with circumstantial details of the projected French rising. The shock to Catherine was extreme. 'Amazed' as she put it, 'and unable to see any reason for so infamous an enterprise which involves the subversion of the entire state and endangers the life of the King' she ordered the Court, which was staying in an open undefended château, to the comparative safety of Meaux and summoned the Swiss from their headquarters at Château-Thierry, thirty miles away. She wrote another letter to Spain: 'You may imagine with what distress I see the kingdom returning to the troubles and afflictions from which I have so laboured to deliver it.' She realised at last that the international aspect of the power of Huguenotism was not a figment of Philip and Alva's over-sensitive diplomatic imagination, but that it was indeed epitomised by Philip's recent angry answer to a protest against the 'cruelty' of Alva's administration: 'Why talk of seventeen hundred put to death—and many of them vile men—and not about the thousands who would die in the Netherlands if they succeeded in transplanting the Huguenot wars there from France, as they are trying to do?' Also Catherine found it hard to forgive herself that, in the years since La Renaudie's conspiracy, she had alienated the best Catholics in France by her policy based on the initial mistake of assuming Coligny to be honest.

At Meaux, where there were further reports that all the roads were alive with horsemen, the Council debated the advisability of a return to Paris as the only certain safety in a situation of unknown danger. The difficulty was that, ignorant of the disposition of the rebel army, they might by doing so run into a prepared trap.

Colonel Pfeiffer, in command of the Swiss, said to the King: 'May it please Your Majesty to trust your person and that of the Queen-Mother to our valour and fidelity. We are six thousand strong and with our pikes will open a way through the army of your enemies wide enough for you to pass through in safety.' Some of the Court were still undecided. They agreed with the Venetian Ambassador's strictures that 'the Swiss looked like a set of disreputable street-porters who had neither the knowledge nor the power to use arms.' But the King and his mother supported by the Cardinal of Lorraine insisted and the Ambassador was forced to change his opinion: 'When ranged in battle they seemed to me to be other men. Thrice they turned and faced the enemy; they threw at them whatever came to hand, even bottles; and, lowering their pikes, they ran at them like mad dogs at full speed and they did it with such zest for a fight that the enemy did not dare to attack.'

APRILVS.

C'eſt en Auril que le ſoleil s'aduance
D'herbes produire, & taire les châps beaux,
Et lors chacun ſe met en diligence
Apres le Cerf, ou au vol des Oyſeaux:

On voit auſſi ſortir à grans troupeaux,
Beufz, & Moutons, pour aux châps paſturer,
L'hôme eſt trop plus expert a telz trauaux,
Qu'à ſon ſalut ou il doit aſpirer.

A hunting-party of Catherine's day.

By nightfall on September 28 the Court was safely in the Louvre and the disappointed Huguenots, reinforced by another army under Montgoméry, ravaged the countryside, burnt the mills, captured most of the strategic points on the river and the roads and, on October 2, occupied Saint-Denis.

Catherine sent a messenger to them asking them to state their grievances. They replied by demanding that, as aristocrats, they should be exempt from taxation and, as Huguenots, they should have freedom to practice their religion publicly without any restriction whatever.

Furiously she then dispatched a herald to order them to appear before the King as the rebels they were. Their answer was to lay siege to Paris, having cut off the city's supplies.

The Constable, who was now seventy-five, prepared to give battle, urged to haste by the clamour of the hungry Parisians and the information that Coligny was arranging for the return of the Germans. The engagement on the plain of Saint-Denis on November 10 was a formless affair of skirmishes and mass-killings rather than an organised battle. The Huguenot cavalry had so much freedom of movement that Coligny was able to enter the city and fire the matchless Sainte-Chapelle which St. Louis had built on his

169

return from his crusade as a reliquary for the Crown of Thorns. On the battlefield itself the Constable, fighting on foot, was dazed by four wounds in the face and a blow on the head when a Scot, Robert Stuart, raised a pistol. The old man, expecting to be taken for ransom, called out: 'I am the Constable'.

'That is why I am killing you', said the Scot and fired.

The Constable fell but still had the strength to strike his adversary hard enough to break his jaw before he lost consciousness. Three of Montmorency's sons who were fighting with him bore him dying back to the city; and returned to lead a ferocious, avenging charge which sent their cousin, Condé and Coligny, fleeing from the field.

The defeat at Saint-Denis made the Huguenot position near the capital untenable and the rebels retreated eastward to meet the ten thousand German mercenaries at Pont-à-Mousson on the Moselle a few miles south of Metz. After they had joined forces they started for Paris again, choosing their route through Burgundy which had so far escaped the ravages of war and could offer them both food and pillage. But this return of the *reiters* and the destructive bestiality that their presence was now known by grim experience to mean rallied the ordinary Catholics of France as nothing else could have done. Everywhere they formed themselves into local 'Leagues', semi-secret societies on the model of the Confraternity of the Holy Spirit which Marshal Tavannes founded that year at Dijon, pledged to support the Catholic Faith and the house of Valois on the lines of the old Triumvirate all of whose members, with the death of the Constable, were now dead.

The Huguenots, too, slowly discovering that in reality they were regarded by the great mass of their fellow-countrymen not as the purifiers of religion but as a despicable company of traitors, began to lose heart, while those who had volunteered in the army, restless, homesick, unpaid and hating their enforced allies, deserted in droves.

Meanwhile Catherine, unwilling to avail herself of Alva's offer of help on the grounds that 'it is quite easy to bring the Spaniards in: the difficulty would be to get them out' wanted above all things the cessation of strife even if it could not be construed as a lasting settlement. From the moment when, the day after the battle of Saint-Denis, some courtiers had petitioned the King 'to cast eyes of pity on his subjects' she had continued to negotiate wherever it was possible.

Her first action, however, was unconnected with diplomacy. It was to restore the Sainte-Chapelle after Coligny's men's damage and desecration of it. Quite apart from pious and aesthetic considerations, she had St. Louis much on her mind. Giovanni Correro, one of the ablest and most perceptive of the Venetian ambassadors with whom Catherine was on terms of personal friendship, reported how she told him that in her recent travels 'she had read at Carcassonne a manuscript history which told about the mother of St. Louis, Blanche of Castile, left a widow with a son only eleven years old, and how the nobles had risen in arms objecting to the rule of a woman and a foreigner at that. To accomplish their designs they had united with the Albigensian heretics who, like those of her day, did not want priests, monks,

Anne de Montmorency in his old age; he has mellowed considerably since the date of the engraving on page 46; but the great Constable of France retains both his strength and his courage.

171

While Catherine visited Spain, Egmont and Horn (whose arrest is here depicted) were fomenting Protestant rebellion in the Netherlands.

masses, images in churches, etc. They also called in a king of Aragon to help them and it was necessary to meet them in a pitched battle. Toulouse, their stronghold, was dismantled and finally, at the suggestion of the Queen, a peace was made which conceded many of their demands. However, the King, grown strong with the lapse of time and the counsels of his mother, finally took that vengeance on his rebels which they deserved.

'Then she showed how all these details exactly matched her own situation. She was a widow and a foreigner with no one to trust and with a son eleven years old. The nobles had risen under pretext of religion but really against her government, calling in the Queen of England and the Germans to help them. There was war and victory and Orléans was taken and dismantled, like Toulouse. Peace was made by her advice, to the advantage of the Huguenots. She admitted she had granted them the advantage, hoping to gain by time what she could not gain without great bloodshed by force of arms.

'At this point I said: "Madame, Your Majesty ought to draw consolation

172

The Duke of Alba, whom King Philip II sent to put down the rebellion in the Netherlands.

from this history which is not only a picture of the events of your day but a prophecy of the final outcome." (I was alluding to the eventual punishment). She laughed very loudly (as she does when she hears anything that pleases her) and said: "I should not want anyone to know that I have read that chronicle because they would say that I am imitating Queen Blanche who was a Spaniard!"'

Catherine's present efforts for peace were successful through no action of her own but because Condé once more became her ally as he saw no other way of preserving his family estates and possessions in Vendôme from the attention of the Germans. On 23 March 1568 at Longjumeau a treaty was signed by which the Edict of Amboise was reaffirmed without alteration and the Huguenots undertook to restore all the places they had captured during the war and to dismiss the Germans. Coligny alone denounced the arrangement as 'a bloody peace full of infidelity' and violently urged the continuance of the rebellion.

173

'War of Devils'

The uneasy peace did not last six months. On St. Bartholomew's Eve, 23 August, 1568, Condé and Coligny issued a call to arms and set out for La Rochelle to establish themselves in that Huguenot fortress, difficult to capture, rich with the spoils of pirates and easily in touch with England. In the first days of September the Queen of Navarre and her son Henry, also arrived. She had twenty gold medals made and inscribed: *Ou paix assurée, ou victoire entière ou mort honneste*, and gave them to her friends. Then, with her own hands, she armed Henry in the presence of the rebel forces and presented him to them as their leader, to take his place with Condé and Coligny. Condé, on his part, made his long dream come partially true by having coins struck with the legend: *Louis XIII, premier roi Chrétien de France.*

Condé's rapid defection from Catherine after having secured the departure of the Germans and so preserved his estates was due to the appointment of Henry of Anjou as Lieutenant-General of the Realm. Now that the Constable was dead, Catherine determined that never again should any of the great families have control of the army to the possible detriment of the Crown. The King, who was now eighteen, agreed to his brother's appointment with considerable reluctance because of his own desire for military glory, but he saw the force of his mother's argument that, as King of France, he could not possibly lead the army against a body of his own subjects as only too probably the Lieutenant-General would have to do at any moment.

Anjou's appointment led to another strain in family relations. With the prospect of long absences from Court, it was natural that he should commit his interests to his sister. He and Margot, in their mutual adoration, had become virtually a secret society of two and, early that summer, when they were staying at Plessis-lès-Tours, he made a proposal to her.

'My brother of Anjou', she recorded, 'begged me to take a walk with him in a green alley, apart, and once there spoke to me thus: "My sister, you know that of our family you are the one I love most and you feel the same for

174

me. Till today we have had no aim but the joy of being together. But now our childhood is over and childish things have passed away. You know the great offices to which I have been called and, believe me, I will never have greatness or possessions which you do not share. But my strength lies in keeping the Queen our mother's good graces and I am afraid my absences will do me harm. The wars will keep me constantly away and our brother the King is always at her side, flattering her. I fear that in the long run I shall suffer; for the King will not always find amusement in hunting, but will soon want to chase men instead of beasts. Then he will deprive me of my Lieutenancy and go to lead the army himself. So it is absolutely necessary that I should have someone to uphold my cause with the Queen. Who is better fitted for this than you, who are my other self? You must never fail to be at her *lever*, in her study, at her *coucher*; in a word all day and every day"'.'

Margot, torn between her desire to please him and her fear of Catherine, which had grown rather than decreased with the years, reminded him of the difference in their mother's affection for them. It was not that she was jealous of Catherine's obsessive preference for him; she was only afraid of her own reactions to her mother's scarcely-concealed dislike of her and she had more than her share of the filial awe which the Queen-Mother inspired in all her children and which made even Elisabeth confess that she never got a letter from her without trembling before she opened it lest it should contain an angry word or a reproof for some offence unwittingly given.

So now Margot explained to Henry: 'It is not only that I dare not open a conversation with her, but when she looks at me I almost die of fright in case I have done something to displease her.' Anjou brushed it aside with: 'I will speak to her about it. I will make her understand your ability and the comfort and help you could be to her. I will beg her not to treat you as a child any longer but in my absence to look on you as if you were me. On your part, you must stop being afraid of her. Speak to her with the same assurance as you do to me and, believe me, you will get on very well together.'

Margot promised. 'The instant my brother spoke like this', she wrote, 'it seemed to me I was quite changed—that I had become something better than I had been before.'

'You were quite right to be sure of me', she said. 'There is no one in the world who loves you as I do.'

Henry on his part fulfilled his promise and discussed the matter with Catherine who sent for Margot almost immediately and said to her: 'Your brother has told me of his conversation with you. To him you are no longer a child, nor shall you be one to me. I shall talk to you as if I were talking to him. Only obey me and never be afraid to discuss things openly with me. That is my wish.'

'These words', wrote Margot when she recorded the incident, 'made me feel what I had never before felt—a measureless content—so that I now looked on the sports of my childhood, dancing, hunting, friendships, as something long past. I obeyed her wishes and never failed to be first at her *lever* and last at her *coucher* and she did me the honour sometimes of talking to me for three or four hours together.'

Catherine, during those months of uneasy peace, was suddenly but not unexpectedly, called on to deal with the affairs of her daughter-in-law. In the May of 1568 she received an urgent message from Mary Queen of Scots. Mary's seven-year sojourn in her native kingdom had been a bitter disaster. Her bastard half-brother, James Earl of Moray, with his associates, had succeeded as he had planned to do in dislodging her from the Throne before her twenty-fifth birthday (when she had the right to revoke earlier grants made during her minority to men who, like himself, had proved themselves

Mary Queen of Scots wearing the white mourning she adopted when her husband, Francis II, died.

traitors) and he was now Regent of Scotland while she was a prisoner of the Calvinist Lords of the Congregation. She now begged Catherine, in a letter written while her gaolers were at dinner and smuggled out by a faithful page, to send some French troops, 'for it is by force alone that I can be delivered. If you send never so few troops, I am certain great numbers of my subjects will rise to join them; but, without them, they are overawed by the power of the rebels'.

Moray's first attempt to get rid of Mary had been by playing on the ambition of her second husband, Lord Darnley, whom she had first met in France. Darnley had turned out to be a drunken weakling in the control of her English enemies. Darnley, furious that Mary denied him the Crown Matrimonial of Scotland she had granted to Francis II, led a band of nobles to murder her Italian secretary before her eyes in the palace of Holyrood in the hope that the shock, as she was seven months pregnant, would kill both her

Henry Lord Darnley, Mary Queen of Scots' second husband.

and the child and leave him King of Scotland, with Moray as his chief minister.

As both Mary and the child survived the experiment he made another attempt to get rid of her a year later. He tried to induce her to spend the night with him at a house on the outskirts of Edinburgh where he was recovering from syphilis. Gunpowder filled the vaults and his intention was to leave her sleeping to be blown to eternity after he and his favourite page had made their escape and ridden from the city.

Fortunately for her, the Earl of Bothwell, who had been her faithful friend since her days as Queen of France, discovered the plot, persuaded her to stay in Holyrood House instead of remaining with her husband at Kirk o' Field and ensured that Darnley died instead.

'The matter is horrible', Mary had written to Catherine the following morning, 'and so strange as we believe the like was never heard of. This night past, a little after two hours after midnight, the house wherein the King was lodged was in an instant blown in the air, he lying sleeping in his bed, with such vehemency that of the whole lodging, walls and other, there is nothing remaining, no, not one stone above another. It must have been done by force of powder and appears to have been a mine. By whom it has been done and in what manner appears not yet.'

Catherine had been disturbed and asked Mary's uncle, the Duke of Aumale, to pay a family visit to the Scottish court to find out, if he could, what was going on. But by the time of Aumale's arrival, the situation had been exploited in a way which Catherine, for all her reputation for 'Italianate cunning' could not have foreseen.

Moray and the Calvinist lords decided to accuse the Queen of Scots of having murdered Darnley and, in order to give an air of credibility to so improbable a falsehood, they proceeded to urge Bothwell to become her third husband. Such an action would allow the Earl to be represented as Mary's secret lover and the murder of Darnley as a *crime passionelle*. To encourage it, they formed themselves into a 'bond', backed by Queen Elizabeth of England, pledged to support the marriage 'considering how our Sovereign, the Queen's Majesty, is now destitute of a husband, in the which solitary state the Commonwealth of the Realm may not permit Her Highness to continue.'

The difficulty was that, as Mary showed no enthusiasm for a new marriage, he had had to abduct her. In her next letter to Catherine she had reported how Bothwell 'awaited us by the way with a great force and led us to Dunbar. And when he saw us like to reject all his suit and offers, and when never a man in Scotland made any attempt to procure our deliverance, he never ceased till by persuasions, accompanied by force, he has finally driven us to the end he thought might best serve his turn.'

The fatal marriage had already taken place when Aumale had arrived in

John Knox, Calvin's rabid and sex-obsessed Scots disciple, who wrote The First Blast of a Trumpet against the Monstrous Regiment of Women, *directed against Catherine, Mary Queen of Scots and Elizabeth I of England.*

Edinburgh and the French Ambassador had to report to Catherine: 'It is too unhappy. On Thursday the Queen sent for me when I perceived something strange in the mutual behaviour of her and her husband. She attempted to excuse it and said: "If you see me melancholy, it is because I do not choose to be cheerful; because I shall never be so and wish only for death." Yesterday, when they were both in a room with the Duke of Aumale, she called for a knife to kill herself so loud that the persons in the antechamber heard it. I believe that if God does not support her she will fall into despair.'

She had reason for despair. Moray's plot had been entirely successful. Urged on by Calvin's most bitter and self-righteous disciple, the sex-obsessed John Knox, the godly rose up against her as an adulteress and a murderess and, under a banner on which Darnley was painted lying dead under a tree with the young prince, James, kneeling by the body praying: *Judge and revenge my cause, O Lord!*, had challenged the royal forces at Carberry Hill just outside Edinburgh.

The French Ambassador, acting on Catherine's instructions, had advised Mary to leave Bothwell and trust herself to the Calvinist nobles. The Queen of Scots, reflecting that her mother-in-law, even with her experience of the Huguenots, could have no real understanding of the Scots traitors, had at first furiously refused, pointing out that those who were now in arms against Bothwell were the very men who, a few weeks before had signed the 'bond' supporting him and urging him to marry her. But eventually she had decided that the wisest course in the interests of the peace of her kingdom was to trust herself to the confederate Lords in return for a safe-conduct for her husband. So, after their farewell between the armies, he had ridden off to Dunbar and she had been taken to Edinburgh, amid shouts of 'Burn the whore! Burn her! She is not worthy to live!' Her captors had immediately broken their word and imprisoned her in Moray's castle of Lochleven, where she had miscarried Bothwell's child.

And now, after eleven months imprisonment, she wrote to Catherine asking for French troops to help her regain her kingdom.

Such a course was obviously impossible, but Catherine was saved the unkindness of refusal by the course of events at Lochleven. Hard on the heels

of Mary's letter came a dispatch from the French Ambassador telling of her escape the day after she had written it: 'All Scotland is in motion, some declaring for the Queen and some for the Earl of Moray. With regard to her flight, it is judged here, by those who know the site and how closely she was guarded that her escape was most miraculous.'

Mary's intention was to gain the shelter of Dumbarton Castle, commanding the Clyde estuary where the French troops could be landed or from which she, should the situation become desperate, could take ship for France. Men flocked to her standard and her improvised army soon outnumbered the Calvinist force by 6000 to 4000. But among those who joined her by far the largest contingent was that led by Moray's brother-in-law who naturally defected in the battle and ensured that the Queen suffered a decisive defeat and, the way to Dumbarton now barred, fled southward.

One of her servants, John Beaton, managed to get to France to give Catherine the news personally and to carry a letter from the Queen of Scots

The island castle on Loch Leven where Mary Queen of Scots was imprisoned by her half-brother under the care of his mother.

to her uncle, the Cardinal of Lorraine. In it Mary described her plight: 'I have endured injuries, calumnies, imprisonment, famine, cold, heat, flight not knowing whither, ninety-two miles across the country without stopping or alighting, and then I have had to sleep upon the ground and drink sour milk and eat oatmeal without bread and have been three nights like the owls.'

On the afternoon of Sunday 16 May, as she was crossing Solway Firth in a fishing-boat on the last stage of her flight, Mary suddenly realised the peril in which she was putting herself and ordered the boatman to see that she was taken, whatever the risk and cost, to France. But the wind and tide were against her and the men put in at the little Cumberland port of Workington where she was recognised and installed in the castle 'with posted guards on all sides.'

The fall of the Queen of Scots, leaving Calvinism visibly triumphant in Scotland and providing Protestant England with an unrivalled hostage, was, quite apart from its personal implications, a severe blow to Catherine's policy. It gave such encouragement to the forces of rebellion in France that Coligny, within a month of receiving the news, came up to Court to urge the relaxation of the Edict.

Charles interrupted his long list of grievances with: 'Today you wish to be our equals. Tomorrow you will wish to be our masters and drive us out of the realm.' Then, rushing from the room in one of his rages, he went to his mother and shouted: 'I am now of the Duke of Alva's mind. Heads like these are too high for the State.'

Catherine was reluctantly coming to the same conclusion. To prevent another civil war, it might be wise to arrest and imprison Coligny and Condé.

Before she could arrive at a decision, the Queen-Mother received a blow which almost prostrated her. She had been ill but had left her sick-bed to attend an important meeting of the Council. When she entered the room, the King was already seated. Charles had insisted that no one but himself should give her the news that he and most of the Court had known for twenty-four hours—that Elisabeth had died in childbirth.

Catherine said nothing but retired immediately to her oratory to face alone the misery that 'the best and dearest of daughters' had left her. An hour later she returned, completely self-controlled, to the Council Chamber.

'Messieurs,' she said, 'God has taken away all my hopes in this wor'd. But the Huguenots should not be too quick to rejoice, or to suppose that by this death our friendship with Spain will be broken. King Philip will certainly marry again. My own wish is my daughter Marguerite shall take the place of her sister.'

The proposition, though it was obliquely discussed, came to nothing and the French Ambassador in Madrid eventually wrote: 'I must tell you plainly what I think; it is my opinion that there is nothing in these people here except bad will. They reckon that your civil war keeps them at peace and the impoverishment of your kingdom in men and in money is the strengthening of theirs.' Philip had little desire and less need to marry France a second time.

The rebellion had started in August, but Charles was not able to put an immediate army into the field, owing partly to the shortage of money to pay the Swiss and partly to the method of organisation which allowed the regular cavalry to live in their own houses and attend to their own equipment and horses. As regards money, Catherine did her best to raise it by seeking foreign loans and giving her own jewels as security, but the process was necessarily slow and, though six regiments of the regular troops of the line were put in the field, they were so hopelessly outnumbered that within a month of the arrival of the Huguenot leaders at La Rochelle, the rebels had forced the surrender of the important city of Angoulême where they slaughtered priests and women, and continued victoriously in the same vein. At the surrender of Pons, in spite of the terms of capitulation, four hundred soldiers were killed. In the neighbourhood of Bourges they pillaged and burnt the churches and killed the priests. At Lignières, they massacred the garrison, pillaged the town and desecrated the churches, even opening the tombs to melt down the lead of the coffins for cannon-balls. They closed the proceedings by killing the parish-priest and throwing his body in the river. After the storming of Aurillac they tortured and hanged the magistrates. The Vice-Admiral of the Huguenot pirate fleet based at La Rochelle captured seven Portuguese ships on the way to Brazil, carrying sixty-nine Jesuits on a mission to the New World, all of whom were thrown into the sea.

Even Beza, the leader of the Calvinists since Calvin's death, deplored the outrages: 'Certainly defence by arms is just and necessary, but the arms have been so badly used that we must pray God that He will teach us to handle them in a more holy manner. May His church be rather an assembly of martyrs than a refuge for murderers and brigands.' And La Noue, one of the best of the Huguenot leaders, confessed: 'We fought the first war like angels, the second like men and the third like devils.' The appropriateness of 'angels' may indeed be questioned, but no one could dispute 'devils'. It was as if, into the two years between the August of 1568 and the August of 1570 the atrocities of many wars were crowded and all the tales of them were true. 'In the name of Heaven' was a Catholic comment, 'the Huguenots brought Hell to earth.'

From the rank and file, especially the 17,000 Germans, led this time by William of Orange, unspeakable things were only to be expected; and such phenomena as the fashion of making necklaces of priests' ears and using the bones of dismembered nuns as drum-sticks caused no more surprise than the slaughter of garrisons who had surrendered on promise of quarter or the systematic rape and massacre of women and children. But savagery this time spread to the leaders who, with the exception of the Queen of Navarre's friend, the Baron d'Andrets, with his accustomed aura of torture and death, had hitherto attempted to observe an honourable code of warfare. It was Coligny now who improved on the usual method of sacking an abbey by forcing the monks to hang each other for the amusement of his troops. It was Coligny who ordered the decimation of all the peasants of Périgord in retaliation for a small local outbreak.

When the Pope, at the beginning of the new uprising, wrote to Henry of Anjou as Lieutenant-General: 'Your brother's rebels have disturbed the public peace of the realm, have subverted the Catholic religion, have savagely slain the priests of Almighty God, have committed innumerable crimes and they deserve the full penalties of the law', he was only stating the incontrovertible truth in its simplest form. What he did not allow for was that the Catholic populace had started to reply to the massacres of priests and the destruction of shrines and churches with counter-massacres and that in the mounting fury, Catholic barbarities began to equal, if not to exceed, those of the Calvinists. Judged by their actions there was nothing to choose between Catholic loyalists and Calvinist rebels, nor was it possible to exaggerate France's desolation.

An English traveller that year reported: 'The fate of France is lamentable, the meaner subjects spoiled everywhere and the greater neither sure of life nor living in any place where murder is no cruelty or disobedience any offence, bathing in one another's blood, making it custom to despise religion and justice and any sacred bond of either divine or human institution; where the victor may bewail his victory and the native be in danger of being overrun by the stranger he calls to his defence; having consumed the store of the last year and wasting that on the ground which should serve for the year to come, so that a present desperation and a piteous mourning doth invade every sort, as if their calamities should have no end but at the end of their lives. And with all the dreadfullest cruelties ever in the world, plague, hunger and sword—which God in His mercy cease in them and preserve us from! And to this is joined an incredible obstinacy on either side, ever hardening their hearts with malice and fury to the utter extermination one of the other.'

Coligny, Condé and Montgoméry, leading the Huguenot forces, and young Anjou, under the tutorship of the old and experienced Marshal Tavannes, leading the royal forces, were all disinclined for a full-scale autumn campaign and when winter came moved thankfully into winter

Labels on image: Der Spanschen besatzung · PARIS · Mer Brison President · Der Franſoſen besatzung

Battles, massacres and fighting in the streets of Paris.

quarters, Anjou at Chinon, Coligny at Niort, where he received some welcome munitions from England.

In the spring they moved out to battle and on Sunday 13 March 1569 at Jarnac to the south of La Rochelle, with Anjou leading the Royal attack, the Huguenots were defeated and Condé killed. The Prince, after Coligny and Montgoméry had both fled from the field, led a last desperate charge, crying 'Louis de Bourbon goes to battle for Christ and his country' and almost cut his way through to Anjou. But the weight of numbers told and it was soon clear that Condé was doomed though 'all his men', as one of them put it, 'struggled for the honour of making a rampart for him with their bodies.' Wounded and surrounded by Royalist soldiers, he offered 200,000 crowns ransom money, but as two of Anjou's squires stepped forward to take him into their protection, the Captain of the Guard, who had fought at Saint-Denis and had not forgotten the manner of the Constable's death, raised his pistol and shot Condé in the face, blowing out one of his eyes.

Thus was fulfilled the prophecy of Nostradamus (who had now been dead for two years):

> *Bossa sera esleu par le conseil*
> *Plus hideux monstre en terre n'apperceu.*
> *Le coup voulant crevera l'oeil*
> *Le traistre au Roy pour fidelle receu.*

The verse (III. 41 of the *Centuries*) may be translated: 'The hunchback will be elected to the Council. A more hideous monster was never seen on earth. An intentional shot pierces the eye of the traitor who had sworn to be faithful to the King.'

A band of drunken soldiers put Condé on the back of a she-ass and led it from the battle. When Anjou heard of it, he had the body taken to his house and decreed death for any further outrage. A few days later he sent the body to Henry of Navarre for burial at Vendômen the ancestral crypt of the Bourbons.

> *L'an mil cinq cens soixante neuf*
> *Entre Jarnac et Chateauneuf*
> *Fut porté mort sur une ânesse*
> *Le grand ennemi de la Messe*

they sang exultantly in the streets of Paris.

Catherine, at the time of Jarnac, was on the eastern frontier at Metz. She had caught a prevailing epidemic and the doctors were seriously anxious. Margot for remembrance left an account of a strange occurrence: 'Round my mother's bed stood King Charles my brother and my brother and sister of Lorraine and divers gentlemen of the Council, and many ladies and gentlemen who thought she was at the point of death and would not abandon her. And she, dreaming, kept telling them what she saw, all in order as it happened. "Look how they flee!" she said suddenly. "My son has the victory. *Hé, mon Dieu*, set my son on his feet again—he has fallen. Do you see the Prince of Condé? He is dead in that hedge!"

'All those present thought she was dreaming and that, since she knew that my brother Anjou meant to give battle, it was the thought of that which was haunting her. But a few nights later there came M. de Losses with the news of the victory, thinking that he was bringing most welcome tidings and deserved a reward at her hands. But all she said was: "You are tedious to come waking me for that. I knew it well already. Did I not see it all?".'

Left: *Louis of Navarre, Prince of Condé in his armour.*

Right: *The armour worn by King Charles IX of France.*

Charles, however, welcomed the detailed confirmation of his mother's second sight and, after a special *Te Deum* in the Cathedral, instructed the Cardinal of Lorraine to write to the Pope, promising to send the ensigns captured in the battle if the Pope would agree to have them hung in St. Peter's as a memorial of the first decisve French victory over heresy. They duly arrived there—twelve of them—on April 23 when, an eye-witness of the ceremony reported, 'the Pope hath joyfully received them and this day joyfully triumpheth in the victory.'

During the summer, while the main war settled down into a series of sieges, Coligny sent Montgoméry south to drive the Royal forces out of Navarre which, with Jeanne's absence at La Rochelle, they had largely over-run.

The turning point of Montgoméry's campaign was his capture of Orthez which was surrendered on 18 August 1569 by the Lord of Terride on Montgoméry's pledged word that all lives should be spared. Nevertheless on St. Barthomolmew's Day, August 24, Montgomáry, in the words of a contemporary historian, 'having returned victorious to Pau and having caused the prisoners to be brought there, he had them stabbed in cold blood, although they had only surrendered on condition of their lives being saved. This cruel deed was done on the Feast of St. Bartholomew. The news strongly angered King Charles, who from that day resolved in his mind that he would have a second St. Bartholomew in expiation of the first.' Though the ascription of definite purpose suggests the neatness of hindsight—Favyn did not publish his *History of Navarre* till well after the event when the coincidence was too dramatic to escape notice—it is not improbable that the first Massacre of St. Bartholomew, as it was called, was in the minds of both Charles and Catherine (because it was Montgomáry's action) when the second was being discussed three years later.

The key to the summer campaign elsewhere was the city of Poitiers, whose size and strategic importance made Coligny besiege it with an army of 25,000 men—an action which provoked Catherine at last to accept the assistance of 4000 Spanish troops from Flanders.

The defender of Poitiers was the eighteen-year-old Henry Duke of Guise who, after his refusal to be reconciled to Coligny at Moulins three years ago had prepared himself for a war for the Cross by getting his uncle, the Cardinal of Lorraine's, permission as soon as he was sixteen to join the Emperor in his crusade against the Turks and had returned from it only when the death of Suleiman the Magnificent brought the war to an end. In the siege of Poitiers, which began on July 25, 1569, Guise was fully aware of the ferocity he was undertaking. For Coligny, the fall of the city would secure the whole of Poitou for the rebels, but even greater than the military value would be the satisfaction of securing the person of the feared and hated avenger who was defending it. Yet the young Duke fought with that gay *panache* which was part of the Guise temperament. When a breach was made in the walls and a bridge of boats was made across the river by which it could be entered, Guise led a night expedition which not only destroyed the improvised bridge but dammed the river so that it overflowed into the surrounding meadows, drowning many of the besiegers, and sent a herald to Coligny to point out

Opposite: *The Château of Amboise.*

Overleaf: *The Battle of Montconcour on 3 October 1569, where Henry of Anjou, Catherine's favourite son, defeated the Huguenot forces, composed mainly of Germans, and brought the third 'war of religion' to an end.*

Der herr von noue

Der herr von acuer
gefencklich

that his command as Lord Admiral did not extend to an inland freshwater sea.

Yet, though on September 3, the defenders managed to repulse a violent triple attack, Guise knew that without reinforcements he could not hold out indefinitely. He sent a request to Anjou to draw off some of Coligny's forces. Anjou thereupon commenced the siege of a Huguenot fortress and within four days Coligny abandoned the attempt on Poitiers.

A month later, when the Admiral was starting to move south to join forces with Montgoméry, Anjou forced a battle at Montcontour which resulted in an even greater victory than Jarnac. Anjou himself was unhorsed and nearly lost his life, but he insisted on quarter being granted to the French in the Huguenot army, ordering: 'I will not countenance Frenchmen slaughtering Frenchmen.'

Anjou, Tavannes and Guise would have preferred to have continued the war to the complete victory which they believed, not without reason, they could now win; but Catherine was determined on a settlement. And it was Catherine who counted. The new Venetian Ambassador described her, as she entered her fifty-first year: 'Her industry in affairs causes a general wonder and astonishment. No step, however unimportant, is taken without her. Scarcely has she time to eat or drink or sleep, so great are her harassing cares. She runs here and there between the armies, doing a man's work, without a thought of sparing herself. Yet she is loved by no one in the land— or, at least, by few. The Huguenots say she has given them feigned words and fine promises but all the time she has been treating with the Catholic King [Philip II] for their destruction. The Catholics, on the other hand, declare that if she had not exalted and favoured the Huguenots, these latter would not have been able to do what they have. It is a marvel to me that she has not become confused and given herself to one of the parties, a course of action which would have ended in the total ruin of France. When she has not been able to have her way she has compromised here and there and it is from these forced compromises that ill-considered measures have arisen.'

In the matter of a compromise peace, she was able to have her way the more easily because of the growth of the *Politiques,* led by Coligny's cousin, Montmorency,—those lukewarm Catholics whom grim old Tavannes characteristically described as 'preferring the repose of the kingdom and their own houses to the salvation of their souls; who would rather the kingdom remained at peace without God than at war with Him.' The alliance of the *Politiques* and the Huguenots, combined with Charles's maniacal jealousy of his brother who, because of Jarnac and Montcontour, was now a popular

Opposite: *A watercolour from 'Habits de France', published in 1581, showing a horseman of the time of Catherine.*

193

hero and had gained the military glory the King himself coveted, and the general war-weariness of the country, led to the peace of St. Germain by which there was the now conventional reaffirmation of the Edicts of Toleration. This time, however, there was an additional clause. The Calvinists were, as a guarantee that the Edicts would be observed, to be allowed the two-year tenure of La Rochelle and three other towns which they might hold as 'cities of refuge'.

To La Rochelle Coligny immediately retired and refused to leave it for eighteen months. He made it a little republic on the model of Geneva with himself as dictator, and fashioned a new policy for the triumph of his cause— to persuade France, with England as an ally, into war with Spain on behalf of the Protestant rebels in the Netherlands.

Family Affairs

It was at this time that Catherine's relationship with her children assumed an importance which was to influence the rest of her life and, incidentally, to mould the course of French history. To the Spanish Ambassador she confessed: 'I no longer have the same authority as I did. My sons are men now and I do not have the controlling hand in affairs which I once had.'

Her rival in the struggle to control Charles was to be Coligny who once more laid himself out to capture the King's affection. In Henry's case it was to be for the rest of his life and hers his succession of *mignons*. Her attitude to the King showed a wisdom which was lacking in her passionate possessiveness of Anjou. Provided she could direct Charles's policy she was content to allow him to grow away from her and when he fell in love with Marie Touchet, the daughter of a minor Court official, she not only encouraged it, but gave the girl—who herself asked for nothing—the manor of Belleville, near Vincennes, where Charles was so often in residence on his hunting expeditions.

Marie, warm, simple, generous, completely without ambition, was, so Catherine came to the conclusion after penetrating observation and extensive inquiries, the one person at Court who cared for Charles for himself. She had no great beauty, but her plump little face, her full mouth, her honest, untroubled eyes gave the King promise of understanding and peace which the sad, neurotic boy could find nowhere else. When he stole away from the Louvre to her little house in a high-walled garden in the Rue de la Mortellerie, he went, so he said, from Purgatory to Paradise.

Charles was a physical and a mental misfit. His powerful body was supported by over-long, spindly legs. His muscular arms hung from bowed shoulders. He loved music and poetry, but he was prone to insane, murderous anger and his passion for the chase was, in part, as he insisted on seeing the spurting blood of the stag, an attempt to exorcise murderous fantasies. When hunting was impossible, he would turn blacksmith and beat out

195

weapons for his armoury until he was prostrate with exhaustion. Then he would turn to his lute or join in part-songs with the choristers of his private chapel. Or he would practise poetry with his adored master, Ronsard, to whom he addressed a poem beginning:

Tous deux également nous portons des couronnes
Mais, roi, je la reçus; poète, tu la donnes.

In the autumn of 1570, Catherine arranged Charles's marriage with Elizabeth of Austria, the younger daughter of the Emperor (and thus sister-in-law of Philip of Spain), a gentle, pious child, unworldly and quite uninterested in politics. When he first saw a portrait of her, the King said: 'She will not give me a single headache' and Marie Touchet assured him: 'I am not afraid of the Austrian.' They were both kind to her. They respected her piety and both approved of her habit of spending most of the night in prayer. At her coronation which, instead of taking place in the morning was, through unforeseen delays, postponed till three in the afternoon, she refused the canonical permission to break her fast before communicating lest she might faint at the arduous ceremony, and, says the record, 'received the Body of the Lord at six in the evening as upright and gay as though it were six in the morning.'

When Coligny visited Blois for the first time after the Peace of Saint-Germain, his arrival involved Elizabeth in a crisis of behaviour. She accepted the judgment of her brother-in-law Philip, who had written: 'We cannot

Pierre Ronsard in old age.

Opposite:
Marie Touchet, the mistress of Charles IX and the mother of his son Charles de Valois to whom Catherine left much of her fortune. Marie herself lived to the age of eighty.

cease to deplore that the King has let himself be persuaded to permit such a wicked man as the Admiral to appear in his presence unless it were to secure and behead him, which would be an act of great merit and honour; but I do not think they have the resolution or courage for it.' On the other hand, she was Queen of France and her husband was obviously in a welcoming mood. It was very difficult and she prayed earnestly for guidance. When the moment came and Coligny, ordered by the Queen-Mother to make his obeisance to the Queen, 'fell on his knees and would have kissed her hand, she flushed and drew back'—according to Margot who was observing the scene with a certain amusement—'and would never allow him even to touch her.'

Charles and Elizabeth had one child, a girl who died at the age of five-and-a-half. The child's one recorded *mot* is often cited as an illustration of the excessive pride in ancestry which Catherine instilled into all her family from their earliest years. Her governess, who was Brantôme's aunt, told how 'that little princess would often say she was descended from the two greatest houses of Christendom, France and Austria, and she could name her remote ancestors as well as any herald in France. Once when she was sick her uncle Henry came to see her. She pretended to be asleep and kept her face turned to the wall, although he called her three times. When her governess turned her round she would scarcely speak to him and after he had left her governess scolded her. She answered "Why should I receive him graciously when he has not sent to inquire after my health—I who am his niece and the daughter of his elder brother and one who does not dishonour the family?" '

The pride of birth was also prominent in the precocious princess's half-brother, Charles, Charles's son by Marie Touchet, who lived on into the reign of Louis XIV. He coined money in his own province, altering the superscription, and le *Roi Soleil* did not interfere out of respect for the blood of the Valois.

Catherine's relationship with Charles was basically simple nor had she serious need to fear that she would ever really lose control of him. As Tavannes, closely observing things, remarked: 'The Queen-Mother, knowing how entirely she possessed her son, did not care a jot for his opinions, certain as she was that she could change them in an instant.' But Henry was a very different matter. For one thing, he was much more intelligent than Charles. Also—and more importantly—his temperament raised problems which, it would seem, his mother never properly understood. Obviously she was not able to appreciate that, as a Freudian age would interpret it, it was her intense maternal dominance that was the major cause of his homosexuality,

Opposite: *Elizabeth of Austria, Queen of Charles IX, who became one of the stays and comforts of Catherine's old age.*

but even on the ground of simple common-sense, she showed a certain obtuseness in supposing that one totally averse to women could be 'cured' of his antipathy by being entertained at a banquet where the servitors were all female nudes. Also it appeared that Catherine deceived herself—a most rare thing for her to do—by rationalising her objections to Henry's continuous stream of lovers. Of the Spaniard Lignerolles, the lover of the moment under whose influence Anjou had turned *dévot*, hearing three Masses a day and fasting to excess, Catherine complained that he had induced Henry to adopt an asceticism which had made 'his face grow pale from the strain and I would rather see him turn Huguenot than thus endanger his health.' On the other hand she told the Ambassador of Spain that her objection to Lignerolles was that he was a spy of Spain.

To a courtier she attributed her anger to Lignerolles's attempt to discredit her with the King, while to the English Ambassador she blamed the *mignon's* interference with her project of marrying Anjou to Elizabeth of England. Whatever the reason, when Lignarolles was murdered in broad daylight in a street not far from the Louvre, Catherine was generally suspected of having encouraged his assassin by suggesting to him that the deed could be done with impunity and without fear of punishment; and this is one of the two murders —the other being the later killing of Coligny—from which her fiercest partisans do not attempt to exonerate her.

Family relationships were further complicated at this time by the estrangement of Margot and Anjou and the entrance of the youngest brother, Francis (*né* Hercules), who was now sixteen, on the political stage. The reason for the dramatic change from love to hate between Henry and his sister was due to the fact that Margot fell in love with Guise. They were discreetly spied upon by another of Henry's *mignons*, Louis de Béranger, Sieur du Guast, who one night discovered the lovers' rendezvous in an unused bedroom in a far corridor of the Louvre. De Guast reported to Anjou who felt it his duty to report it to the King. It was five in the morning, but Charles was not asleep. When he heard the news, his conduct was such that his brother thought it wise to retire immediately. The King rolled on the floor, tearing his hair, screaming blasphemies and vowing to kill Guise for his presumption. When the fit had spent itself, he went to his mother's apartments, woke her and demanded to know whether she was aware of the *liaison*. Catherine had in fact suspected it from hints Anjou had dropped and she saw at a glance that a pretence of complete surprise would only make matters worse. The King sent de Retz to fetch Margot and when he returned with her, the picture of injured innocence with a white robe flung over her shoulders and her hair streaming down her back, the King ordered him to post himself outside the door and let no one enter. Then, the room being

A miniature from a Book of Hours showing Charles IX with his new wife Elizabeth of Austria.

cleared of all but the family, Charles threw his sister to the ground and, aided by Catherine, beat her into insensibility.

His rage exhausted, he flung out of the room, leaving his mother to repair the damage they had done. It was daylight now. At all costs, Margot must not be seen in this condition at the *lever*. For an hour Catherine, with genuine solicitude, dressed her wounds, restored her dress, rearranged her hair and, as they faced the courtiers at the opening function of the day, they appeared their relaxed but inscrutable selves, purring with mutual affection.

Guise, at Margot's entreaty, had escaped by the window before Retz had arrived at the bedroom and had returned to the family mansion to give his uncle, the Cardinal of Lorraine, the unwelcome news. The Cardinal took a sufficiently grave view of the situation to write immediately to Guise's mother: 'Your son is in deep trouble here and you and I will share it.' He warned the Duke that he must be prepared to get married immediately, a solution on which everyone was agreed. The bride selected was one of Catherine's god-daughters, the recently widowed Princess of Porcien, whose eccentricity it was to have miniature pictures of her lovers painted as crucified in her Book of Hours. At the wedding banquet given at the Guise hôtel, (where the table was set with a hundred thousand crowns worth of silver and crystal belonging to the Cardinal of Lorraine) Anjou paid the bridegroom a series of elaborate compliments ending with a whispered aside: 'If you so much as look at my sister hereafter, you will get a knife between your ribs.' As for Margot, she took the first opportunity that presented itself to have de Guast assassinated.

'Margot'. Marguerite de Valois, youngest daughter of Catherine, wife of Henry of Navarre. Her nymphomania and intrigues alienated her mother.

The cleavage between Margot and Anjou was complicated by the emergence of Francis, Duke of Alençon, who was well described by a Spanish observer as 'a vicious little chap who says he is a Catholic but keeps himself surrounded by atheists.' In fact his ambition, as he confessed in a secret letter to Elizabeth of England, was 'to become leader of the Protestants of the world against all comers'. For this it was necessary first to become leader of the Huguenots in France and—if possible—to displace Anjou in the royal succession. Any principles he might ever have possessed were sacrificed to his ambition; and his natural dynastic envy of his elder brothers was reinforced by personal hatred because of their lack of sympathy for his sensitivity over his squat, pock-marked, bulbous-nosed appearance. He was thus an ideal instrument for Margot's campaign of vengeance against Henry and Catherine. By the mere act of giving him sympathy and understanding and lavishing on him in public to a point where there was court-gossip of incest, the affection she had once given to Henry of Anjou, she enslaved him completely. Francis of Alençon henceforth was to become little but the agent for Margot's designs.

The tensions with her mother were increased by Catherine's decision to marry her to Henry of Navarre and when the news was first given her, Margot made such scenes as to irritate Catherine intensely. For hours she lay crying, stretched comfortless on a wooden coffer, while her mother alternately stormed and coaxed. Sometimes she remained silent for days. She loathed the idea of the marriage for several reasons. For one thing she was still in love with Guise and now that he was married and back at Court she had every intention of arranging more—and this time much more careful—clandestine meetings. In the second place, she and Henry of Navarre had known each other during their growing-up at least well enough to be aware that they had no glimmer of sexual attraction for each other and even domestic accommodation was imperilled by such differences as her liking for at least one bath a day and his aversion to more than one a year. Also he always stank of garlic.

Eventually her mother won, as she had always done, and by the time the Queen of Navarre arrived in Paris to conclude arrangements for her son's marriage. Margot was ready to exercise the diplomacy of her house. On one thing, however, she remained adamant. When Jeanne asked her when she was going to change her religion, before or after the wedding, Margot replied: 'I have been brought up in the Catholic Faith and that I will never renounce, not even for the greatest monarch on earth.'

'That's not what I was told', said Jeanne. 'If I had known this I should not have come. I have been deceived' and wrote to Henry, who had remained in Navarre: 'Do not budge from Béarn until you get another letter from me. If you have started, invent some excuse and return home.'

She never saw him again. Before all the preliminaries had been settled the exasperating, indomitable woman was dead at the age of 43. A post-mortem revealed that she was in an advanced state of consumption and that one of her lungs had long been useless; when the head was opened several small sacs of water were found in it. The cause of death, in fact, was a sudden attack of pleurisy and of phthsis, aggravated by the fetid air of Paris.

The Huguenots announced that she had been poisoned. In the pamphlets they disseminated, they denied that the head had been opened and maintained that the examination of the body was only a blind, since the effects of poison sniffed through the nose could be detected only in the brain. Within a few days it was an article of faith among Calvinists that the Queen of Navarre had been murdered by Catherine de' Medici, using a subtle Italian poison by her official perfumier, René, with which a pair of gloves had been impregnated.

The day before she died, Jeanne sent for Coligny, who was at Châtillon, only a few hours' ride away and to his care she confided her son, beseeching Henry in her will 'to live all the course of his life according to God's Word and never permitting himself to be turned aside by the allurement of the pleasures of this world.'

Jeanne d'Albret, Queen of Navarre, who became Margot's mother-in-law.

The Massacre of
St. Bartholomew

Coligny's return to Court heralded a more intensive attempt on his part to induce the King to declare war on Spain. The plan tempted Charles if only because it would give him an opportunity to fulfil his greatest ambition—to emulate his father by leading a victorious military campaign and, in doing so, to detract from Anjou's reputation won at Jarnac and Montcontour. Coligny's most powerful ally, indeed, was Charles's jealousy of Henry which he took so little pains to hide that when the Court poet Dorat presented him with some complimentary verses the King struck the paper from his hand and shouted: 'This is nothing but lies and flatteries, for as yet I have done nothing that deserves praise. Henceforth write nothing for me. Keep your fine words—you and all the troop of *Messieurs les poètes*—for my brother.'

Catherine on her part, who had needed the Admiral's co-operation in the matter of the marriage, had told him bluntly: 'We are both of us too old to try to take one another in. I know that you do not trust me any more than I trust you. Have you not offended my son, the King, by taking up arms against him? Well, we will let that rest and I assure you that if you will now be his loyal servant you shall have my favour.' But now that the marriage was arranged and Jeanne was dead, Catherine saw no reason for further tactful pretences or for not considering Coligny as the enemy he in fact was. At all costs his attempts to involve France in a war with Spain which would inevitable lead to a defeat as disastrous as Pavia must be stopped.

Tavannes was present at the crucial interview when she reasserted her control over her son. 'The King goeth forth to hunt at Montpipeau', he left on record, 'and the Queen his mother hasteneth after him. Of a sudden she bursteth into tears. "After all the pains" quoth she, "that I had to bring you up and to preserve your crown—the crown which Huguenots and Catholics alike did their best to snatch from you—after having sacrificed myself for you and run a thousand dangers, how could I ever have dreamed that you would treat me so miserably? You wrench yourself from my arms which have guarded you to lean on the arms of those who once desired to kill you. I know that you hold secret counsels with the Admiral. I know that you wish to plunge us rashly into war with Spain. I know you offer your kingdom, yourself and your family as a prey to those of 'the Religion'. Grant me leave, I pray, before this grief cometh to pass to retire to the land of my birth. And send away also your brother who may indeed consider himself unfortunate in that he has spent his life to preserve yours. At least give him time to escape from the enemies he has made in your service—the Huguenots who, while they prate of war with Spain, really wish for another war in France and for the ruin of all states so that they alone may flourish".'

The King immediately capitulated 'asking pardon and promising obedience' and Coligny returned temporarily to Châtillon where his greatest consolation was his daily study of the Book of Job.

The Admiral came back to the capital at the beginning of July 1572 to welcome Henry of Navarre who was accompanied by eight hundred horsemen all in deep black for Jeanne d'Albret. Though the making of another marriage-contract, giving Henry his new style as King of Navarre, was speedily concluded, the actual date of the marriage could not be fixed because the bridegroom's uncle, the Cardinal of Bourbon, who was to perform the ceremony, refused to do so until the dispensation from Rome (which was necesssary because Henry and Margot were within the forbidden degrees) had not yet arrived.

That same week, one of the Huguenot leaders, the Sieur de Genlis, with a force of 4000 infantry and 800 cavalry, was leaving to join the rebels in the Netherlands. As many of the Huguenots visiting Paris went with him—and this, rather than the royal wedding, was the real object of their journey to the capital—the departure of the expedition kindled high hopes and higher emotions among those who were left. Genlis's anticipated victory would justify Coligny's war policy in the eyes of the court and Council and thus lead directly to the triumph of Huguenotism in France.

On July 21 news arrived that Alva's Spaniards had annihilated Genlis's force. Three thousand Huguenots were dead on the field and many others were slaughtered by the peasants. Genlis himself was among the six hundred prisoners.

'Poor Genlis!' was Coligny's only comment as he set to work to make redoubled efforts to induce the King to declare war on Spain. One thing was now in his favour. Catherine was away. She had left Paris at the end of July to visit her elder daughter, Claude, who had been taken ill as she was travelling to the wedding.

The Admiral took every advantage of the Queen-Mother's absence. He never left the King's side and played unceasingly on Charles's obsession for

Gaspard de Coligny at the time of the Massacre of St Bartholomew.

military glory. 'He was made absolute master of affairs', wrote the Venetian Ambassador, 'and the whole court followed in his wake.' He prevailed on Charles to call a secret council which lasted from eleven at night until two in the morning at which only himself, his Montmorency cousin who was leader of the *Politiques* and a Secretary of State were present and from which Anjou was carefully excluded.

The Secretary of State, however, was M. de Sauve, whose wife, Charlotte, was a leading member of Catherine's *Flying Squadron*. She immediately sent post-haste an urgent messenger to Catherine with the result that, on August 3, the Queen-Mother unexpectedly arrived back in Paris, exhausted and in a towering rage, in the face of which Charles, as usual, capitulated.

Having recovered her balance, she enquired of the Admiral his reasons for urging a war with Spain. He explained that he considered it wiser to unite France by a foreign war against a traditional enemy than to allow her again to drift into civil war. The moment was propitious. In the Low Countries France had traditional claims on Hainault, Flanders and Artois and the people there, oppressed by Spain would welcome an invasion in which the French could join forces with William of Orange whom they were already welcoming as a liberator. If the King of France made war as a friend of the land and an enemy of its enemies, as the avenger of tyranny and the restorer of liberty, the hearts of the Netherlands would be won and the rest would be easy. 'Besides', he concluded, 'war is inevitable, either now, when we are ready, or later, when Spain is ready.'

In reply, Catherine spoke directly to Charles, not even glancing at the Admiral. 'My son', she said, 'there is no proof whatever that King Philip's subjects in the Netherlands have any desire to submit to you and it is certain, whatever claims the lawyers may draw up, that Flanders and Artois are hostile to France. If you won those territories you could only hold them at such a vast expense that you would have to tax them more heavily than they are taxed now in order to make both ends meet. In any case, an attack on Spain would mean a long and bloody war which would reduce us to poverty and we are not likely to win such a war because King Philip is wise, powerful and rich. William of Orange may have an army, but he has no money and without money no army can move. As for saying that we and Spain must some time fight, it is impossible to foresee the future in that respect.'

Unable to resist her logic, the King announced that in no circumstances would he countenance a war against Spain.

Coligny said: 'But Your Majesty will not take it ill, I trust, if, having promised the Prince of Orange every aid and favour, I attempt to keep that promise wich such friends, relatives and servants as I can, and even with my own person?'

Charles did not reply and the Admiral turned to Catherine with: 'Madame, the King refuses to enter on one war. God grant that another may not befall him which which he will not have it in his power to withdraw.'

To this threat of a new Huguenot rebellion, Catherine answered simply: 'Though you have filled the land with your soldiers, my son is still able to govern in peace.'

Coligny wrote to William of Orange that despite Genlis's defeat and the hesitations of the French Council he was bestirring himself and could promise 12,000 harquebusiers and 3000 horse. There were already 3000 Huguenots on the frontier, who would soon be reinforced by those who had assembled for the approaching wedding.

Meanwhile Paris was full to overflowing. It seemed to the Parisians, explosive with hatred, that every Huguenot in France had invaded the capital and with them many soldiers come to enlist under Coligny and students taking this opportunity to enlarge their education by studying the French Court. Every lodging was crammed. Unendurable tensions, combined with the stifling air of August, made it imperative to get the wedding over as soon as possible and as the dispensation had still not arrived, it was decided to proceed without it and the date was fixed for Monday August 18, whether or not permission arrived. The one danger was that Catholic Paris, which was clinging as a last straw to the hope that the Pope would forbid the hated marriage, might riot if the truth were discovered. Catherine regretted more than ever that her original attempt to have the ceremony in the royal chapel at Blois, where the crowds would have been negligible because of the limited accommodation, had been over-ruled by Jeanne who considered that it would have been an insult to the house of Navarre. However she did what she could. She wrote to the Governor of Lyons, a city through which any messengers would pass on their way from Italy to France: 'M. de Mandelot, I write you this brief letter to tell you that, insomuch as you love serving the King my son you are to allow to pass no courier coming from Rome until Monday be past. And do it as secretly as you can without giving rise to any rumours.'

On August 18, a stiflingly hot day, the crowds were able to witness the actual wedding because, since it was a mixed-marriage—at which there had been protests from all the pulpits of Paris for weeks—the ceremony was performed outside Notre Dame. The King of France and the King of Navarre, Anjou and Alençon and young Condé were all dressed alike as a sign of perpetual amity in suits of primrose-coloured satin, covered with raised silver embroidery, 'enriched with pearls and precious stones.' Anjou's dislike of conventional conformity was expressed in his cap, in which he wore thirty-two pearls worth twenty-three thousand gold crowns.

Margot herself was elaborately dressed in purple velvet, with a cape of spotted ermine which covered the front of her bodice, 'I shone with crown jewels', she noted, 'and glistened in my wide blue mantle with its four yards of train.' Catherine, for once laying aside her usual mourning, was in velvet of a darker shade than her daughter's.

When the Cardinal of Bourbon put to the bride the question of her consent to have Navarre for her husband she did not reply. The spectators saw Guise —who by reason of his great height was easily distinguishable—gaze at her

This detail of a tapestry in the Uffizi Gallery in Florence shows (left to right) Henry of Navarre, Margot, and Catherine, at the time of Margot's wedding to Henry, where she had almost to be dragged to the altar.

intently. As she returned the look and still said nothing, her brother the King stepped forward and angrily pushed her head down in token of assent.

That evening Coligny wrote to his wife: 'Today was concluded the marriage of the King's sister with the King of Navarre. The next three or four days will be passed in pleasure, in banquets in masques, in ballets and tourneys; after which the King (so he assures me) will devote several days to the hearing of the complaints which arise in many parts of the kingdom because of the violation of the Edict. In this matter I am constrained to labour to the utmost of my power. I had far rather be with you than stay at Court, but we must put the public good before our private happiness. As for the rest all I have to say at the moment is that it was past four o'clock this afternoon before the nuptial Mass had been said; and in the meantime the King of Navarre and I, with certain gentlemen of our Religion strolled outside the church.'

During their ostentatious 'stroll' to demonstrate their refusal even to enter the Cathedral while Mass was in progress, they pretended not to hear the vociferous insults of the crowd, and when the service was over and they went to fetch the bride Coligny pointed out to an English Envoy those banners from Jarnac and Montcontour which had not been sent to Rome but kept to hang in the nave of Notre Dame, and remarked: 'In a short time these will be torn down and replaced by others better to see.'

The Englishman suggested that, as far as he had been able to judge, Frenchmen were by no means united on the advisability of war with Spain.

'He who prevents the Spanish war', retorted the Admiral, 'is no true Frenchman but has a red cross [the emblem of Spain] in his belly.'

'In the days after my sister's wedding', Anjou confided to his diary, 'my mother and I noticed three or four times that when the Admiral had a private interview with the King (which happened frequently, the two of them holding long conferences alone), if we were approached the King when he had left, we found him strangely moody and impatient, harsh in his manner and more so in his replies, which were not such as he was accustomed to make to my mother nor expressed with the respect and honour he ordinarily showed her. After comparing all our impressions, observations and suspicions and our memory of past incidents, we were all but certain that the Admiral had given the King certain sinister opinions of us and we determined there and then to be rid of him and to arrange the means with Madame de Nemours, the only person in whom we thought we could confide because of hatred for him.'

The Duchess of Nemours had been before her second marriage the Duchess of Guise, wife of the murdered Duke. The Duchess, during the wedding festivities, had been living in a house near the Louvre which, in earlier years, the Guises had provided for the tutor of the present Duke and his younger brothers. Its front entrance was on the street by which the Admiral was accustomed to return to the du Bourg mansion, which he had rented, in the Rue de Béthisy a few hundred yards further on.

The Duchess and her son had often discussed the possibility of accomplishing their long-delayed vengeance by shooting Coligny from one of the windows of the house and when she had asked who should fire the shot, he had always said: 'That honour, Mother, should surely be yours.' She had refused, not on any humanitarian grounds—for life had hardened her into something far other than the sensitive girl whose tears Catherine had had to reprove during the executions at Amboise twelve years ago—but because she did not consider herself a good enough shot. Guise himself, though for years his one desire had been to kill his father's murderer in battle or in a duel, would not violate his rigid code of honour by himself resorting to

Ambroise Paré, surgeon to Charles IX, who successfully extracted the bullet from Admiral Coligny's arm.

assassination—though he was at this moment for political reasons prepared to condone it—and now that the Queen-Mother had approved this method of ridding France and herself of the Admiral, the question of the gunman called for immediate decision.

On Wednesday, August 20, the Duchess moved to the Hôtel de Lorraine so that Guise might instal in the empty house the best marksman among his retainers whom he summoned from Joinville and who arrived in Paris on the Thursday. On Friday, which marked the end of the wedding-festivities and the resumption of the work of the Council, Coligny was shot but, as he happened to bend down to adjust an uncomfortable over-shoe just as the marksman fired, he was only slightly wounded and was able, assisted by his friends, to walk home to his lodging.

The King was playing tennis with Guise and Téligny, Coligny's son-in-law, when the news was brought to him. Flinging down his racquet with a string of his usual blasphemous oaths, he shrieked: 'Am I never to have any

A bas-relief of the school of Bernard Palissy.

peace?' and hurried to his private study and refused to see anyone for the rest of the morning, after sending his own surgeon, Ambroise Paré to the Admiral. Guise took immediate refuge in the Hôtel de Lorraine and Téligny rushed to the bed-side of his father-in-law.

Catherine was about to dine when she received the news. Without a word or any change of countenance, she left the table and sent word to Anjou to meet her in the garden of the Tuileries. As was her habit she trusted only the open air and the evidence of her eyes that no one was within earshot when dangerous matters were to be discussed.

In a corner of her new garden she had created a little world of fantasy, a grotto guarded by yews cut to resemble Adam and Eve and approached by paths scented by thyme, marjoram and rosemary. The surrounding flower-beds were embellished by Bernard Palissy's wonderful enamel creations—toads, snakes and fabulous reptiles as well as life-sized men, curiously attired—which she and the designer had placed there. This spot she regarded as

213

'far enough removed from the crowd to be most suitable for a council' and here Anjou, accompanied by Tavannes and Retz met her to discuss how to retrieve the dangerous situation. With the Admiral wounded but not dead, anything could happen.

They still had reached no conclusion when the Sieur de Bouchavannes, Catherine's most trusted secret agent who so successfully posed as a Huguenot that he was in Coligny's confidence, arrived with the news that the King intended to visit the Admiral at half-past two. At Anjou's suggestion they hurriedly prepared themselves to accompany him.

Meanwhile, in the three hours since the assassination attempt, the house in the Rue de Béthisy (on the site of what is now 144 Rue de Rivoli) had become a focal point of Paris. Huguenots with drawn swords hastened to it from every quarter, forming an unofficial guard about it, and over two hundred 'captains and gentlemen', including Montgoméry, upon whom the military leadership of the Huguenots would fall in the case of Coligny's death, had crowded into the house itself, noisily discussing plans of vengeance.

When the royal party arrived, Charles went to Coligny's bedside and embraced him with genuine emotion, saying: '*Mon père*, though you have the wound, I have the perpetual pain. I renounce my salvation if I do not take so terrible a vengeance that it will be remembered for ever.' He explained that he had already set up a tribunal for the full investigation of the circumstances and that two people found in the house from which the shot had been fired had already been arrested.

'I suspect no one', said Coligny, 'but M. de Guise.'

'Who was playing tennis with me when the shot was fired', said Charles.

'But the real assassin', said Catherine, 'does not always fire the shot.'

'Nevertheless' said the King, 'M. de Guise will be questioned.'

'My only regret', said Coligny, 'is that my wound should prevent me working for Your Majesty at such a time. The war in Flanders is begun. Do not disown it, sire. Do not force us to break faith with the Prince of Orange. And your Edict is being violated every day. It is a disgrace . . .'

'We will put everything to rights, *mon père*, and I have already sent Commissioners into the Provinces.'

Coligny asked that he might have private speech with the King. 'The King made a motion to my mother and myself to withdraw', reported Anjou, 'which we did, standing in the middle of the room for their private talk,' Eventually Catherine went over to the bed and interrupted the conversation, with: 'You must leave the Admiral to rest, my son!'

'This is the bullet which M. Paré has taken out of his arm', said Charles, showing it to her.

Catherine took it in her hand and estimated its weight.

'I am very glad', she said slowly to Coligny, 'that it has not been left inside you, for I remember when M. de Guise was murdered near Orléans, the doctors told me more than once that if the bullet had been extracted, even though it was poisoned, there would have been no danger of his death.'

With this, the Royal party left and, once in the street again, Catherine walked beside Charles the short way back to the Louvre asking inexorably: 'What did he say to you, my son? What did he say?'

Just as they reached the gates of the palace, the King's nerve broke and he screamed at her: '*Mordieu*, Madame, since you insist on knowing, the Admiral said I was never to trust you, that in your hands all my power has gone to pieces and that great evil for me and my kingdom will come of it. That is what he said.' And with another oath Charles rushed away from her and shut himself in his study once more.

On the way to it he met Guise who had come to ask his permission to leave Paris. 'Go where you like, to Hell if you want' said the King, his face twitching. 'I shall know how to find you if I want you'. So Guise left the city in some state by the Porte-Sainte-Antoine on the road to his grandmother's at Joinville and as soon as it was dark doubled back quickly with only one attendant and returned to the Hôtel de Lorraine.

In the Rue de Béthisy, Coligny held a Council of War at which Boucha-vannes was present and was subsequently able to give Catherine the details of what decisions were come to. The Huguenot plan to take Paris, occupy the Louvre and capture the King had received by Coligny's wounding a set-back and the date now set for the attempt was August 26, though Téligny had argued hotly for its postponement to the 30th to give more time both for the Admiral's recuperation and for 'recruits' to be brought into the capital. But the council was unanimous that every opportunity should be taken im-mediately to heighten the tension in the city.

Within an hour armed bands of Huguenots were parading the streets demanding justice and indulging in scuffles with the retainers of Guise. Shops were hastily closed and barricaded against trouble and Armand de Pilles and Jean de Pardaillan, who in the late rebellion had held St. Jean d'Angely against the King, swaggered into the Louvre, brawling with the King's Guard who, according to instructions, tried to stop them, so that they might be the first at the *coucher* to demand vengeance on Guise.

The King did his best to secure order. He placed fifty of his own Guard in the Rue de Béthisy, across which chains were now stretched, and had the houses near that of Coligny (who refused the reiterated offer of safety in the Louvre) filled exclusively with Huguenots. He ordered each Alderman to have the city-gate for which he was responsible manned by ten responsible citizens 'to see and learn who shall enter and who pass out and with what arms and force'. He reinforced the civic authority by military backing. The Captain of Archers with all his men guarded the Hôtel de Ville, and the Captain of the Royal Guard with a strong detachment the tower on the Quai St. Bernard containing the city's supply of gunpowder, and a cannon was placed on the Place de Grève. Finally, in order to have some idea as to where, should these precautions fail to preserve order, rioting was most likely to occur, the King ordered a list to be made of all the houses at which the visiting Huguenots were lodging.

All the instructions were obeyed, but the tensions did not ease. Early next morning, Saturday 23 August, the King was informed that during the night armed men had been roving the streets. 'What is happening?' he said. 'The people in an uproar and arming! What of my orders?' He sent Anjou, as Lieutenant-General, to make a tour of Paris in his coach so that he could obtain a first-hand impression of the state of the capital.

Catherine had at last made her decision. Though she still shrank from the idea of murder, she had been forced to realise that had she followed Alva's advice at Bayonne and deprived the rebels of their leaders, tens of thousands of dead Frenchmen would still be alive and the pitiful countryside unscarred by the 'war of devils'. Now her knowledge of the Huguenot plot made action imperative. The ethics of assassination were banished by the intrusion of political necessity. To save the throne and the country a lightning counter-stroke was essential. She herself would have been prepared to accept no more than half-a-dozen 'salmon'. The number could even be reduced to three— Coligny, Montgoméry and the Vîdame de Chartres, for Henry of Navarre and young Condé must not of course be touched—and Catherine in later years always insisted that she had on her conscience only five or six Huguenots. But before any details could be settled, the King must be convinced. He alone could initiate action.

A short while after noon, Catherine, with Anjou, Retz, Tavannes and Biragues, waited on him with details of the Huguenot plan. At first he refused to believe it, saying angrily: 'Only the greatest fool in the world would believe that a Huguenot plot would begin by trying to kill the Admiral.'

Tavannes explained that that was a mere coincidence. 'We all know M. de Guise's blood-feud with the Admiral, sire', he said. 'It happened that the wedding offered the occasion.'

Retz then gave an account of the Huguenot conference of the previous day, reporting the arguments which had taken place between those who advised an immediate attack on the Louvre with what forces were at present in Paris and those who favoured the removal of Coligny to Châtillon so that, as soon as he had fully recovered, he might raise another rebellion in the

René de Biragues, Chancellor of France; a medal by Germain Pilon.

country. Biragues followed with details of the thousands of Germans and
Calvinist Swiss Coligny was recruiting. He included in his report the exact
number from each commune and the source of sums available for payment.
Anjou elaborated the intended seizure and possible murder of the Royal
family.

Charles, who had been dazed by the statistics he could not contradict
(since they had been taken from the Admiral's files by Petrucci, the Florentine
colleague of Bouchavannes) broke out into a passionate repudiation: 'It is all
a lie. The Admiral loves me as if I were his son. He would do nothing to
harm me.'

'Have you forgotten so soon', said Catherine, 'how he tried to take us all at Meaux and how we fled through the night to escape him? And how you wept at the shame of it?'

Charles, who could never bear the episode mentioned, said: '*Mordieu,* Madame, be silent!'

'How can I be silent at such a moment when your life and your kingdom are at stake? Will nothing cure your blindness? Cannot you see why the Admiral tries to make you distrust me?'

Charles saw clearly enough even if he would not admit it and the realisation of Coligny's cozening of him brought him near to tears. He said 'What do you advise me to do?'

Tavannes, according to his own account, answered by a question: 'What do you do, sire, when in the chase a wounded boar turns on you?'

'You know well enough, Marshal. I take my firmest stance, await him and stab him in the throat with my sword.'

'You must regard the Admiral, sire, as the boar.'

'I have given my word for his safety. I will not have him touched. I will not have him touched. I will have justice done. My troops shall guard the city and the enquiry shall be continued until the attacker of the Admiral is found.'

Catherine played her last card. 'And when the enquiry sifts all the evidence who do you think will be left behind the attack?'

'M. de Guise, of course.'

'And behind M. de Guise?'

'Who should be behind M. de Guise? We all know that his house—'

'I', Catherine interrupted, 'am behind M. de Guise.'

Charles stared at her incredulously. '*You!* But why—why?'

'If I have given France a king so worthless as to plunge his kingdom into ruin, I must make what amends I can to save us all.'

For seconds that seemed to those watching an infinity, mother and son looked at each other. Then the King lowered his eyes and muttered: 'I will not have the Admiral touched. I will not—' Suddenly his voice broke into an hysterical scream and a thin foam of blood appeared on his lips as he gave his authorisation: 'Kill the Admiral if you wish; but you must also kill all the Huguenots, so that not one is left alive to reproach me. Kill them all! Kill them all! Kill them all!'

'If till this hour', Anjou recorded, 'it had been hard to persuade my brother, our difficulty now was to restrain him.' The distracted King, in his anger, his alarm and above all his disillusion, would indeed have killed every Huguenot in Paris, whereas Catherine wished to kill only their leaders and Anjou wanted only to ensure that, after the death of Coligny, on which everyone was agreed, his troops could contain any insurrection. Retz, Biragues and

Charles IX; engraving by Moncornet.

Tavannes, on the other hand, urged a general massacre. Throughout the afternoon the discussion continued until, about five o'clock, the King summoned Marcel and Le Charron, the past and present Provosts of Paris and explained to them that proof had come into his hands that 'those belonging to the new Religion intended to rise against him and the State and to disturb the repose of his subjects and of his city of Paris.' Therefore for the safety of his family and his subjects and for the 'peace, repose and tranquillity and the kingdom and the city' and to prevent the said conspiracy from succeeding, the King instructed Marcel to organise as many loyal Catholic citizens as possible to reinforce the military. Every man capable of bearing arms was to arm himself and to 'stand ready' in their own districts and at all the cross-roads of the city. In order that they might know each other in case of a *mêlée,* each man was to wear an armlet of white linen on his left arm and a white cross on his hat.

To Le Charron, as the Provost in office, the King gave additional instructions. He was to take possession of all the keys of all the gates of the city, being careful that no one should enter or leave, and he was to see that all the boats on the Seine were drawn up and fastened with chains so that no one could cross to the Left Bank and thus have freedom to escape to the open country of the south.

Finally, every Catholic house was to have a light burning in the window.

It was nearly midnight when Marcel and Le Charron returned to the Louvre to inform the King that all his instructions had been carried out and that the city was alert and guarded by loyal citizens. Charles then issued his final orders. He explained to them that Montgoméry had been ordered by Coligny to collect 4000 men and next Tuesday, the 26th, Huguenots were to enter the Louvre in small bodies, so as to escape notice and at mid-day when the guard was careless, one of their number was to present an insulting memorial from Coligny which was calculated to throw the King into a passion.

'And when I' said Charles, 'answer this as it deserves, I am to be set upon and slain, with my brothers, my wife and my mother and the rest of the Court, every Huguenot having arranged beforehand which of us he shall kill. It is to avert this that we must strike first. This you will make known to the loyal citizens and you will tell them that when they hear the usual dawn-tocsin sound from the Hôtel de Ville it is my wish that they should take what measures they see fit.'

And with this licence to kill, he dismissed them to disseminate the news, which was received by the Parisians 'with great joy'.

In the Louvre that midnight, Margot was the only member of the family who was in ignorance of what was happening. 'I was at the *coucher* of the

Queen my mother', she wrote, 'sitting on a chest with my sister of Lorraine, who was very depressed, when my mother spoke to me and sent me to bed. As I was making my curtsey, my sister caught me by the sleeve and detained me. She began to weep and said '*Mon Dieu*', sister, you must not go. My mother, noticing it, called my sister and spoke to her sharply, forbidding her to say anything to me. I learnt afterwards that my sister said it was not right to send me away like that to be sacrificed because, if they discovered anything, they would probably avenge themselves on me. My mother replied that, God willing, I should come to no harm; but in any case I must go for fear of awakening their suspicions. I could see they were arguing, though I could not catch the words. My mother then sharply commanded me to retire. Then the King my husband sent me word that I should come to bed, which I did. I found his bed surrounded by thirty or forty Huguenots, who as yet were strangers to me as I had been married only a few days. All night long they talked of the accident to the Admiral, deciding to go to the King as soon as it was day and demand justice on M. de Guise and, if it were denied them, to take it into their own hands.'

About midnight, most of the Huguenots in the Louvre started to go back to their lodgings in the city. Almost the last was La Rochefoucauld who had been spending much of the evening with King Charles. As his friend began to make his *adieux*, the King, anxious to save him, pleaded: 'Don't go, Foucauld. It's very late. Let's go on talking for the rest of the night.'

'One's got to sleep sometime', said La Rochefaucauld, yawning.

'In that case, stay here and sleep with my *valets de chambre*.'

'Their feet stink. Good-bye, *petit maître*.' And La Rochefoucauld went back to his lodgings in the Rue Saint Honoré, after spending an hour with his mistress, the widow of Prince Louis de Condé.

The remainder of the dark hours passed slowly. Charles, intolerably restless, suddenly sent for the Bishop of Orléans, who was asleep in bed. The Bishop, though a member of the Council, had been absent from the recent discussions and when he was now told of the Huguenot plot, 'such fear seized his heart' that he sat down 'quite stunned' and for a time was unable to speak 'for want of breath'.

Charles told him of the counter-measures and asked his judgment on them. He 'wept and sighed' and eventually said that 'if indeed what was reported was true, then all Huguenots should be killed in accordance with the King's wish.'

Suddenly a pistol shot was heard. There was no means of telling what it was or who had fired it but 'the mere sound so wounded us and entered so deep into our spirits'—the words are Anjou's—'that it did hurt both our senses and our reason.'

The Cour Carée of the Palace of the Louvre, where the royal family remained throughout the events of St Bartholomew.

Catherine, in a panic lest a Huguenot rising might after all have forestalled them, sent over to St. Germain l'Auxerrois across the road—the parish church of the Louvre—an order that the three silver bells in the south tower were to be rung immediately. It was two hours before the dawn-tocsin would be sounded from the Hôtel de Ville, but she dared not wait.

It was half past two in the morning of Sunday 24 August, the feast of St. Bartholomew.

As soon as the church bells sounded, Guise with his uncle Aumale set out for the Rue de Béthisy with a small force of Guise retainers and the Swiss Guard, wearing Anjou's colours. The Colonel of the Royal Guard was still on duty there, but he had received from the Louvre instructions that his rôle was now changed and that he was not required to protect Coligny but rather to aid his attackers if necessary.

One of Navarre's Swiss was patrolling the courtyard of the house when Guise arrived and explained that he had been sent by the King to visit the Admiral. The Swiss unlocked the gate and was at once killed by the Colonel's dagger. As the attackers streamed across the courtyard, the rest of Navarre's Swiss, realising the position, started to barricade the staircase with coffers, chests and wardrobes so that, when at last the outer door was broken down, the intruders found themselves in front of a blocked stairway defended by several Protestant Swiss whom Anjou's Catholic Swiss, putting nationality before religion, refused to attack. At this point the Colonel appeared once more. Brandishing his sword, he ordered one of his harquebusiers to shoot a defending Swiss, who fell 'stricken stark dead out of hand'. The others were similarly dealt with; the barrier was broken down and the troop of armed men, led by Jan Yanowitz, a young Bohemian in Guise's service, made their way up to the Admiral's room, which was the third on the first floor.

In the grey half-light preceding dawn they could not see Coligny's features and Besme (as he was known because of his nationality) demanded: 'Are you the Admiral?'

'I am, and you should respect my age and my wounds. At least let me be killed by a gentleman and not a blackguardly boy like you.'

They were his last words. With seven dagger wounds, Coligny fell dead against the chimney-piece. In the courtyard below, Guise and Aumale heard the noise of the fall and Guise called out loudly: 'Besme, is it done?'

Opposite: *The first attempt to assassinate Gaspard de Coligny, by shooting him; this is the right-hand half of the picture on page 228.*

Overleaf: *Painting by François Dubois of the Massacre of St. Bartholomew on 24 August 1572.*

'It is done', shouted Besme and threw the body out of the window for his master to identify it. The corpse fell at Guise's feet. The face was so blood-covered that the Duke had to dismount to wipe it with a piece of linen before he and Aumale could recognise it.

At that moment the great bell sounded from the Hôtel de Ville and with the dawn the streets leapt to life.

'Now for Montgoméry!' said Guise, as he led his men away.

One of Anjou's guard put the Admiral's body in the stables of the house, while upstairs Petrucci who had accompanied the murderers took immediate possession of all Coligny's files, the whereabouts of which he knew. The documents revealed that the plot was even better organised and more dangerous than Bouchavannes had been able to discover. It extended to the setting-up of 'a republic within the kingdom' and Henry of Navarre himself was to have been murdered with the rest of the royal family to make way for Coligny as head of it.

In the Louvre Charles sent for Navarre and Condé and offered them their lives on condition that they returned to 'the Catholic Faith into which we have all been baptised.' In their replies the blood of their fathers was apparent in the cousins. Henry of Navarre, as charming and complaisant as Antony, was 'as meek as a little lamb', but Henry of Condé, who was only sixteen, had inherited the valour of the little hunchback, Louis, and said: 'I cannot believe, sire, that Your Majesty can break the promise you have so solemnly sworn in the Edicts. Religion cannot be commanded. My life and my pos-sessions are in your hands and you may do what you will with them, but the fear of death will never make me change my faith.'

La Rochefoucauld was killed in his lodgings by the brother of Chicot, the King's jester. Téligny was shot as he tried to escape over the roof of his house next to the Admiral's. But Montgoméry, with about sixty leading Huguenots, including the Vîdame de Chartres, who were all lodging on the Left Bank, managed to escape into the open country and, though Guise and his men followed them in a whirlwind pursuit and managed to shoot many of them, Montgoméry himself, mounted on a particularly fast Spanish jennet, managed to escape.

In the Rue de Béthisy, the Paris mob, now thoroughly aroused, took the body of the Admiral from the stable where it lay. It was kicked, spat upon and mutilated—castrated, decapitated and the right breast and arm hacked off—and dragged to the gallows at Montfaucon where it was hung in chains, with a horse's tail fixed where the head had been. Many of those who thus insulted

Opposite: *Two days after he was first shot at, Coligny is successfully assas-sinated on the instructions of the King, and his body is abused.*

the dead body were women and children, who numbered at least three hundred. The men had other work to do.

With all law and order at an end, the hordes of thieves and professional murderers lurking in the hovels of the closely packed streets emerged to acquire unimagined booty. The word 'Huguenot' had meaning only as an excuse for killing. Every feud, every private grudge, every law-suit and money-quarrel, every rivalry in love and every obsession of hatred, could now be resolved by murder. Debtors sought out their creditors, merchants their competitors, academics their rivals. Huguenots and Catholics were impartially slaughtered.

A world-famous Greek lecturer of the University of Paris was killed by an envious lecturer who wanted his Chair and the body given to the rival's students who dealt with it in such a fashion that one who saw their handiwork fainted in horror. The students, predictably, were the worst of the mob. One of their sports was to kill a pregnant woman, disembowel her and beat the embryo to pulp. But there were more mature ruffians, like the goldsmith who 'showing his naked arm boasted that that arm had cut the throats of 400 men that morning' and the printer who superintended deaths of booksellers and binders by suspending them over a fire made of their books and, when they were half-dead cutting them down and drowning them in the Seine.

Though plunder was the prime motive of the mob, killing for killing's sake was not despised. Two thousand people were killed that morning and, according to Tavannes, 'there was no alley in Paris, however small, in which they did not assassinate someone.' In the narrow streets leading down to the river there were 'torrents of blood as if it had rained heavily' and 'blood and death ran through the streets in such horror that His Majesty himself could hardly keep from fear in the Louvre.'

At half-past-ten, Marcel and Le Charron sought an audience to urge that the defensive measures taken the previous evening to forestall a Huguenot rising no longer applied to the promiscuous carnage and pillage in which it seemed that the whole of Paris was taking part. The mob was totally out of control.

'They are killing everybody', said Marcel, 'stripping them naked, dragging them through the streets, plundering the houses and sparing not even the children.'

Charles ordered the immediate disarming of all who had been called to arms the night before and by the patrolling of the streets by the military. But as the citizens and the soldiers were all now indiscriminately assassins and looters, the order was useless and the King began to fear the demon he had roused.

Only Catherine remained unshaken. The Savoy Ambassador who had an interview with her at mid-day wrote to his master: 'She looks a younger woman by ten years and gives the impression of one who has recovered from a serious illness or escaped a great danger.' She was the first to acknowledge it. 'I have never before', she told him, 'been in a situation where I had so great a reason for feeling terrified and from which I have escaped with greater gratitude.'

The envoy suggested that the price she had paid might by some be considered excessive.

'It was better that it should fall on them than on us' she replied. 'What has been done is no more than is necessary.'

On the Monday, it seemed that Heaven agreed with her. A hawthorn planted at the foot of a statue of Our Lady, in a cemetery, which for the last four years had shown neither fruit, flower nor even a leaf, suddenly burst into flower. The crowds flocking to see it, crying 'A miracle! A miracle!' were soon so great that guards had to be placed round the cemetery. Church bells rang and people went through the city, beating drums and crying out that 'the Catholic religion and the Kingdom would now flower anew and recover their past splendour'. An Italian visitor reported, in a letter written the following day, how he had seen it 'covered with flowers', adding: 'I piously touched it with my rosary.' Later in the day the 'Thorn of the Holy Innocents' was visited by the King, with his mother, his brothers and his sisters as well as several noblemen 'each of whom made it his duty to pay his devotions to the image of Our Lady'. Soon three Masses were said there every day and crowds of the sick came to touch the Thorn for healing. Many, it was testified, were cured.

The same day—through which the killing sporadically continued—the King wrote to the various provincial governors reporting the massacre and, lest there might be other similar outbreaks 'at which I should feel a wonderful regret', ordered them to ensure the strict maintenance of the Edict and see that 'none take up arms but that all remain quietly in their houses.'

In the greater part of France, he was obeyed. In Champagne and Burgundy, which were under the strong rule of Guise and his uncle Aumale, there was not a single murder. (In Paris, Guise himself on his return from his abortive pursuit of Montgoméry, had busied himself in saving Huguenots and given over a hundred of them refuge in the Hôtel de Lorraine). And Lower Normandy was kept calm under the rule of Matignon in whom Catherine confided more than in any of the governors of provinces. But in Meaux, Troyes, Orléans, Bourges, Angers, Lyons, Rouen, Toulouse, Bordeaux and other cities where religious feeling ran high, massacres took place, sometimes three or four weeks after St. Bartholomew's Day.

The total number killed is difficult to estimate but, as Lord Acton said, 'no evidence takes us as high as 8,000' (Huguenot propagandists put it at 110,000) and the most probably estimate is 7,000 for the whole of France, of which between 2,500 and 3,000 were in Paris.

The reception of the news abroad depended on the varying religious predispositions. Philip of Spain necessarily applauded it and is said to have laughed for the only recorded time in his life. The Pope ordered an immediate *Te Deum,* 'rendered to God the thanks due for so happy a success,' commissioned Giorgio Vasari, Catherine's friend who had painted her portrait just before she left Florence for her marriage, to paint a series of scenes to hang in the Vatican as a reminder of the Church's deliverance from a dire peril, and eventually struck a commemorative medal. In Geneva, Beza spoke of it as 'that horrible and most execrable massacre, a cruelty so barbarous and inhuman that as long as the world shall be the world and after the world has perished, so long shall the authors of this enterprise be held in perpetual execration'. And Elizabeth of England, anxious to maintain a diplomatic neutrality, tactfully supposed the event to be 'some strange accident'.

Catherine herself, speaking with formal dignity to the Venetian Ambassador, pronounced what was both the objective truth and her own self-justification: 'I wish to advise you that I have done nothing, counselled nothing and permitted nothing except what the honour of God and my duty and love for my children command, since the Admiral, ever since the death of my husband, King Henry II, has shown by his acts that he was aiming at the subversion of the state. The King my son has done what became his dignity and, as the Admiral was so strong, so powerful in this kingdom, he could be punished for his rebellion in no other way than that which we were constrained to take both against him personally and against those who were his partisans; and we deeply regret that, in the commotion, a number of other persons of his religion were killed by the Catholics who were smarting from the infinite afflictions, pillage, murder and other wrongs that had been inflicted on them.'

Theodore Beza described the Massacre as 'a cruelty so barbarous and inhuman that as long as the world shall be the world and after the world has perished so long shall the authors of this enterprise be held in perpetual execration'.

Queen-Regent once more

Of the practical results of the massacre there was no doubt at all. The fourth Huguenot rebellion started immediately. From La Rochelle the Calvinists hurled defiance at the Crown. The Rochellois wrote to Elizabeth of England offering to acknowledge her 'their sovereign queen and natural princess' if she would protect 'her people of that Guienne which had belonged to her from all eternity.' All that came of the suggestion was the sending of Montgoméry, who after his escape had taken refuge in England, with a small fleet to keep open the sea-approaches to La Rochelle.

Catherine's diplomatic counter-stroke was to persuade La Noue, a Huguenot leader of such unquestioned integrity that he was known as 'the Bayard of the Religion' to accept the post of Royal Governor of La Rochelle. As a long-term plan to neutralise England, she began to negotiate for a marriage between the Virgin Queen and Alençon.

As the Rochellois refused either to accept La Noue, whom they regarded as a traitor, or to negotiate with the King (who offered them total freedom of worship in La Rochelle) on the grounds that 'it was impious to enter into any compact with murderers', Charles and his mother 'resolved on making a great effort for the destruction of the last haunt of heresy' and sent the army, under the command of Anjou, to reduce the city. With him in camp were Navarre and Condé—now both practising Catholics—and Alençon, already determined to bid for Coligny's place as leader of the Huguenots and doing his utmost to procure a victory for the Rochellois. He tried unsuccessfully to persuade Navarre and Condé to join him in inducing the four hundred or so ex-Huguenots in camp to organise a general revolt and desert to the defenders. When they refused on the grounds of the stupidity and certain failure of such a plan, he went up to Paris and with engaging simplicity asked Catherine to persuade the King to put him in command of the fleet blockading La Rochelle. Were this granted he could, so he imagined, join Montgoméry and, having raised the siege, sail for England. Catherine, though she did not at that point

—as far as can be ascertained—suspect such treasonable intentions, asked him what had put such an idea in his head and assured him he was much too young for such a command.

He replied that he was tired of always being ignored in favour of Anjou. 'Your precious Henry was no older than I am when you and the King made him Lieutenant-General of the Realm', he sobbed (no one except Henry of Navarre could so easily produce tears on any occasion) and went to seek consolation from Margot.

It was Margot's brain which made Alençon dangerous. She set to work to weld together widely differing forces into a coherent company—her husband; his subjects in Navarre; the four Montmorency brothers, sons of the old Constable, who led the *Politiques;* Louis of Nassau, brother of William of Orange, just over the eastern boundary of France; Montgoméry and the Rochellois. As her trusted agents she chose two of Alençon's favourites, the Provençal Comte Boniface de Lérac de la Mole, a notable debauchee, and the Piedmontese Comte Annibal de Coconnas, a paid spy for Spain whose wanton cruelty in the massacre had earned him Catholic contempt as well as Huguenot hatred. Possibly to ensure efficiency, Margot took de la Mole as her lover.

Her ultimate objective was to make it possible for Alençon to displace Anjou as Charles's successor to the throne. A change in Huguenot propaganda made such a strategy feasible. As it was now essential for the Huguenots to ally themselves with the *Politiques* who were at least nominally Catholic, the emphasis had to be shifted from the religious to the political. Religion had never been, except in special cases, anything but a convenient cloak for a secular revolution. Now the pretence was abandoned even in theory. Francis Hotman, a professor of Roman Law in exile at Geneva, had written a book *Franco-Gallia* to prove that the French crown was elective, not hereditary, and that the States-General had the power both to choose and to depose the King; and this was now accepted as the basis of Huguenot policy. The circumstances of the time were propitious. Anjou had just obtained the elective crown of Poland. King Charles's health was failing so rapidly that, in spite of his youth, he was unlikely to live long and, should Anjou be in Poland when he died, there would be time to secure the crown of France for Alençon before Anjou could get back to Paris.

The candidature of Anjou for the elective crown of Poland had been desultorily discussed since 1571. The originator of the idea had been Catherine's Polish dwarf, Krassowski, whose wit and intelligence made him a great favourite with her. Like all her entourage, he knew of her ambitions for her children, so that when he received the news from his father, who was Keeper of one of the Polish royal castles, that King Sigismund of Poland was mortally ill, he had remarked to Catherine: 'There, Madame, will soon be one crown for the Valois taking.'

The Queen-Mother, after having examined the practicalities of the situation, sent her most trusted diplomat, the Count-Bishop of Valence, who had led sixteen memorable embassies to the Vatican during which his understanding of all the *nuances* of ecclesiastical chicanery had become unrivalled, to canvass the electors of Poland. She provided him with as much money for bribery—even pawning some of her personal jewels—as she could raise, knowing that he would know how to use it to the best advantage and sent him off to Poland on 17 August 1572, the day before the marriage of Margot and Navarre. He had arrived in the autumn and between then and the meeting of the Election Diet in the spring he worked so successfully with his comparatively limited resources and by oratory, argument and persuasion that on 11 May 1573, amid scenes of violence and confusion, Henry of Valois, Duke of Anjou, was proclaimed in Warsaw King of Poland.

By the time Catherine received the news from the Count-Bishop, she had already known it for three hours. The dwarf Krassowski, having had it from a Polish messenger, had greeted her with: 'I come to salute the mother of our King of Poland', and Catherine had wept tears of joy.

Charles wrote to Anjou in camp: 'My brother, through God's grace you have been elected King of Poland. I am so happy that I don't know what to say. Forgive me, but sheer joy prevents me writing more.' Margot and Alençon were, for their own reasons, even more joyful. Only Anjou was bitter at the acquisition of what was 'nothing but the presidency for life under the title of King' of 'a desert worth nothing, where the people are brutes'. He decided to postpone as long as possible his impending 'exile'.

One reason for Anjou's disinclination to leave France was Marie, the youngest daughter of the Duke of Nevers who had been killed at Dreux and sister of Guise's wife. She was now the wife of the young Prince of Condé, whom she had married a fortnight before the massacre—a match which had been the subject of the caustic comment of Jeanne d'Albret when she was negotiating the other and more important Catholic-Huguenot marriage of her son and Margot: 'If you cannot make love better than your cousin Condé', she had written to her son, 'you had better give it up altogether.'

It was not however the relationship between Marie and her clumsy young husband which was of any interest to anyone, but the fact that she was the one and only woman who appealed to Anjou. Surrounded by an increasing number of male lovers, of whom du Guast was still the *maître-en-titre*—if such a phrase may be used—and the latest infatuation, from whom Anjou would not be parted, the seventeen-year-old Jacques de Lévis, Comte de Quélus. Anjou, who had not yet finally resigned himself to his temperament, importuned Marie, in whom he thought he had found one who could give him his manhood, with a kind of desperation. He implored her to become his mistress. He wrote passionate love-letters to her, signed in his blood. He besought her eldest sister to plead his cause: 'I beg you as you are my friend do what you can for me. I am mad for love of her. I swear to you that my eyes have been wet with tears for two hours'. He even contemplated turning to Guise, her brother-in-law, for help. But Marie's only response was to visit Condé in camp, so that Anjou might at least have the solace of being near her, and Quélus, who had the honour of dealing with Anjou's arm when he wanted blood for a signature, was not at all disturbed.

Meanwhile Catherine busied herself with the English alliance and sent a deputation to London to inform Elizabeth that Alençon would shortly come to woo her and that she as his mother would be proud to become the mother-in-law 'of the grestest, the most intrepid Queen that human eyes have ever seen'. Then, wondering whether her envoys had been right in advising her that the Queen of England's vanity was such that it was impossible to flatter her too much, she added a touch of simple femininity by informing her that, during his service at La Rochelle, Alençon had grown taller and had managed to grow a beard 'which much helps his imperfections'.

Elizabeth in reply pointed out that the raising of the siege of La Rochelle was an indispensable prelude to an official alliance between England and France.

The raising of the siege was necessary for other reasons. Already in the fierce fighting there had been considerable casualties, including Tavannes and Guise's uncle, Aumale; but the over-riding consideration was that it would be disastrous if the official embassy from Poland arrived to find their new king, who had been chosen partly by reason of his sympathetic understanding of the relations necessary between the Catholics and Protestants of Poland and partly on account of his military reputation as the victor of Jarnac and Moncontour, engaged in war against the Huguenots and unable, after six months at the head of an entire army, to reduce a single city. Accordingly on June 24, the Rochellois were granted very favourable terms. Only one mark of submission was demanded. The chief magistrates were required to pray the King of Poland—as Anjou was now everywhere termed—to enter their city, a prayer which, it was privately arranged, His Polish Majesty would refuse.

The entry of the Polish embassy into Paris on August 19 was magnificent.

The arrival of the Polish ambassadors in Paris. **Opposite:** *Catherine attends the entertainments.* **Overleaf:** *A different part of the same Florentine tapestry shows the entertainments, including the bringing of an elephant on to the terrace at Blois; on the right are Margot, Hercules and Henry.*

The Parisians, wrote a contemporary historian, 'gazed with admiration on the stately bearing of the Polish magnates, their majestic carriage, their long beards, their caps sparkling with rare gems, their scimitars, their bows and quivers full of arrows, their wide boots studded with spikes of iron, their shaven heads.'

On the gates and bridges of the city were paintings of the three royal brothers, Charles depicted wearing the crown of France, Henry the crown of Poland, while an angel reached down to the head of Francis with the crown of England.

In the great hall of the Louvre a platform of state had been erected on which were two thrones, one surmounted by the lilies of France, the other by the eagle of Poland. The envoys, led by the Duke of Guise as Grand Chamberlain deposited at the feet of Charles a silver-gilt casket containing the Decree of Election and asked permission to present it to his brother. On the receipt of it Henry seated himself on the throne of Poland to a prolonged flourish of trumpets and beating of drums.

In the evening Catherine gave a reception in her new palace of the Tuileries, justifiably happy at what, indubitably, was her triumph.

Henry's coronation at Cracow was fixed for October 3, but the new king was still in Paris in September, and showed no disposition to start his exile. Only when Charles threatened to have him escorted to the frontier under military guard did Anjou set St. Michael's Day, September 29 as the date of his departure. This matter settled, Charles and Catherine set out for Villers-Coterêt, about forty miles from Paris, to receive a Huguenot deputation who were demanding a revision of the Treaty of La Rochelle.

Fortified by their new alliance with the *Politiques,* the Huguenots so overreached themselves that Catherine could hardly believe her ears and, too angry even to dissemble, she said angrily: 'If your great leader, Louis Prince of Condé, has been alive and had held Paris with seventy thousand troops, he would not have demanded half of what you are daring to ask.' Then, quickly recovering herself she asked whether the leaders of the *Politiques* had authorised their requests. The Huguenots had to admit they had not even been told of them. 'When you have their opinion', said Catherine, 'you may return and tell me of it.'

On their return to Paris, the King of Poland, accompanied by the King, the Queen-Mother, Alençon, Margot and Henry of Navarre with a train of five hundred nobles and gentlemen including many Poles, set out at last for his new kingdom, but at Vitry, about seventy-five miles to the west, Charles

Opposite: *Henry III on horseback; elaborate clothes for himself, and trapping for the horse, were features of Henry's taste.*

succumbed to a fever which raged for thirty hours and left him too weak to continue the journey. The rest of the court continued their way to Nancy for the baptism of Claude of Lorraine's new-born daughter, Christine, to whom Catherine and the Dowager Duchess of Lorraine were god-mothers.

At the end of the ceremony, Anjou suddenly noticed a fair-haired girl of nineteen, Louise de Vaudémont, a cousin of the Duke of Lorraine. For the remaining three days of the visit, Anjou and Louise were inseparable, to the considerable surprise of the French, the Poles and the Lorrainers who could not decide its precise diplomatic import. No one, apparently, not even Catherine noticed Louise's amazing resemblance to Marie.

The final farewells with the King of Poland were taken at Blamont, a ducal estate on the German border where, according to a diarist, 'the Queen-Mother conversed long and earnestly with her beloved son and, with tears and sobs without end, at length suffered him to depart.'

As soon as Anjou was safely over the border, Alençon and Navarre confided to Margot that at a convenient point on their return journey to Paris they intended to ride off to the south and at once put themselves at the head of a Huguenot rising. Margot, who realised that such premature imbecility would ruin the great strategic plan she was constructing, did not argue. She went immediately to her mother and informed her in detail of their intention, explaining that she was doing so out of loyalty to Anjou. Catherine, surprised but gratified that, in spite of appearance, Margot still had Anjou's interests at heart, immediately provided a special guard to ensure that Alençon and Navarre had no privacy and no opportunity whatever to leave the royal party.

Immediately she arrived in Paris, Catherine consulted Guise who, during the Court's absence had been ceaselessly vigilant and had managed to discover some of the ramifications of the vast Huguenot plot.

It was too complex for him to have touched more than the fringe of it, but

Opposite: *Catherine's youngest son, Hercules, re-named Francis after his eldest brother Francis II died. He was, as Duke of Alençon, the suitor of Queen Elizabeth of England, and the subject of the rhyme 'A frog he would a-wooing go' (Elizabeth called him her 'frog'). He became eventually Duke of Brabant and was known in France as Monsieur.*

Below: *Henry of Anjou sets off for Poland, where he has been elected king.*

at least he was able to confirm Catherine's fears and suspicions and put her further on her guard.

The conspiracy already enveloped the country and Anjou's departure was the signal for it to go into action. From England Montgoméry was to land on the coast of Normandy. Louis of Nassau was to invade France from the Netherlands. La Noue was to invest the fortresses of Poitou. The Governor of Languedoc, a *politique,* had promised to maintain a friendly neutrality in his province. The Duke of Bouillon was to open the gates of Sedan, where Alençon would be received as the new titular head of the Huguenots, while Navarre, returning to Béarn, would rouse the south.

When the two royal brothers-in-law failed to escape from court on the way back from Lorraine, this part of the plan had to be changed and the Sieur de Guitry was put in charge of a picked force to make a surprise attack on Saint-Germain.

By one of the strange coincidences of history, unpunctuality—in the sense of being too early—which had ruined La Renaudie's attack on Blois fourteen years earlier again betrayed the Huguenots. De Guitry was ten days ahead of time. During the night of Shrove Tuesday, 22 February 1574, the Royal Guards discovered his force lurking about the château and raised the alarm. Guitry had not only arrived at the wrong time; he had brought the wrong number of troops—too few to force the gates, too many to escape premature discovery.

Catherine, fearing that the attackers were only the advance-guard of the entire rebel army and that their intention was to capture or assassinate the King 'vehemently entreated him to leave Saint-Germain while there was yet time'. Charles wearily agreed. His only comment was: 'It is too cruel. They might have waited till I was dead. It will be such a little time.'

The consternation of Alençon at Guitry's miscalculation was such that his will seemed paralysed. He wept, raved, protested his loyalty and when Catherine questioned him became voluble with terror and betrayed everyone. His mother ordered her coach, bundled him and Navarre in the back like a couple of naughty children and drove to Vincennes where she confined them safely in its strong, square keep.

The King travelled by litter, guarded by his Swiss and Scots, showed himself to the Parisians and in a day or two himself went to Vincennes to die in sight of his favourite forest.

Catherine set herself with even more than her usual energy to crushing the rebellion and unravelling the threads of the conspiracy. Against those already in arms she sent three divisions of royal troops, one into Normandy, one into Guienne, one into Languedoc. In dealing with what came to be known as *'L'enterprise des Jours Gras',* she adopted other tactics. While exercising in fact the strictest surveillance over Alençon and Navarre, she allowed them the illusion of comparative freedom and treated Margot as if she were as innocent as she managed to appear. The result was, as the Queen-Mother intended, that the Princes made an attempt to escape, organised by La Mole and Coconnas. Under cover of a hunting expedition they were to ride away and join La Noue. In the event—it was the Wednesday in Easter week—they found themselves at every turn so hemmed in by Catherine and members of her household that escape was quite impossible and they returned to the château crestfallen to try again another day. But Catherine gave them no chance. On the Friday warrants of arrest were issued for La Mole, Coconnas and some lesser members of Alençon's household and he himself, with Navarre, was subjected to a rigid imprisonment.

La Mole and Coconnas, brought to trial immediately, admitted that part of the Huguenot plan was to set fire to Paris during High Mass on Easter Day but that this had had to be abandoned owing to the vigilance of the citizens themselves. Catherine, however, was more interested in the discovery among La Mole's belongings of a wax image of a royal personage with a needle driven through its heart. It transpired that it had been made by Cosmo Ruggieri, who was immediately arrested. La Mole insisted that this represented not Charles but Margot and that it was a love-charm intended to dispose her heart in his direction. Considering that Margot's *affaire* with him was the talk of the court, her mother might be forgiven for doubting the necessity of such an aid, but the hint of magic increased Catherine's fears that the plot was directed against the life of the King. 'At eleven o'clock in the evening, the 29th of April, 1574', she wrote a note to the Attorney-General bidding him to subject Ruggieri to the greatest pressure to disclose the truth about the King's illness 'and make him undo it if he has thrown any enchantment on the King to injure himself.'

Next day La Mole and Coconnas were executed on the Place de Grève in spite of Alençon's plea that they should be spared the indignity of a public execution. He chose to regard it as a personal insult to himself and refused to speak to either Charles or Catherine for a week.

A month later, on May 29, Catherine received the news that Montgoméry, after an initial success in Normandy, had been captured at the siege of Saint-Lô. She gave instructions that he was to be sent under strong guard to Paris and imprisoned in the Conciergerie to await trial before the Parlement for treason. When she gave the welcome news to Charles, he said no more than: 'I am so near death that all things are of indifference to me. Punish him as you please.' When, after a due trial, Montgoméry was executed in the Place de Grève, Catherine undoubtedly was a spectator from a curtained window nor is there on this occasion need to find an excuse for her action.

May 30 was Whitsunday. At eight in the morning the King sent for his confessor. In his dying confession, which was long and scrupulous, he showed intense remorse for all the sins of his life, but he made no mention of the massacre of Saint Bartholomew. The saving of his realm from heresy was, in his mind, a counterweight of goodness in the scale (which, incidentally, discounts the Huguenot propaganda that he died screaming in terror and remorse, clinging to his Huguenot nurse). After he had received absolution, he said: 'If only Jesus my Saviour will number me among His redeemed!' and asked the Bishop of Auxerre to say Mass for him at an altar placed at the foot of his bed. He died quietly in his sleep, holding his mother's hand, during the afternoon. He was not quite twenty-four.

Catherine wrote immediately to Henry: 'My son, I am sending a messenger to bring you the piteous news that I have seen another of my children die. I pray God may send death to me before I see any more. I thought I should become desperate watching your brother die and seeing the love he showed me at the end. He couldn't let me go. He begged me to send in all haste for you and asked me to administer the kingdom until you arrived. He charged me to execute justice on the prisoners, whom he held responsible for the evils that afflict the country.

'No one ever died in fuller possession of all his senses. He spoke of your goodness and said he was sure you loved him, because you had always obeyed him and done him very great service. He received Our Lord's Body in the morning and died about four o'clock, the best Christian there ever was. His last words were 'Ma mère'.

'The only consolation I have is of soon seeing you in good health, for if I should lose you I should have myself buried alive with you. You know how much I love you; and the thought that we shall never again be parted gives me the patience and strength to bear everything else.

'With regard to your departure from Poland, you must not delay an instant, though it might be advisable to leave someone behind who could conduct the affairs of the country so that the crown may remain in your possession. As for this realm, I will restore it to you, by the grace of God, entire and at peace. It will be a joyous reward for the troubles and sorrows of the past years.'

Margot realised that the success of her plan to keep Henry from the throne now depended on the escape of Alençon and Navarre in a matter of hours. In desperation she suggested that one of them should put on the clothes of one of her women and be smuggled out in attendance on her in her coach. The brothers-in-law were quarrelling animatedly as to which of them it was to be

Opposite: *A public execution in Paris; anonymous wood-engraving.*

when Catherine swept into the room and ordered them both to get into *her* coach to go to Paris.

Once there she took the most rigid precautions against their escape. Neither was allowed to leave the Louvre without a pass signed by herself (which she never granted them); all the doors were sealed up except the principal portal which was guarded by a reliable company of archers and Swiss; all the windows looking on the river were barred. And Catherine provided herself with a master-key by which she could—and did—let herself into their apartments at any hour of the day or night.

Henry, who found some difficulty in escaping from Poland and travelled home slowly, savouring the delights of Italy, did not arrive in France until September 5, exactly twelve weeks after receiving his mother's letter in Cracow. As he crossed the little river that separated Savoy from France, he was greeted by Alençon and Navarre. Catherine, who had arrived in Lyons, had sent them forward so that, according to protocol, the returning monarch might be welcomed by the Princes of the Blood. She had instructed them with severity to acknowledge their faults and ask for pardon. Alençon's manner of obeying was, after kissing hands, to exclaim: 'The King of Navarre and I had every reason to be dissatisfied with our late king who shamefully maltreated us. To our very great regret, this led us to plot certain designs against him which, with his death, we have abandoned and we have now no other desire than to live and die your faithful subjects.'

Henry embraced them both and said: 'Be it so, *mes frères*, The past is forgotten. I restore you both to liberty.' Then he asked the question he had been burning to ask from the beginning: 'Where is mother?.

They explained that she was waiting for him in Lyons. It was with difficulty she had got even so far since her Council had implored her not to leave the capital in a time of such uncertainty. 'The Queen our mother', said Alençon, 'has given orders that gun-salutes should announce your happy arrival throughout France. You have heard the one fired just now. By this time the chain of echoes will have reached even beyond Lyons, and she will know she has not long to wait.'

'I should have preferred', said Henry, 'that you had waited to present yourself until I had embraced her.'

At Lyons Catherine controlled her impatience as best she could. She inspected the troops; she consulted the City Fathers; she made a further effort to persuade the bankers to let her have a loan at reasonable interest; she visited the studio of Corneille de Lyon where she noticed a portrait of herself 'habited in the French fashion in a little cap wreathed with great pearls and a dress with large sleeves of silver tissue lined with lynx' which he had painted over twenty years earlier. The stout, ageing widow stared at it and 'all the company there present amused themselves in watching her.'

Presently Nemours interrupted her nostalgia with: 'Madame, I think that is a very good portrait'.

'I believe, cousin, you remember very well the time and age and fashion of it and can judge better than any of the others here how like it I once was.'

When the gun-fire announcing Henry's arrival was heard in Lyons, Catherine could wait no longer. She set out to greet her son on the road. They met at the little village of Burgoin, about twenty miles from Lyons. Both were in tears (which flowed, according to the Spanish Ambassador for nearly an hour) and Henry threw himself into his mother's arms before kneeling and kissing her hand and saying loudly enough for all to hear: 'Madame, my most dear mother, to whom I owe my life, I now owe to you both my liberty and my crown as well.'

Henry then asked where Marie was. Catherine told him that the Princess of Condé had stayed in Paris for her *accouchement*, which was only a week or two away. Her advanced state of pregnancy made travel unwise.

Next day the royal party entered Lyons, the King riding in an open coach with his mother beside him and his brother facing him and the King and Queen of Navarre on horseback on either side.

The following morning, as soon as he was dressed, Catherine visited Henry for a two-hour secret conference in which she rendered an account of her stewardship and reiterated her advice: 'Above all, from the very first you must show that you are the master.' The great decision to be taken was whether to grant full toleration to the Huguenots or whether to continue efforts to put down their rebellion. To Catherine and Charles it was, of necessity, still a choice. They neither would nor could face the reality as the Spanish Ambassador put it: 'The King cannot make peace because the rebel demands are too great and he cannot make war because he has not a *sou*.' It was decided to continue with even greater energy the campaigns against the Huguenots.

Catherine, determined to teach her son a regular application to state-affairs to counter his propensity to unrelieved amusement, (which was later to earn him the nickname of 'king of buggery and buffoonery') insisted on a part of every morning being devoted to detailed work on despatches. One morning early in October, Henry noticed that Catherine, having glanced through one of the letters, instead of passing it to him threw it on the table in the pile of those already dealt with. This often happened when there was a tedious letter of little importance, but on this occasion something in his mother's face made Henry retrieve it. He read it, rose from his chair in silence, took a step forward and fell unconscious.

Marie had died in childbirth.

Anonymous French school painting of Henry III, King of Poland and France; he is wearing the order of Saint-Esprit, which he founded.

The *Mignons,* the League and the King of Paris

Henry, after a period of prostrating grief and extravagant mourning, during which the court followed his example and had white skulls embroidered on their black doublets, turned his thoughts to Louise of Lorraine and announced to his mother that he intended to make her an offer of marriage. Catherine, who was at the moment negotiating for his marriage to a Swedish princess, could not contain her anger. On every count, she said, Louise was impossible. She was a Guise, which, remembering Mary Queen of Scots, she said had its own dangers. She was of a lowly branch of Lorraine, entirely unfitted to wear the crown of France. And it was unlikely that she possessed the health and constitution 'soon to render His Majesty the father of a son, an event so necessary for the consolidation of the royal authority.'

Henry assured his mother that his objective was the same as hers (as indeed it was, since Louise was the only woman likely to provoke him into paternity) and that whether she liked it or not, he was going to marry Louise 'a princess of my own nation, beautiful, agreeable and one whom I could love and be faithful to.'

Catherine's opposition was overcome by the death of the Cardinal of Lorraine, an event which, she explained, left the house of Guise far less powerful. He died the day after Christmas, from a chill contracted by leading a three-hour religious procession in sandalled feet and carrying the crucifix, in the bitter wind and snow of Avignon. When she was told of his death, she said: 'We have lost the greatest man and most glorious intellect France has ever seen.' The years had softened the early hatred and fear and now, with his death at the age of forty-nine, she felt above all lonely at the loss of the last of the statesmen with whom she had worked since she became Queen of France nearly thirty years ago. He was near enough to her to provoke her second-sight the night he died. She was at supper when her attendants noticed her staring apprehensively at a distant corner of the room. She called for wine, but, shuddering, let the cup drop and whispered: 'M. le Cardinal is over there, gazing at me. He is dead. He passed me just now on his way, I hope, to Paradise.'

From this time, Catherine's attitude to the Guises began gradually to change until it resulted in the alliance between them and her which was to be the determining factor of the coming years; and her new daughter-in-law of Lorraine was to become a loved and trusted friend. Henry's marriage to Louise, celebrated by the Cardinal of Bourbon, took place on 22 February 1575, two days after the King had been crowned at Rheims by the Cardinal of Guise, the dead Cardinal of Lorraine's younger brother. The festivities accompanying the double-event were cut short by the illness of Claude, who was unable to leave Nancy. The royal physicians were immediately sent to her, but they could do nothing and a fortnight later she died—at 27 the longest lived of all Catherine's children. Her mother appeared more grief-stricken than anyone had expected; but to Philip of Spain's letter of con-dolence, Catherine replied: 'I am bound to think God does not wish me to be destroyed by the honours and grandeur of the world which, if I enjoyed them without affliction and evil and sorrow, might perhaps make me forget to honour Him as I ought.'

On the way to his coronation, Henry had discovered that his brother was still plotting against him. Alençon, who now that he was Heir-Apparent insisted on being known as 'Monsieur', a title which emphasised his status, tried to have the King kidnapped as he passed through Huguenot-dominated Burgundy and himself to continue the journey to Rheims to be crowned in his stead. As had become depressingly usual with him, his plan miscarried— this time because Navarre, who as first Prince of the Blood was personally responsible for the King's safety, refused to co-operate with him—but the result was that, by the time the Court returned to Paris, the hatred between the brothers had increased to such a pitch that Catherine realised that her over-riding maternal duty was to reconcile them. Unfortunately she adopted the maternal fiction that, basically, her sons loved each other and only needed to be more in each other's company to realise it. In her desire at all costs to avoid a family scandal (which, in any case, all France knew of and was discussing), she allowed herself to forget that the archetypal brothers were Cain and Abel and tried to remedy matters by treating it as a kind of nursery quarrel which could be mended by sympathetic understanding of both points of view. She so far lost her grip on reality as to trust Alençon to the point of persuading Henry, against his own judgment and du Guast's vehement advice, to allow Monsieur freedom from strict surveillance. The natural result was that, aided brilliantly by Margot at her wiliest, he escaped from the Louvre, taking with him nothing but the blood-stained shirt La Mole had worn on the scaffold which he had sworn to wear when he led an army against the King, and from his hereditary town of Dreux proclaimed himself 'Governor-General for the King and Defender of the Liberties of France.'

Henry immediately sent a detachment of troops 'to arrest Monsieur who has gone to make war on the realm and so to bring him to a sense of his folly'. Having given the order, he turned furiously on his mother and reproached for having persuaded him to ignore du Guast's wise advice.

The Tuscan Ambassador who had witnessed Catherine's recent grief at Claude's death, wrote that he had never seen her so afflicted by anything as by her youngest son's action. Her face was distorted with emotion and she spoke hesitatingly, as if afraid of breaking-down altogether, but she made no attempt to excuse herself and said to Henry merely: 'I will go myself and bring back the wretched boy wherever he may be.'

Her chagrin at the faultiness of her own judgment was intensified by the rightness of du Guast's. It was a defeat she grudged the *mignons*, who constituted a permanent menace to her power over Henry of which she was never

Two war-machines imagined by Agostino Ramelli in a book he wrote and dedicated to King Henry III. On the left can be seen a type of siege-cannon in a basketwork emplacement; on the right an elaborate field-crossbow.

 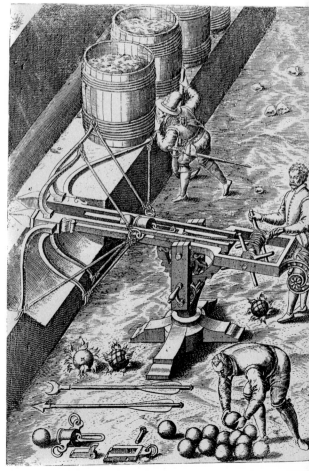

to be free. The simplicity of her original attempt to deal with it, the murder of Lignerolles, could not be repeated, though Margot, for her own reasons, shortly managed to have du Guast assassinated. This, however, only made matters worse. Henry, additionally disturbed by his failure to beget an heir, Louise's satisfactoriness notwithstanding, threw discretion to the winds and publicly advertised his proclivities.

Though one of the *mignons*, Villequier, whom Henry made Governor of Paris, had to retain some dignity, Quélus, who was only too happy to *épater les bourgeois* led gaily through the streets of the capital the most recent additions to Henry's harem—D'O, Saint-Luc, Saint-Mégrim, de la Valette, d'Arques and lesser lights. 'These fine *mignons*' wrote a diarist, 'with their painted faces wear their hair long, frizzed and refrizzed by careful artifice, standing up above their little velvet caps like the whores in the brothel quarter. Their frilled ruffs are half a foot wide and when you see their heads sticking out above the pleats you might think it was John the Baptist's head on Salome's platter. They all dress alike in coats of many colours and they are sprinkled with violet powder and other sweet perfumes.' The Parisians named them 'the Princes of Sodom'.

This anonymous engraving of the period shows a selection of fashions worn by gentlemen of the court of Charles IX.

When they went through the streets, there were jeers, whistles and a long drawn-out 'Piou-piou!'. The students parodied them in paper-ruffs taken from the butcher's shops on which calves' heads were exhibited for sale. Women shouted: 'Tête de veau' and more accurate names. And a libellously satirical pamphlet entitled 'The Isle of the Hermaphrodites', in which Henry's bed was designated 'the Altar of Antinous', rapidly became a bestseller.

From Henry's point-of-view, the *mignons* were chosen for three qualities—their physical beauty, their reckless courage and their brilliant swordsmanship. All of them were daily prepared to die for his interest. In their fashion they loved him and were completely oblivious of their own safety. They would 'draw their swords if a straw blew across the road'. Only one of them—a newcomer, de la Valette, who was eventually made Duke of Epernon—survived their mid-twenties and their heady enjoyment of the freakish moment was the obverse of their expected rendezvous with death. They fought always *à l'outrance*.

The climax of their notoriety was the so-called 'Duel of the Mignons' between Quélus, Livarot and Maugiron and three of Guise's men in which Quélus was mortally wounded and, in spite of Ambroise Paré's skill, died three weeks later in Henry's arms. His last words were 'O mon roi, mon roi', which scandalised some of the bystanders, who put it about that 'he did not mention God or His Mother'. The King, who had never left his bedside, in frantic grief cut off some of his golden hair, for which he had a reliquary of gold and diamonds made, and ordered an elaborate state funeral, which the court attended in full mourning, led by Catherine and Louise.

The *mignons* who remained avenged their dead comrades in their own way. The youngest of them, Paul de Caussade, Comte de Saint-Mégrim, seduced the Duchess of Guise. As he intentionally showed no reticence, the cuckolding of Guise became the talk of the town and the Duke's brother, Mayenne, with thirty ruffians set on Saint-Mégrim and killed him in the Rue du Louvre in the dark. Everyone collaborated in the fiction of 'Persons Unknown', but Henry, who regarded Guise, by promoting the original duel, as the murderer of Quélus, swore that he would have him assassinated and this resolve underlay all his relations with the Duke until, ten years later, he achieved it.

The crucial experience of Quélus's death and the dangerous illness that followed it, coinciding with Henry's twenty-eighth birthday, marked the King's transition to a new manner of life. Even physically the effects were visible. At twenty-eight he was an old man. He became partly bald so that now he never removed his velvet head-dress, even at the Elevation at Mass; several of his teeth fell out; he lost all sexual desire. In public, though his careful make-up ensured that his appearance did not change, his abandon-

*At a ball given at the wedding of the Duke of Joyeuse, Henry III and
Catherine are seated at the end of the row of spectators.*

ment of the ruff for a simple linen collar was a sign to those who could read it.
He became intensely devout. There would be no more *mignons;* but if he no
longer wanted the bodies of his companions, he needed their minds and
abilities and it occurred to him that the very hatred the *mignons* had provoked
by their intimacy with and total dependence on him could be utilised as an
instrument of government. He would take two of the remaining *mignons*
whose heredity suggested that the gift of ruling might be in their blood,
train them and entrust them with power. He chose Arques and de la Valette,
created the one Duke of Joyeuse, the other Duke of Epernon, allied Joyeuse
to the royal family by marrying him to Louise's younger sister at a wedding
which, with its seventeen festivals, exceeded in splendour anything hitherto
seen and cost 'more than two millions in gold', and referred to the Dukes in
public as his 'elder sons'.

Catherine, who saw this action merely as a more outrageous eccentricity
than ever, rated him soundly, only to be reduced to tears by his savage retort:
'By God, Madame, I will raise them so high that, if I die, even you will not be
able to pull them down!' Epernon, who had less charm and more ruthlessness
than Joyeuse, she came to detest more than she had detested any of her son's

256

Henry Duke of Guise in two versions: on the left, before the Battle of Dormans where (right) he received a scar most similar to his father's.

favourites except Lignerolles. She saw him not only as the greedy, grasping, arrogant Gascon that he was but as a symbol of the miseries of France. And more than any other single factor it was Epernon's personal hatred of Guise that prevented the alliance between the King and the new Catholic League which she believed was essential. Politically, it was Lignerolles again, but the earlier solution was no longer possible. As Cavriana, her Florentine physician, said to her: 'You say that Epernon is the obstacle to the reconciliation of M. de Guise and the King, but, Madame, you know that if Epernon were to die, another and yet another Epernon would take his place.' Experience precluded a denial.

The founding of the League in the May of 1576 was the result of Alençon's escape. In spite of all Catherine's efforts to bring 'the wretched boy' to a sense of his responsibilities to the Crown and to return to the King's side, he preferred to put himself at the head of a new Huguenot army under Condé which, about 14,000 strong, was reinforced by 5000 German mercenaries under the Lutheran John Casimir. In spite of Guise's victory at Dormans (where he received a wound on his face which allowed him to inherit his father's nick-name of *'Le Balafré')*, Catherine saw that, to save the country from renewed experience of German atrocities, peace must be made. 'The only thing that concerned my mother', Margot noted, 'was to get rid of the Germans and detach my brother from the Huguenots.' She advised the King to sign a preposterous peace, which became known as the *Paix de Monsieur*, by which Alençon was given the three rich provinces of Anjou, Touraine and Barri as well as a yearly pension of 400,000 gold crowns, Condé received the Governorship of Picardy with Péronne as his capital, Navarre was given Guienne, the leader of the *Politiques* Languedoc, John Casimir the Duchy of Etampes, the principality of Chàteau-Thierry, nine lordships in Burgundy and 40,000 livre a year. In addition, eight more 'cities of refuge' were given to the Huguenots who were granted complete freedom of worship everywhere but in Paris, and Coligny, the elder Condé, Montgoméry, La Mole and Coconnas were declared to have been innocent of all charges brought against them.

Guise supported the King in his refusal to sign this treaty drawn up by his 'rebel kinsmen', but Catherine urged: 'Accept, my son, accept! These articles which I ask you to confirm will work their own destruction. France will rise against the pretensions of these heretics. War will start again, but this time your brother will not be with them and we shall dictate the real terms of a true peace.'

The appointment of Condé as Governor of Picardy, with Péronne as its centre, an intensely Catholic district, was an act of such glaring and monumental folly that Catherine must be presumed to have done it deliberately in order to provoke the reaction she had predicted. The Governor, the Marquis of Ancre, a devout Catholic in command of the royal troops, immediately garrisoned Péronne, shut the gates and refused to allow Condé to enter, and held a series of meetings with the nobles, burghers and ecclesiastics of the district to plan the formation of a secret Catholic League, *La Sainte Union*, to be dedicated to the Holy Trinity, on the lines of the original Triumvirate and Tavannes's *Confrérie du St. Esprit*.

Its object, as stated in the first article, was the restoration and upholding of the sole supremacy of the Catholic, Apostolic and Roman Church and the outlawing of heresy. The second article pledged support to the King, whom the signatories swore to protect against all conspiracies and to obey, the limits of such obedience to be defined by the coming States-General. Every member engaged as his sacred duty, his life and property to accomplish the designs of the League, which was intended as a fighting body under the command of a chief to whom all members were to swear fealty and implicit obedience, whose power was absolute and whose commands were to be carried out irrespective of any other authority.

The formation of the League had one immediate result. The Huguenot leaders in their demands granted by the *Paix de Monsieur* (more properly designated 'the Treaty of Beaulieu') had insisted on the summoning of the States-General because they were certain they would dominate it and thus further impose their will upon the Crown. But in the six months between the signing of the peace and the meeting of the States-General the founding of the League accomplished a silent revolution and the deputies who assembled at Blois on November 17 were overwhelmingly Leaguer. The assembly which was assumed to be going to ask for further concessions to Calvinism in fact demanded its total suppression and the enforcement of Catholicism as the only permitted religion of France.

The burden of defence of a tolerationist policy—which alone would prevent the crown becoming dependent on the Huguenots or the Guises—fell on Catherine herself. At a royal council held before one of the sessions when Henry was being suddenly urged to put himself at the head of the League and lead a crusade against heresy, she suddenly intervened with: 'I am a Catholic and have as good a conscience as anyone here. I have hazarded my person in battle against the Huguenots and I am not afraid to do so again. I am ready to die, being fifty-eight years old and I hope to go to Heaven. But I have no desire to gain credit among Catholics at the price of destroying the kingdom.' But there was an overwhelming vote in favour of exterminating *la religion prétendue réformée* and the war started again.

The new campaign (known in history as 'the Sixth War of Religion') lasted only six months and, as far as Catherine and Henry were concerned, served a double purpose. Monsieur, now detached from his former allies, was put in

These tritons were designed as part of the stage-set for a ballet performed at the wedding of the Duke of Joyeuse, a favourite of Henry III.

command of the Royal troops finally to discredit him with the Huguenots. He accomplished this better than anyone could have anticipated. When he was besieging the Huguenot towns of La Charité and Issoire, he induced the inhabitants to surrender on promise of their lives and then slaughtered them all, including the women and children.

The second purpose the King achieved was, in the new terms of peace, to modify the Treaty of Beaulieu and substitute conditions far less favourable to the Huguenots, as Catherine had predicted he would be able to. The Treaty of Bergerac, which was signed in the September of 1577, he always referred to as 'my peace' and those wishing to please him were careful to call it '*la Paix du Roi*' in contra-distinction to '*la Paix de Monsieur*'.

The following year Catherine set out on her last great undertaking—a journey of pacification in the south, which lasted for sixteen months, though she had hoped to accomplish it in three. She visited Guienne and Languedoc, Provence and Dauphiny, even Navarre itself. Frequently she found the towns and *châteaux* of the lesser nobility had shut their gates against her, but she pitched her camp wherever she could find a suitable site, set up a portrait of the King, summoned the important men of the district and addressed and argued with them. Hostility and suspicion, bad roads and brigandage, plague, her gout and her age—nothing deterred her. The Huguenots who came at her summons were impressed in spite of themselves. Nowhere was she attacked or insulted. She on her part kept her sense of humour and remarked: 'People over forty should not expect comfort in this world but they should try and remain gay while they are in it'. Her only real misery was her absence from Henry from whom she had never been apart, even when he was in Poland, for so long.

A careful observer described her at this time: 'She enjoys work and grows young on it, whence comes the saying: "If the Queen-Mother goes, who stays here; and if she stays here who goes?" She is very stout, but has a fine presence and a strong, erect figure. She is always on the move, which gives her an excellent appetite and, as she takes enough exercise for two, she eats in proportion which sometimes brings on indigestion. She is very proud of the fact that she never lets anyone leave her presence dissatisfied, at least as far as words go, of which she is very liberal. She is very religious, as can be seen not only by her good works—building churches etc—but by the example of her

Opposite: *Anonymous painting of Paul d'Estuer de Caussade, Comte de Saint-Mégrim, one of Henry III's mignons.*

Overleaf: *The room in the Château of Blois which was used for the States General in 1576.*

Catholic life, which makes her most merciful to everyone. She is also so patient that no man remembers seeing her seriously angry and she easily forgives wrongs done to her. But she trusts very few people because, in the past, she has been deceived so often. She spends a great deal of money in building palaces and libraries in order to leave an undying memory of herself in the world.'

Whether or not this was her motive, she never, even on her travels, lost her interest in architecture and in acquiring small manors that appealed to her, as she had done in her earlier journey of pacification. Her ancestry and her training by Francis I made it inevitable. One of the Venetian Ambassadors wrote: 'The Queen-Mother has this much of the temperament of her ancestors that she desires to leave behind her buildings, libraries and antiques. So she has made a beginning in every sort of artistic patronage.' One of her most characteristic actions was asking one of the ministers to entrust some despatches to Rome to the young son of her first architect, Bullant, 'in order that he might go and see for the improvement of his art the beautiful things that are there.'

Architecture remained her favourite art. She added a new wing to the Louvre and started to build the Tuileries, besides building herself another palatial residence in Paris. In her château in Touraine, she laid out a new garden at Chenonceaux and added a grand gallery to the Louvre. At Blois she re-arranged her rooms and decorated them with superb panelling, including her famous secret cabinet, consisting of 180 small oblong panels, decorated with Italian arabesques in red, blue and green on a ground of gold. At the bottom of the panelling on the floor-level, a heavy skirting concealed a number of springs and by pressing one of the hidden knobs Catherine could open certain panels known only to herself behind which lay hiding-places of varying depths. The skilfully combined colours and gilding that covered the cracks made it impossible to detect which of the six panels would open on its unseen hinges. She built the châteaux of Monceau and Chaillot and the country manor of St. Maur in the countryside not far from the capital. She told her favourite architect, Philibert Delorme, that the Louvre was 'dedicated to the Muses'. Her library consisted of 4,550 volumes, including nine hundred manuscripts in Greek, Latin and Hebrew on theology and philosophy and canon and civil law. Her personal reading is best indicated by the twenty-two books which she had specially bound for her in velvet or vellum

Opposite: *Anonymous painting of the French school, showing part of the procession of the League, passing typical houses in the Place de Grève, Paris. Another illustration of the procession of the League is the anonymous engraving shown on the endpapers of this book.*

of black or green Levant morocco. They included works on history, divination, chess, topography and geneaology.

Music she loved and asked the governor of Piedmont to send his violinists to court. She made their leader 'King of the Violins' and allowed him to compose the music for the frequent ballets danced at court for fifteen years. She acquired four hundred and sixty pictures, of which many were of a religious nature, and some were landscapes and historical scenes, but by far the greatest number of them—three hundred and sixty-five—were portraits. This was as it should be. All her life, Catherine's main interest was people and the game of managing them.

The game became too difficult for her as the political dilemma sharpened. She saw clearly enough that Guise was her natural ally. She even discussed with him the possibility of circumventing the Salic Law so that Claude's son should be made Henry's heir and so the two families be united on the throne of France.

The question of the succession became acute after the death of Monsieur who, after an unsuccessful wooing of Elizabeth of England (which gave rise to the popular rhyme 'The frog he would a-wooing go') was made Duke of Brabant and so won a crown of a kind. Inevitably he betrayed his new subjects who consequently expelled him and he came home to France to die, to everyone's relief, until it was realised that his death raised more difficulties than even he had managed to cause when he was alive. For, since it was clear that Henry would die childless, the Heir-Apparent was Henry of Navarre, whom the Pope excommunicated for heresy and whom the people of France as a whole indubitably rejected. No excommunicated heretic would ever be tolerated on the throne of St. Louis. The League, in a desperate bid for national unity, then adopted as its head the Cardinal of Bourbon, as senior Prince of the Blood and now, with the Pope dispensing him from his Orders, the unquestionable Heir-Apparent.

Navarre and the Huguenots called in the Germans and war started again, with the League supporting the King, who himself took the field, with Joyeuse and Epernon, against the invaders. Catherine was again made Regent and remained in Paris, with the Cardinal of Bourbon as her principal counsellor. She organised matters with her usual competence, increased now by experience. It seemed that she went back to the early years, as she used precisely those tactics her husband in his first experience of war as Dauphin, had learnt disapprovingly from the old Constable. She arranged for all the grain in the country through which the German invaders would pass to be collected and stored in strong cities and for all mill-wheels to be made ready to throw into the rivers, the windmills destroyed and the forges dismantled. She was particularly alert in guarding against a Huguenot attack from

The Duke of Epernon, Henry III's influential favourite who controlled his policies and was hated by Catherine and by the Duke of Guise.

Normandy—where, after all, she herself had fought them—ordering the disposition of the troops and not letting them join the King on the more southerly battlefield.

There Henry of Navarre won a battle at Coutras, where Joyeuse was killed, but the campaign as a whole was saved by Guise's two victories at Vimory and Auneau, which brought great delight to Catherine who saw the hand of God in 'what is really a miracle, the defeat of an army of thirty thousand men with so little loss'. Guise was welcomed in Paris as the conqueror he was, while Epernon, who had secretly tried to thwart him and minimise his victory by helping some of the *reiters* to escape, had the mortification of seeing peddled in the streets of the capital a book entitled 'Martial Deeds of the Duke of Epernon against the Heretics' in which each page contained only one one word—'*Rien*'. The hatred between Guise and Epernon, which had been a constant factor since the days of the duel of the *mignons,* hardened into irreconcilability. And it was, as Catherine so clearly perceived, Epernon's control of the King which made impossible Henry's acceptance of the League as what it had become, the patriotic champion of Catholic France. For herself, Guise was '*le bâton de ma vieillesse*'.

Epernon's influence at this point became dangerous and the Parisians, who were fiercely Leaguer, were provoked to the edge of insurrection by the King's continued public insults to Guise. Without Guise's knowledge and certainly against his intentions they formed a secret conspiracy by which the Louvre was to be seized, Epernon brought to trial, the King held a prisoner while the Queen-Mother was once again made Regent and Guise invited to come immediately to Paris as Lieutenant-Governor of the Realm. Though the plot, betrayed to the King, was abortive, Guise decided to go to the capital in spite of the royal prohibition and arrived, without any guard, just after mid-day on Monday 9 May 1588. He was immediately recognised and the first cries of 'Guise is here! We are saved' were taken up by the growing crowds till 'Vive Guise!' became a roar from, it seemed, a city with a single voice. Men and women swarmed round him and, as if he were a saint, pressed their rosaries against him. Others rained flowers on him from the windows and roof-tops.

'Messieurs! Messieurs!' he called 'C'est assez! C'est trop! Criez "Vive le roi!"'.' But no one did.

He made his way not, as everyone expected, to his own Hôtel de Guise but to the Queen-Mother's Hôtel de Soissons. Catherine was chatting with her god-daughter, the Duchess of Montpensier, Guise's sister, who always wore a pair of golden scissors at her girdle in order to give the King the tonsure when he decided to become a monk. At the window one of the Queen-Mother's dwarfs was trying to amuse them by commenting on the passers-by,

Eighteenth-century engraving from a sixteenth-century drawing of the Procession of the White Penitents, an Order favoured by Henry III.

so that when he said that M. de Guise was just dismounting outside the Hôtel, Catherine naturally supposed he was joking. She was disabused when the Duke entered and made his obeisance. She said: 'I welcome you with all my heart, but my joy would have been ten-fold greater if you had come at any other time and not disobeyed the King's prohibition.'

At the Louvre, when the King heard of Guise's arrival, he said: 'By God's Body, he shall die for it' and summoned six of the Forty-Five, a band of ruffians, sworn to do his bidding, even if it included murder, which he had formed as his personal guard four years ago. He now instructed the selected six to hide in a small cabinet, occasionally used for private audiences, which adjoined the room in which he intended to interview Guise. He would leave the connecting door unlocked and when they heard him raise his voice and say 'You are a dead man, M. de Guise!' they were to rush in and kill the Duke.

A messenger from the Queen-Mother arrived, suggesting that Henry should come to see Guise at the Hôtel de Soissons. When the King, in a paroxysm of fury, asked the man how he dared even mention such an insulting proposition, the messenger answered mildly that Her Majesty the Queen-Mother's ailments were now giving her such pain that she had not been able to leave her Hôtel for three weeks and that doubtless she thought that His

Majesty would wish to spare her the discomfort of even so short a journey as that from the Hôtel de Soissons to the Louvre. Henry retorted that there was no need for his mother to accompany the Duke who was quite capable of finding his own way, only to be told that 'Her Majesty seemed to consider it of some importance'.

Catherine, though she had, of course, no knowledge of her son's plan in detail, suspected that Guise's life was in danger and as they made their way through the streets—he walking bareheaded beside her chair—and she saw the extensive military formations, the Swiss, the Scots and the Archers, round the palace, she realised that he was walking into a trap and told him that he must leave as soon as he had made his obeisance.

The King asked the Duke why he had dared to disobey him and come to Paris.

Guise replied: 'I heard that by the advice of Epernon you have planned to murder all the Catholics in Paris and, as the Faith is dearer to me than my life, I came to die with the rest.'

This had, in fact, been what Epernon had urged—a kind of Bartholomew in reverse—but the King, quite truly, denied ever having considered such a thing and counter-charged Guise with disloyalty and ambition to gain control of the Crown. As Henry worked himself up into a rage in which he could utter the words which would be the signal for the Forty-Five on the other side of the door, Catherine intervened and led her son to the window. She told him she was beginning to fear for his mind. He answered that, on the contrary, he had just come to his senses and that it was Guise who was mad—mad to come to the Louvre without a *garde-du-corps*.

'If you have not altogether lost your wits', she said, pointing to the packed chanting crowds outside the gates, 'you will see that the whole of Paris is his *garde-du-corps*.' Very earnestly, she continued: 'My son, I do not know what you are planning, but I do know that unless M. de Guise sets foot safely out there among those who are expecting him, neither your life nor mine is worth a month's purchase.'

Henry, convinced that his mother must by her occult powers know everything, gave his word for Guise's safety and, after having arranged another meeting in the gardens of the Tuileries for the morrow to discuss the affairs of the realm, he dismissed him. When the King heard the deafening acclamations which greeted Guise when he emerged safely into the street, he said to his mother: 'Can I be King of France as long as he is King of Paris?'

Catherine said: 'I am convinced that he has no desire but to serve you and France.'

Nevertheless, in defiance of Catherine's advice and without her knowledge, at four o'clock in the morning of Thursday 12 May, the King, violating

the Parisians' age-old and jealously-guarded constitutional privilege of providing their own defences, introduced 6000 troops led by Navarre's deputy-
governor for Guienne, into the capital. But this attempt to overawe the
citizens was a dismal failure and the ultimate outcome of it was that two days
later, after 'a day of the barricades', the King himself was forced to flee from
Paris, never to enter it again.

Henry's action was a severe blow to Guise, who was thus made to appear
as the King wished to represent him—a rebellious subject who had taken up
arms against the Crown. He issued an immediate manifesto deploring that 'it
had not pleased the King to witness a little longer my respect and filial
obedience and further announcing: 'I have taken the Bastille, the Arsenal and
other strong places into my hands; I have sealed the coffers of the Treasury
in order that I may return them into the hands of His Majesty when he is in
the pacific mood which we hope to bring about by our own prayers to God, the
intercession of His Holiness the Pope and of all Christian princes.'

Catherine remained in Paris as the King's representative, continuing to
negotiate with Guise and receiving her old friend the Cardinal of Bourbon,
who entered Paris in lay dress and took up his residence in the Hôtel de
Guise as the recognised Heir-Apparent.

Eventually Catherine's diplomacy brought about at least a temporary solution and on July 1, the King, who had made Chartres his headquarters signed
an Edict of Union which conceded to the League all the points which Guise
had discussed with Catherine in the meantime and which made it the power
behind the Throne to enforce the Edict of Pacification. A *Te Deum* was sung
in Notre Dame in the absence of the King, who refused to return lest his
gesture should be interpreted to signify that he had forgiven Paris 'the day of
the barricades'.

A fragment from the grotto in the Tuileries garden, by Bernard Palissy.

The Death of Catherine

The Edict of Union, which was signed on 1 July 1588, was Catherine's last act of power. Old and ill as she was, she had ensured a compromise which at the same time faced the realities of the situation and restored Henry to his place as Catholic King of France. The States General was to meet in October at Blois: Guise was to be made Lieutenant-General of France to continue the war against heresy; Henry of Navarre was to be debarred from the succession; Epernon was banished and Paris was pardoned for its rebellion.

Henry signed, but secretly made two resolves. He would undermine once and for all, his mother's control of the Royal Council and, at the first opportunity, he would have Guise murdered. He accomplished the first when suddenly and without any explanation on September 8th he dismissed eight of his best councillors and replaced them by nonentities who could be relied to do whatever he wished. Catherine was both hurt and angry. 'She resents this action the more', wrote the Venetian Ambassador, 'because most of those dismissed had been appointed by her during one of her regencies; and seeing a thing of such importance done without her knowing anything about it, she is entirely beside herself.'

The Court noticed that none of the new ministers went near the Queen-Mother, and Henry, in a fit of combined conscience and caution decided to make an *amende* when he opened the States-General. 'I cannot pass over in silence', he said in his Speech from the Throne, 'the infinite pains which the Queen my mother has taken to meet the evils which afflict the State and I think it right to render her in this illustrious assembly, in my own name and in the name of the nation, public thanks. If I have any experience, if I have been educated in good principles, whatever piety I have, above all the zeal I have for the establishment of the Catholic Faith and the reformation of the State—I owe them all to her.

'What work she has undertaken to appease the troubles that have arisen and to establish everywhere the true worship of God and public peace! Has

Catherine two years before her death; miniature from a Book of Hours.

her advanced age been able to induce her to spare herself? Has she not for this cause sacrificed her health? It is indeed from her example and training that I have learnt to devote myself to the cares inseparable from government. I have convoked this States-General as the surest and most salutary remedy for the evils with which my people are afflicted and it was my mother who confirmed me in this decision.'

Catherine sitting at his right hand listened with no visible sign of emotion, though she smiled an acknowledgement of his bow. In the long speech that followed Henry pledged himself to observe the Edict of Union and said that he claimed no mausoleum more superb and honourable than one reared on the ruins of heresy, but he also announced his determination to destroy 'all leagues, associations, practices, schemes, intelligences, raising of men or money without the King's permission' which Guise took as an oblique reference to himself. As soon as the sitting was over, the Duke hurried to the apartments of the Cardinal of Bourbon, who had been prevented by a sudden illness from attending it, to ask him what course should now be followed. The old Cardinal, who had not quite grasped the meaning of the recent changes, gave his accustomed reply: 'Consult the Queen-Mother'.

Catherine, however, had nothing to suggest. '*You* know, M. de Guise, how far I am from having the influence with which my son credited me in his speech. As he misled the deputies in that, so he may have done in your matter.'

'You can say no more than that, Madame?'

Catherine gave him one of the half-smiles which he knew how to interpret. 'Is the speech printed yet?' she said.

When Henry was told, a day or two later, that the printers refused to set up the speech, he resumed, almost without realising it, his life-long habit of consulting Catherine. She was at her most matter-of-fact. 'The decision, my son, has been made for you. If the printers will not print there is an end of it. Would it not be better to strike out what offends them and so get some of it printed?' Her tone became self-mocking. 'I should not wish your testimonial to me to be lost to posterity.'

The subsequent tensions at Blois were temporarily dispelled by the great social event of the Christmas season, the marriage-by-proxy in the chapel of Catherine's favourite grand-daughter, Christine of Lorraine, to the young Duke of Tuscany. As a wedding-gift, Catherine gave the girl, whom, after Claude's death, she had brought up and had come to love more than any human being except Henry, all her property in Naples, including the Medici palace in the Via Larga. She said to her wistfully: 'How lucky you are to be going to a land at peace and not staying here to see the ruin of my poor kingdom.'

At the festivities Catherine insisted on joining in the dancing, with the result that, becoming overheated in the freezing weather, she caught a heavy cold which, combined with her gout and her obesity, her recurring cough and undulating fever—'and with seventy years on top of that', as the Papal Nuncio observed—forced her to take to her bed ten days before Christmas.

Her last action before retiring was to make the King and Guise swear friendship. Henry swore upon the Host at the altar, according to an historian who witnessed the events of those days, 'a perfect reconciliation and friendship with the Duke and oblivion of all past quarrels. And furthermore he declared that he was resolved to abandon the reins of government to the Duke of Guise and the Queen Mother, since he desired to concern himself with nothing but prayer.' To give some verisimilitude to the unlikely story he had some special cells constructed on the roof which he said were for Capuchin friars, but which were in reality to harbour those members of the 'Forty-Five' who were to carry out the assassination of Guise.

Guise's sister, the Duchess of Montpensier, hearing rumours of the King's intention, implored her brother to escape while he could. He said only: 'What can I do, being who and where I am? If I saw Death coming in at the door, I should not try to escape by the window.' The Duchess then appealed to her godmother, the Queen-Mother, who tried to reassure her namesake with: 'As long as I am here, Catherine, you need have no fear for your brother.'

His mother's indisposition was a considerable relief to Henry who intended to use the same men and, in outline, the same method to murder Guise as that which she had foiled in the Louvre in May. There was now, as she was firmly confined to her bed, no chance of her unexpectedly and inconveniently visiting his apartments and again thwarting his plan.

On Thursday 22 December, the King and Guise visited her in her bedroom and stayed for some time chatting, eating sweetmeats and discussing plans for the Christmas season. There was the appearance of the greatest amity between the two men, although Guise the previous day had received no less than ten anonymous notes warning him that the King was making plans against his life. Charlotte de Sauve was supping with Guise that evening and promised to let the Queen-Mother have any additional information she might manage to glean.

At half-past-six the following morning Guise was summoned to a special meeting of the Council in the King's apartments. Foolishly, he came from the wing of the château he was occupying accompanied by no one but his page. As he obeyed the summons to attend the King in his private cabinet, he was set on by his murderers. One seized his legs to hamper his movement, one threw his cloak over his sword, others stabbed him in the breast, the throat and the back. The captain of the Forty-Five carefully thrust his sword into his groin. With ten wounds and his life fast ebbing, Guise's immense physical strength and power of will was such that he broke the nose of one of his assailants with his comfit-box and managed to drag himself, having for a moment thrown them all off, through the door of Henry's bedroom. As he advanced with outstretched arms, blinded by the blood pouring from the wound on his forehead, the Captain of the Forty-Five, laughing to the others, held his scabbard low enough for him to trip over. Guise fell to the ground at the foot of the King's bed, faintly breathing the words: '*Mon Dieu! Mon Dieu! ayes pitié de moi!*' and so died.

Henry, assured that he was dead, said: 'I did not realise that he was so strong!' and kicked his face. Then, with special care, the King dressed in his most elaborate and festal attire to go and hear Mass. On the way out he visited his mother, who had been enquiring what the noise was.

Catherine's chest was giving her great pain and she was finding difficulty

A German narrative picture of the murder of the Guise brothers, and the subsequent burning of their bodies.

in breathing. The Bishop of Paris was reading his breviary to her. Henry asked her how she felt. She had to admit that she felt worse than she had the day before.

Henry replied: 'You will be pleased to know that I have never felt better. I am King of France at last. I have just had M. de Guise killed. God has inspired and aided me to do it, Whom I am now going solemnly to thank in church.'

She seemed not to understand him, so he repeated: 'I have had the King of Paris killed. I am at last King of France.'

In a tone of utter despondency she answered: 'God grant that it may be as you hope and that you have not made yourself King of Nothing.'

When the news of the murders (for Guise's younger brother, the Cardinal

276

of Guise was also killed later in the day) arrived in Paris, processions of men, women and children, barefoot despite the frost, chanted the *Miserere* and carried lighted torches which on the *parvis* outside Notre Dame they dashed on the ground, crying: 'So may God extinguish the House of Valois!'

Despite the terrible shock, Catherine's health during the next week improved slightly and her physician, Dr. Cavriana, could write: 'In spite of the great trouble of her mind and her inability to see any way of meeting the dangers of the hour, the Queen-Mother is convalescent and in a week we hope she can return to her ordinary way of living.' Next day, however, January 2 she insisted on leaving her room to go to Mass in the chapel of the château and afterwards to visit the Cardinal of Bourbon, confined in another wing, to tell him he was now free.

The Cardinal was so overcome with emotion at seeing her that he threw himself on his knees, kissing and clasping her hands and weeping copiously. She answered his tears with her own and tried to speak comfortable words. But gradually his mood changed and he accused her of having lured Guise to trust the King and thus to have come to Blois at all: 'Madame. Madame, this is your device! You have slain us all.'

At first she was too taken aback to answer, but as he continued his maundering accusations, she replied angrily: 'Listen to me, Monseigneur, it has nothing whatever to do with me. I knew nothing of what my son intended and if I had I should have done everything in my power to prevent it.' The Cardinal would not listen, but continued shouting: 'You have lured us all to death,' Catherine said to her chair-bearers: 'O God, this is too much! I have no strength left. Take me away!' They carried her back to her room and put her to bed.

Next day she made her will, disinheriting Margot and leaving her personal estates in France to her grandson, Charles of Valois, Charles IX's son by Marie Touchet. She then asked for a priest, as her own chaplain had, with many others, fled precipitately from Blois after the murder. They found her the Abbé of Charlieu, Julien de Saint-Germain, who heard her confession, gave her absolution and was able to comfort her greatly until she asked him his name. When he told her, she said emphatically but without any fear: 'Then I am certainly dying.' A year ago Ruggieri had warned her to 'beware of Saint-Germain as it would betoken her death.' In consequence she had been careful never to visit Saint-Germain and she has even left her apartments in the Louvre, which was in the parish of St. Germain l'Auxerrois, for the Hôtel de Soissons.

During the whole of Wednesday 4 January Catherine lay insensible but in the night her sufferings became intense and, though conscious, she did not regain the power of speech. She died in Henry's arms about midday on the

This narrative copperplate shows, on the left, the stabbing of Henry III by
Clément, who is himself killed, on the right, by Henry's guards.

This anonymous engraving shows Henry III on his deathbed acknowledging
Henry of Navarre as his legitimate successor to the throne of France.

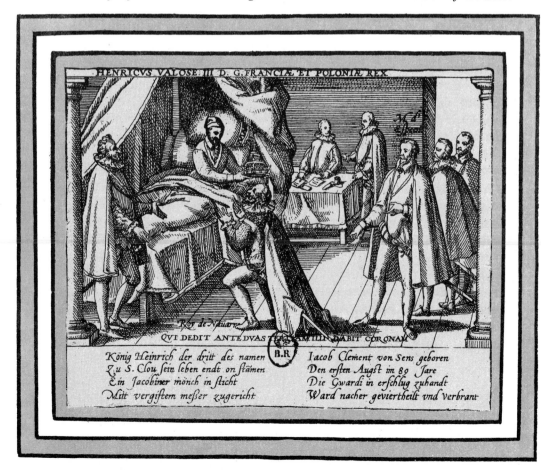

Thursday, the eve of the Feast of the Three Kings. She too could claim her place in her family procession, bearing the gold of kingship, the frankincense of devotion and the myrrh of tears.

An autopsy performed that evening established that her death was due to what her physician describes as peri-pneumonia which brought on apoplexy. But it also revealed 'a condition of health in her bodily organs which, if the grace of God had kept her from pleurisy, would have given her many years of life.'

Catherine was killed, literally and symbolically, by the Cardinal of Bourbon. Her exposure to the cold, damp passages of the château on that bitter January day had precipitated the crisis of her illness, quite apart from the unendurable strain of the conversation. And, in a deeper sense, the fatal interview had destroyed her will to live, for it epitomised her failure. Her idolised son, for whom she had spent her whole life, had, at this last, destroyed all that she had built, rejected everything she had taught him.

At a time when the unification of France as a Catholic country was for the first time in his reign a practical possibility he had chosen to prevent it in the interests of his private and personal feud with the only great man the turbulent times had produced. In her support of Guise, she had given the Valois monarchy its last chance of survival. By the murder of Guise, her son had not only revealed himself as everything his enemies accused him of being, but he had made himself, as she had heart-brokenly forseen, 'King of Nothing'. She, even had she the strength, could do nothing to avert the doom of France, faced with an interminable civil war. It was best to die.

As soon as she was dead, Henry took into his own keeping the celebrated talisman she wore round her neck which was reputed to confer the power of divination. It was said to be made of several metals fused together under astrological combinations based on the date of her birth, and mixed with her blood and the blood of a horned animal. It was covered with drawings and magical formulae. A few days later the King had it broken in pieces.

As Paris was in the hands of the League which, despite the Queen-Mother's recent popularity, now shared the Cardinal of Bourbon's mistake about her implication in Guise's death, Catherine could not be buried beside her husband in the exquisite tomb which Pilon had made for them in the Valois chapel at Saint-Denis. Her body was temporarily interred in a niche near the High Altar of St. Saveur in Blois.

Dr. Cavriana, the night of her death, wrote what may be considered her justest epitaph: 'She died with great repentance of her sins against God. We all remain without light or counsel or consolation and, to tell truth, with her died what kept us alive. The King will suffer more than can be imagined without his greatest and most necessary support. God help him!'

*The King of Navarre accompanies the corpse of Henry III from St. Cloud
to Poissy on 2 August 1589; anonymous wood-engraving.*

One of the preachers of the League proclaimed 'The Queen-Mother is
dead. In her life she did much good and much evil. The question is whether
the Catholic Church should pray for her, since she often supported heresy,
although at the end she is said to have upheld our Holy League and not to
have consented to the death of our good Duke. So I shall say this. If you wish
to say a *Pater* or an *Ave* for her, you may do so. If not, it does not much matter.
I leave it to your own judgments.'

The death of the Guise brothers was avenged on 1 August 1589, when a
dedicated young Dominican friar, Jacques Clément, assassinated Henry III
who, with Henry of Navarre and an army of 20,000 German *reiters,* 12,000
Swiss and 3000 mercenaries raised by Epernon, had camped at St. Cloud to
move against Paris, defended by only 10,000 Frenchmen under Charles of
Mayenne, the remaining Guise brother and now head of the League.

On the evening of the last day of July the two kings had looked down on
the doomed city.

'It is almost a crime', said Henry of Valois, 'to destroy so fine a city.
Nevertheless there is nothing else for it. Only so can the League be taught
obedience.'

Henry of Navarre, now King of France, on horseback before Paris;
anonymous painting on copper, Flemish school, sixteenth-century.

Henry of Navarre, reflecting on the ironic turn of events by which what
had once been regarded as the ultimate enormity of the Huguenots—
Coligny's calling in of the German *reiters* to sack Paris—was now the official
policy of the French crown, could not resist saying: 'I can assure you brother
that our *reiters* will give the Parisians a lesson they will never forget.'

It happened otherwise. Next morning, which had been fixed for the final
assault, Henry of Valois was stabbed by the young Dominican who had
gained access to his bedside. Clément was immediately killed, standing
quietly with his arms outstretched in the form of a cross and making no
attempt to escape. Henry, after naming Navarre as his heir and imploring
him to return to the Catholic faith—'Paris is worth a Mass'—died in the arms
of Epernon and Charles de Valois, Marie Touchet's son. The army melted
away and Paris was, so it seemed, miraculously saved.

For four years, Henry of Navarre was kept from taking the Crown by
Mayenne and the army of the League and, in the end, as the only way of
entering his capital, on St. James's Day, 25 July 1593 he abjured Calvinism,

heard Mass in Notre Dame and henceforward became not only a practising but a proselytising Catholic. The Cardinal of Bourbon had died in 1590 leaving nothing but some 'Charles X' coinage and a few acts signed by him.

When peace and a semblance of unity were restored, the undisputed Henry IV allowed his mother-in-law's body to be brought from Blois to lie in the tomb she had made in the chapel of the Valois at Saint-Denis, beside her husband.

London, Feast of St. Ignatius Loyola 1972

Above: *After Catherine's death, and when her body finally rested at Saint-Denis, Pilon made a bust to match the one he had made for Henry II.*

Opposite: *The lid of the tomb of Henry II and his wife Catherine.*

ACKNOWLEDGMENTS

The Publishers wish to express their thanks to the following museums, libraries, other institutions and private individuals from whose collection works have been reproduced. Bibliothèque Nationale, Paris: 1, 2–3, 32, 45, 49, 50, 56, 58, 61, 63, 65, 66, 68, 70, 74, 79, 80, 82, 83, 93, 95, 97, 99, 101, 107, 110, 113, 115, 117, 119, 120, 121, 125, 126, 130, 143, 151, 153, 161, 169, 172–173, 176, 177, 185, 187, 192, 197, 201, 202, 204, 207, 212, 217, 219, 242, 243, 253, 254, 257, 259, 267, 269, 273, 276, 278, 280; Bibliothèque Publique et Universitaire, Geneva: 156; Collection Ira Spanierman, New York: 10; Hermitage Museum, Leningrad: 196; Galleria degli Uffizi, Florence: 13, 17, 32, 210, 237, 238; Galleria Palatina, Florence: 28; Kunsthistorishes Museum, Vienna: 165; Musée de l'Armée, Paris: 107, 187; Musée Carnavalet, Paris: end paper, 264, 281; Musée de Cluny, Paris: 83; Musée Condé, Chantilly: 71, 73, 240; Musée de Dijon: 53; Musée de l'Histoire du Protestantisme français, Paris: 18, 75, 78, 135, 139, 147, 149, 179, 190, 225, 228, 232; Musée historique des Tissus, Lyons: 43; Musée de Lausanne: 226; Musée du Louvre, Paris: 36, 38, 40, 41, 60, 61, 95, 103, 199, 261; Musée de Versailles: 80, 93, 145; Museo di 'Firenze Com'era', Florence: 22; Museo del Prado, Madrid: 45; Palazzo Medici-Riccardi, Florence: 25; Palazzo Pitti, Florence: 33; Palazzo Vecchio, Florence: 15, 26, 34; Villa Medicea del Poggio a Caïano, Florence: 51.

All the photographs reproduced with the exception of those listed below, are from the Park and Roche Establishment archives (photographers: C. Bablin, M. Carrieri, R. Henrard, L. Joubert, R. Remy, J. Willemin).

Alinari, Florence: 51; Giraudon, Paris: 71, 111; Scala, Florence: 13, 23, 28, 34; Snark International: 256.